D0464854

# THE BOOK OF
# REVELATION
*Plain, Pure, and Simple*

# THE BOOK OF
# REVELATION
## *Plain, Pure, and Simple*

# MICK SMITH

Bookcraft
Salt Lake City, Utah

5|99
19.95

Library of Congress Catalog Card Number: 98-73888

ISBN  1-57008-564-1

First Printing, 1998

Printed in the United States of America

# CONTENTS

# ABBREVIATIONS

The following abbreviations have been used to simplify references in the text of this work. All other sources are cited by author or title. Publication details on each source cited are listed in the Bibliography.

| | |
|---|---|
| *AGQ* | Joseph Fielding Smith, *Answers to Gospel Questions*, 5 vols. |
| *CHMR* | Joseph Fielding Smith, *Church History and Modern Revelation*, 4 vols. |
| CR | Conference Report |
| *DNTC* | Bruce R. McConkie, *Doctrinal New Testament Commentary*, 3 vols. |
| *DS* | Joseph Fielding Smith, *Doctrines of Salvation*, 3 vols. |
| *HC* | Joseph Smith, *History of the Church of Jesus Christ of Latter-day Saints*, 7 vols. |
| *JD* | *Journal of Discourses*, 26 vols. |
| *Life and Teachings* | The Church of Jesus Christ of Latter-day Saints, *The Life and Teachings of Jesus and His Apostles* |
| *MD* | Bruce R. McConkie, *Mormon Doctrine* |
| *Strong's* | James Strong, *The New Strong's Exhaustive Concordance of the Bible* |
| *TPJS* | Joseph Smith, *Teachings of the Prophet Joseph Smith* |

# PREFACE

In 1842 the Prophet Joseph Smith wrote, "Our missionaries are going forth to different nations, and in Germany, Palestine, New Holland, Australia, the East Indies, and other places, the Standard of Truth has been erected; no unhallowed hand can stop the work from progressing; persecutions may rage, mobs may combine, armies may assemble, calumny may defame, but the truth of God will go forth boldly, nobly, and independent, till it has penetrated every continent, visited every ear, till the purposes of God shall be accomplished, and the Great Jehovah shall say the work is done" (*HC*, 4:540). The Prophet taught no greater principles than these: 1) that the work of the Lord was upon the earth; 2) that he, the Prophet, was merely an instrument in the hands of the Lord to bring the work along; 3) that no one could stop the work from progressing; and 4) that the work, the gospel in its fulness, would be restored to the earth, including all of the saving ordinances, thereby bringing about the dispensation of the fulness of times.

We are told to search the scriptures continually (see John 5:39), to ponder the things we have read and heard (see 3 Ne. 17:1–3), and to feast upon the words of Christ (see 2 Ne. 32:3) so that the Lord will make the truth of all things known unto us by the power of the Holy Ghost (see Moro. 10:3–5). By experience I have found the promises of these scriptures to be true. Through study and prayer, the Lord has revealed his truths to me and has confirmed the verity of the words taught and written by prophets of all dispensations.

My first experience with Revelation was shortly before my

mission and, to say the least, I was confused and bewildered as I tried to understand the symbolism and message of the book. For years I felt that Revelation and Isaiah were books that only the most-inspired members of the Church could understand. I was certain that I did not fit the bill.

When I was first hired as a full-time seminary teacher in the Idaho Falls area, I was again confronted with John's intimidating book. I was hired at the end of the New Testament year and fearfully I approached Revelation with the normal skim-over tactics. Four years later, when the New Testament course came around again, I decided to allay my fears and really try to teach Revelation.

As I began to research the subject, I gradually gained a great appreciation for John the Beloved and his writings. I began to see that John would testify of Jesus Christ and his gospel at every opportunity. As I probed Revelation it became apparent that instead of being a confusing agglomeration of beasts and angels, the book was basically a detailed testimony to the divinity of our Savior and an account of his triumph over wickedness.

A methodical reading of Revelation will unlock the mysteries of this often-misunderstood scripture. Two valuable sources for a serious study of Revelation are Elder Bruce R. McConkie's *Doctrinal New Testament Commentary*, volume 3 and Richard D. Draper's *Opening the Seven Seals*. Both have been very beneficial to me throughout my study of Revelation.

The Lord has taught many of the principles contained in Revelation to prophets throughout the ages. Daniel, Ezekiel, Joel, Nephi, and Joseph Smith were all shown many of the things that John saw. Many revelations and teachings are contained in the other works of scripture that shed valuable light on the book of Revelation. By using the scriptures and following the promptings of the Spirit I realized that the books which seem most difficult to understand at first are actually filled with "hidden treasures of knowledge." To unlock such mysteries, one needs only to search diligently.

My desire in writing this book is to provide a commentary to the book of Revelation that is simple to understand and easy to use. I have tried to clarify hard-to-understand terms and phrases in a manner that is accessible to the general membership of the Church. This book allows you to look up a specific verse or phrase from Revelation and find a simple explanation to, as well as latter-day applications of, the principles taught in that section.

I believe that the goals I had in writing this book have been met. I have gained a great appreciation for the things of the Spirit. I am humbled by the understanding that the Spirit of the Lord has provided me with and I am completely indebted to him for all that I have learned. John's book is truly a revelation of the Lord Jesus Christ. It is a record of the Savior's love for and dealings with his faithful followers here on the earth.

I want to thank my wife, Diane, for her constant faith in and support of me throughout my work on this project. I also thank Marsha Jacobson who was a tremendous source of direction and evaluation. I am indebted to my eternal friend Alonzo Gaskill, a colleague who has offered ideas and suggestions that have helped me stay focused on the matters-at-hand. Many ideas found in this book were inspired by Alonzo's observations. I also want to recognize the people at Bookcraft, especially Cory Maxwell for his encouragement in the early stages of the process and Preston Draper for his untiring editorial expertise as the project progressed to fruition. Finally, I wish to express my sincere gratitude to my father, Doyle George Smith, and to my grandfather, Doil Asa Smith, for whom I was named. I thank my mother, Phyllis Smith, for her constant support. Without the support and teachings of these good people I would not have been able to accomplish any of the things that I have done.

Throughout this book I have tried to avoid speculation, and have strived to follow the leaders and official doctrines of The Church of Jesus Christ of Latter-day Saints. Unless otherwise noted, all of the conclusions and assertions in this book are my own and do not represent official Church doctrine.

# PROLOGUE

The Revelation of St. John is a scripture for our day. A Church manual describes the book of Revelation as "a picture of Christ's dealings with men throughout the ages of earth's history. In particular, for modern man it mirrors the second coming of Jesus, the judgment of mankind, the destruction of the wicked, the Millennium, and the ultimate celestialization of the world" (*Life and Teachings*, p. 450). Because of the relevance Revelation has in our lives, I offer this book as a commentary to John's plain, pure, and simple text. I hope that it will serve to help you better comprehend Revelation and more fully appreciate its hidden treasures.

When John received this revelation, he was instructed to eat it, that is, internalize its truths and blessings. We also must eat of Revelation, in effect, "feast[ing] on the words of Christ" (2 Ne. 32:3). By receiving the things that are contained in this scripture, we can be prepared for the second coming of our Savior and we will be sustained in our times of trial.

Revelation, itself being in the form of "letters" to the Church, supposes that readers will be acquainted with the gospel of Jesus Christ and with the ways of God. It is, however, helpful to have some keys or guidelines as we study the book of Revelation.

According to the Prophet Joseph Smith, we are not held accountable for knowing things that have yet to be revealed (see *TPJS*, p. 291). In that spirit, I have not tried to expound upon or speculate about the mysteries of the kingdom. My true desire is to provide you with a greater understanding of this unique scripture by: 1) outlining the basic structure of Revelation, 2) incorporating prophetic guidance to the book as given in various dispensations, 3) providing historical information about the seven churches in Asia, 4) attempting to identify the blessings promised by the Lord to the faithful, and 5) including a Symbols Guide that clarifies the symbolic use of numbers, colors, and so forth. With these helps, I hope that you will find Revelation to be "one of the plainest books God ever caused to be written" (*TPJS*, p. 290).

Elder Bruce R. McConkie also offered some helps to the student of Revelation. In the September 1975 *Ensign*, Elder McConkie gave seven basic guidelines:

"1. Know that the book of Revelation deals with things that are to occur after New Testament times, particularly in the last days."

"2. Have an overall knowledge of the plan of salvation and of the nature of God's dealings with men on earth."

"3. Use various latter-day revelations which expand upon the same subjects in similar language."

"4. Study the sermons of Joseph Smith relative to the book of Revelation."

"5. Use the Inspired Version [Joseph Smith Translation] of the Bible."

"6. Reserve judgment on those things for which no interpretation is given."

"7. Seek the Spirit" (pp. 88–89).

The purpose of my book is to give you a starting point from which to engage in a study of Revelation. This book provides information from a variety of sources and commentators that help to clarify the many images recorded by John. A vast treasury of knowledge and insight concerning Revelation can be had in the resources listed in the Bibliography.

I do not claim to be a great scholar, but I do know the power the Spirit has to teach. If you prayerfully seek for guidance and inspiration as you read Revelation, much knowledge will be unfolded to you. Mormon taught that "the Spirit of Christ is given to every man, that he may know good from evil" (Moro.

7:16). The Spirit will provide guidance as you ponder the marvels of Revelation.

When the Savior visited the New World following his resurrection, he taught four simple principles to spiritual comprehension: 1) "go ye unto your homes," 2) "ponder upon the things which I have said," 3) "ask of the Father, in my name, that ye may understand," and 4) "prepare your minds for the morrow" (3 Ne. 17:1–4). I suggest that you follow the Lord's counsel as you study the book of Revelation: study at home, ponder its words, ask for understanding from the Father in Christ's name, and prepare your mind for your next reading.

As you study Revelation, you will realize that now, in the latter days, we are facing many of the challenges that the Saints of John's time confronted. Satan's tools and methods have become more efficient and advanced, but our knowledge of the things of God has also been enhanced. We have the words of God at our disposal. The scriptures are available to each of us individually. We must make every effort to understand and obey the words of the prophets. If we endure, we will be rewarded in the great day of our Savior.

The book of Revelation can answer many questions you may have as you seek to return to the presence of our Heavenly Father and his Son. Many great treasures of eternal life are promised to those who are faithful. I hope that this commentary will aid you in a productive and enlightening study of Revelation.

# 1

## THE REVELATION OF JESUS CHRIST TO JOHN THE BELOVED

The Prophet Joseph Smith once said, "The things which John saw had no allusion to the scenes of the days of Adam, Enoch, Abraham or Jesus, only so far as is plainly represented by John, and clearly set forth by him. John saw that only which was lying in futurity and which was shortly to come to pass" (*TPJS*, p. 289). At another time he stated, "John had the curtains of heaven withdrawn, and by vision he looked through the dark vista of future ages, and contemplated events that should transpire throughout every subsequent period of time, until the final winding up scene" (*TPJS*, p. 247; see Draper, p. 18).

It is from the aforementioned teachings that we realize that the first chapter of the book of Revelation is an introductory chapter that tells us who is giving the revelation, his authority to do so, and those who are to receive the revelation once it is written. This book is truly a "Revelation of Jesus Christ" showing things which must come to pass, now and eternally (Rev. 1:1).

### REVELATION 1:1–8

1 ¶ The Revelation of Jesus Christ, which God gave unto him, to shew unto his servants things which must shortly come to pass; and he sent and signified it by his angel unto his servant John:

2 Who bare record of the word of God, and of the testimony of Jesus Christ, and of all things that he saw.

3 ¶ Blessed is he that readeth, and they that hear the words of this prophecy, and keep those things which are written therein: for the time is at hand.

4 John to the seven churches

which are in Asia: Grace be unto you, and peace, from him which is, and which was, and which is to come; and from the seven Spirits which are before his throne;

5 And from Jesus Christ, who is the faithful witness, and the first begotten of the dead, and the prince of the kings of the earth. Unto him that loved us, and washed us from our sins in his own blood,

6 And hath made us kings and priests unto God and his Father; to him be glory and dominion for ever and ever. Amen.

7 Behold, he cometh with clouds; and every eye shall see him, and they also which pierced him: and all kindreds of the earth shall wail because of him. Even so, Amen.

8 I am Alpha and Omega, the beginning and the ending, saith the Lord, which is, and which was, and which is to come, the Almighty.

## Verse Commentary

*1:1.* The accounts of both the King James Version (KJV) and the Joseph Smith Translation (JST) say "of" Jesus Christ—indicating the importance of this vision. The term **signified it** symbolizes being given by a sign or token. The angel gives a token to John to "signify" that this message is indeed of Jesus Christ (see Draper, p. 26). Notice how we do the same thing when we "signify" in ward meetings. This is one form of witnessing something.

**Shortly** actually refers to "before long," as in God's own time, or a complete fulfillment of all things in their entirety (see Vincent, pp. 407–8).

**Servant** is speaking of the prophetic office which John holds—revealing prophecy of the Lord to the Saints of the Church (see D&C 1:37–38).

*1:2–3.* Testimony is to be read and we are to **hear** the words, specifically we are to listen. John also delivers his message, with a blessing to all, of what he saw, to those who read, hear, understand, and "keep [these] things" (ponder or remember sacredly) for the coming of the Lord.

*1:4.* The number seven symbolizes completeness and is highly symbolic in many aspects of scripture (see Symbols Guide). Hence, the **seven** days of creation and many other instances of the number in the Old Testament. Seven also occurs as a sacred number in the New Testament. According to Marvin R. Vincent there are seven beatitudes, seven petitions in the Lord's prayer, seven parables in Matthew 13, seven loaves, seven statements from the cross, seven deacons, seven graces as in Romans 12:6–8, and seven characteristics of wisdom in James 3:17. Then in Revelation we find seven spirits (1:4; 3:1; 4:5), churches (1:4, 11, 20; 2–3), golden candlesticks (1:12), stars in the right hand (1:16, 20; 2:1), lamps of fire (4:5), horns and eyes of the Lamb (5:6), seals of the book (5:1; 6:1), thunders (10:3), heads of the dragon (12:3), angels with trumpets (8–9), plagues (15:1; 21:9), and mountains at the seat of mystic Babylon (17:9) (see Vincent, pp. 410–11).

Finally, Vincent identifies seven types of witnesses found in the scriptures, particularly in the Gospel of John, and they are as follows: 1) the Father (5:31, 34, 37), 2) Christ himself (8:14; 18:37), 3) the witness of works (5:17–36; 10:25; 14:11; 15:24), 4) scripture (5:39, 40, 46), 5) the forerunner (1:7; 5:33, 35), 6) the disciples (15:27; 19:35; 21:24), and 7) the Spirit (15:26; 16:13–14) (see p. 42).

This letter of Revelation, although to the **seven** churches, is therefore, to the whole, complete Church. The **spirits** mentioned in the KJV are interpreted in the JST as servants. The servants would be the leaders over those churches. This then indicates that the Revelation is to the members of the whole Church, through their leaders who have the responsibility of sharing the message with the Church. The same is true of today.

*1:5.* A **faithful witness** is one who has sealed his testimony with his blood, his is the most persuasive testimony one can give. The **first begotten of the dead** is the same as the firstfruits of them that shall rise and is in reference to Jesus Christ being the first mortal to overcome death (see Draper, p. 29).

Christ was not the first to rise from the dead, many people had died before him and their spirits had risen from their bodies and ascended to the world of spirits, but he was "the first who so rose that death was thenceforth impossible for Him (Rom. 6:9)" (Vincent, p. 415). It could not keep his body from his spirit as it had done to all those who had died before him (see D&C 138:11–17).

*1:6.* Made us **kings and priests**—kings have power over earthly things and priests have power over heavenly things. Those who are made kings and priests and queens and priestesses will have power over temporal and spiritual things through all eternity, specifically the worlds that they themselves create. Imagery is the best possible teacher here. The Savior loved us. He washed (cleansed, or more concisely, bathed and ransomed) us from our sins in his own blood. He then made us kings and priests unto **God, his Father.** According to Elder Bruce R. McConkie, "Those so attaining shall have exaltation and be kings, priests, rulers, and lords in their respective spheres in the eternal kingdoms of the great King who is God our Father." (*MD*, p. 425).

*1:7.* Notice that **every eye shall see him.** Compare this to his birth when only an elect few were there to witness his coming. Although there were heavenly hosts who sang out at the time of the birth of the Savior, and those who had passed away were almost certainly observing from their place in the world of spirits, few actually witnessed his mortal birth in a lowly stable in Bethlehem. This part of the verse also helps us recognize where he shall come from as he returns and it describes who he is and where his glory comes from. In addition, the verse promises of Christ's eventual return when he shall come with **ten thousands of his saints** (JST Rev. 1:7).

**Kindreds** are actually tribes. "As the tribes of Israel are the figure by which the people of God, Jew or Gentile, are represented, so unbelievers are here represented as *tribes,* 'the mocking counterpart of the true Israel of God' " (Vincent, p. 419).

*1:8.* Christ is **Alpha and Omega, the beginning and the ending.** Alpha and omega are the first and last letters of the Greek alphabet and represent the beginning and ending of all things. Jesus Christ is truly the beginning of all things, in that he created the earth as Jehovah, and he is the ending as he returns in his glory as the resurrected Christ to dwell in celestial glory with the faithful Saints here upon the earth. It is interesting to note that he uses the term twice here at the beginning (1:8, 11) and twice at the end of the book (21:6; 22:13).

## Applicability

One of the greatest truths any person can ever receive is a testimony of Jesus Christ, that he is a personal Savior, and that he is the literal Son of God. It is vital to consider that the first thing John receives in his Revelation is a more sure witness of Jesus Christ, with a command to share this testimony with the seven churches in Asia.

The whole underlying message of verses 1–8 cannot be lost to the reader. It is that Jesus Christ, who paid an infinite atonement for us, has given *us* the opportunity to be kings and priests and queens and priestesses to God (Jesus Christ or Jehovah) and *his Father* (Elohim). We must always remember this glorious promise. The covenants of the Lord are already in place and it is now up to us to receive the promised blessings. It is also imperative to remember that the resurrected Lord shall return in glory with "ten thousands of his saints" (JST Rev. 1:7) and will take his rightful place here upon the earth.

## REVELATION 1:9–11

9 ¶ I John, who also am your brother, and companion in tribulation, and in the kingdom and patience of Jesus Christ, was in the isle that is called Patmos, for the word of God, and for the testimony of Jesus Christ.

10 I was in the Spirit on the Lord's day, and heard behind me a great voice, as of a trumpet,

11 Saying, I am Alpha and Omega, the first and the last: and, What thou seest, write in a book, and send it unto the seven churches which are in Asia; unto Ephesus, and unto Smyrna, and unto Pergamos, and unto Thyatira, and unto Sardis, and unto Philadelphia, and unto Laodicea.

## Verse Commentary

*1:9–10.* John now explains the time, setting, and spiritual events as he received the Revelation. These verses also tell us that John was **in the Spirit on the Lord's day** and heard the voice, **as of a trumpet,** which always heralds some message, proclamation, or coming royalty. It is also interesting to note that from the isle of Patmos one has a sweeping view of the surrounding area, much like the view John will have of the history of the earth.

*1:11.* This is the listing of the seven churches. Although each letter is sent to a specific branch of the Church part of each message may be applied to the whole Church.

## Applicability

The message of the Lord is to go to the whole Church. The applicability of the letters to the seven churches is that though a branch of the Church may not be currently experiencing a particular problem, they are not immune to it and should be prepared for every eventuality. This Revelation was not written just for the Saints in John's time, but is expressly written for all members, throughout the ages. This Revelation comes on the Sabbath, giving us some idea of the value of Sabbath scripture study and of being engaged in other good works on the Lord's holy day.

### REVELATION 1:12–18

12 And I turned to see the voice that spake with me. And being turned, I saw seven golden candlesticks;

13 And in the midst of the seven candlesticks one like unto the Son of man, clothed with a garment down to the foot, and girt about the paps with a golden girdle.

14 His head and his hairs were white like wool, as white as snow; and his eyes were as a flame of fire;

15 And his feet like unto fine brass, as if they burned in a furnace; and his voice as the sound of many waters.

16 And he had in his right hand seven stars: and out of his mouth went a sharp twoedged sword: and his countenance was as the sun shineth in his strength.

17 And when I saw him, I fell at his feet as dead. And he laid his right hand upon me, saying unto me, Fear not; I am the first and the last:

18 I am he that liveth, and was dead; and, behold, I am ·alive for evermore, Amen; and have the keys of hell and of death.

## Verse Commentary

*1:12.* The proclamation of the Lord is to be sent through the **candlesticks** (churches) to the complete Church. Remember that a candlestick holds or carries light but does not give it. The candle or lamp must be lit and then placed on the candlestick, which merely carries the light, thereby implying that the message of Revelation and the light that it brings will come from the Savior and will merely be carried to the world through the Church. The Greek term *luchnos* implies a lampstand upon which were placed lamps that used oil (see *Strong's,* Greek Dictionary, p. 45). The oil is always representative of the Spirit and so the message is sent through the Spirit to the seven churches. This also relates to the parable of the virgins (see Matt. 25:1–13) and the oil in their lamps. The oil (Holy Ghost) is not something that can be purchased at a time of need, it must already be in the lamp (us).

*1:13–18.* Vision of the Savior—It is important to remember that the Savior is in the center, middle, or focal point, and is sending light, by his presence and John's description, out to the Church. In verse 18 the Savior is the one who **has the keys** and Satan is in subjection to the Lord. The only reason Satan is even allowed to come to the earth is that the Lord has unlocked the door. One of the greatest messages of Revelation is that the Savior has the keys of hell and of death, and Satan is powerless to do anything without the Lord *allowing* him to do so.

*1:13.* Some scholars have said that when one **girts** himself it is in reference to putting on special robes, or encircling oneself in robes of power, righteousness, or priesthood; which is especially typified by the Savior girding himself. This underscores the importance of the temple endowment. When we receive our endowments, we then are eligible to receive all of the blessings associated with priesthood power and "girt" ourselves in robes of power.

What a glorious description! The Savior sets the example for us by being **clothed with a garment down to the foot, and girt about the paps with a golden girdle.** The garment the Savior wears stretches down to his foot, similar to a robe, symbolic of priesthood robes. Being girt about the paps (breast) with a golden girdle is indicative of the priesthood robes worn anciently by those who officiated in the ordinances of the temple.

*1:14–15.* **His head and his hairs were white like wool, as white as snow; and his eyes were as a flame of fire; And his feet like unto fine brass, as if they burned in a furnace; and his voice as the sound of many waters.** The brightness, or radiance, of the Savior is unparalleled and his whole appearance is that of light. Even his feet give off a radiance of the glow of fine polished brass being purified in the fires of a furnace. His voice is so powerful that it attracts the immediate attention of the listener.

*1:16.* In his **right hand** he holds **seven stars** and **out of his mouth went a sharp twoedged sword.** The right hand is the covenant hand and always represents the covenants of the Lord and the Father unto their people. The seven stars are the seven spirits who are the leaders of each of the seven churches in Asia, but truly represent the leaders of the Church in every part of the world. The "sharp twoedged sword" which proceeds from the mouth of the Savior is that word of God that is used to judge the nations of the world, and that both cuts and heals, blesses and curses.

*1:17.* John sees the Savior, **falls at his feet** as **dead** and then is blessed by the **right hand**, the covenant hand. We will also experience the same occurrence when we enter the Savior's presence and are allowed to see him as he is. John is so overwhelmed by the glory and power of the Lord that he is overcome by the Spirit and is rendered as dead, or in such a state that he appears dead. Moses, Paul, Joseph Smith, Alma, and King Lamoni went through similar experiences.

*1:18.* The Savior proclaims his own resurrection and eternal life, and also states that he is the one in possession of **the keys of hell and of death.** This concept is vital for our understanding because it means that Satan and his servants are powerless in comparison to Jesus Christ. More of this idea is expressed in chapters 9, 11, 17, and 20.

## Applicability

Who can even comprehend the glory of the Lord? How many prophets have testified of the same things to us today? Can we continue to disbelieve so many witnesses when they each testify that Jesus Christ lives, and has appeared to them in his glory? If he appeared to Moses, Abraham, and many of the Old Testament prophets as Jehovah and to Mary and his Apostles as well as thousands of others (500 near Jerusalem and 2,500 in the Americas) as the resurrected Lord, does it not seem logical that he can appear to prophets of God upon the earth today? Yes! There is no question that Jesus Christ lives and is the resurrected, literal Son of God who will soon return again to the earth in his glory. We would be well-served to heed the words of the book of Revelation and apply what is found in its messages.

### REVELATION 1:19–20

19 Write the things which thou hast seen, and the things which are, and the things which shall be hereafter;

20 The mystery of the seven stars which thou sawest in my right hand, and the seven golden candlesticks. The seven stars are the angels of the seven churches: and the seven candlesticks which thou sawest are the seven churches.

## Verse Commentary

*1:19–20.* John receives the commandment of what to write and whom to write it to. The **seven stars** are in the right hand, are controlled by the Lord, and are his servants in the churches. The term **mystery** comes from the Greek *mustĕriŏn* and is specifically referring to "silence imposed by initiation into religious rites" (*Strong's*, Greek Dictionary, p. 49) rather than to unknown things. Notice that the Savior is the one who reveals the mystery to the servants. Those who knew and could teach the truths (mysteries) taught them to others who were prepared to receive them.

## Applicability

What greater thing can be learned about the value of journals and written records than to see that John was commanded to write what he saw? How often do we have "visions and dreams" of immeasurable teaching value to our children? If we do not record them, after a time the message is dimmed and eventually lost. The Revelation is to the whole Church, not just in John's time, but throughout history, and his message is specifically to us in these latter days. A testimony of the written record of the Lord should always be found in our hearts. Keeping a journal of our earthly experiences is one manifestation of our testimony of the value of written records.

## SUMMARY

It was part of John's mission to receive the Revelation of the Lord. The prophet Nephi saw the same things as John, but he was commanded not to write them being told that it was John's mission to receive and record this vision. Nephi writes, "for the Lord God hath ordained the apostle of the Lamb of God that he should write them. And also others who have been, to them hath he shown all things, and they have written them; and they are sealed up to come forth in their purity, according to the truth which is in the Lamb, in the own due time of the Lord, unto the house of Israel. And I, Nephi, heard and bear record, that the name of the apostle of the Lamb was John" (1 Ne. 14:25–27).

It is wonderful to consider that the Lord has revealed his will to prophets throughout the ages and has shown them the great plan of happiness and the eventual victory of good over evil. This first chapter should help establish within our hearts that the Lord is in control of all things and all things are subject unto him.

# 2

# THE LETTERS TO THE CHURCHES AT
# EPHESUS, SMYRNA, PERGAMOS,
# AND THYATIRA

The following two chapters are concerned with the message of the Lord to the whole Church even though the letters are directed to seven specific groups of Saints. We understand that the number seven symbolizes wholeness or completeness (see Symbols Guide) and this suggests that the book of Revelation is to the whole Church. Although Revelation was written about 1,900 years ago, it is extremely applicable to what we encounter today.

It is important to have an understanding of the challenges facing each of the branches of the Church in John's time, as well as accepting that this Revelation is written to the whole Church, including us. We must realize that although we may not face each of these challenges in our particular situation in the Church today, nevertheless, members throughout the worldwide Church in this dispensation will encounter some of the same type of problems as did the Saints of the seven churches.

Richard Draper observes that, "from the content of the letters, the Church's spiritual life foundered in six areas. Two were external: a willingness to compromise with paganism and a denial of Christianity due to Jewish harassment. Four were internal: the acceptance of unauthorized leaders, approval of false doctrine promulgated by pseudoprophets, halfheartedness and indifference, and a loss of love for the Church and her master" (p. 37).

It is important to develop an understanding of the letters to the seven churches because these letters declare the commendations, rebukes, counsel, and promised blessings of the Lord to

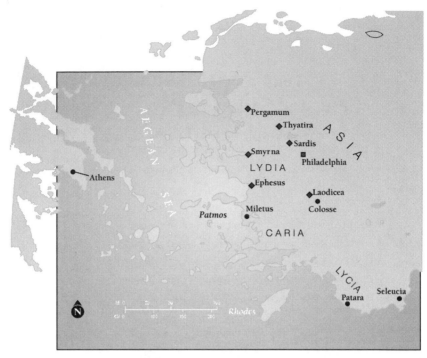

**MAP OF SEVEN CITIES**

his Saints. The central message of the book of Revelation is that Jesus Christ will overcome all things. Revelation also promises blessings to those who are faithful witnesses and who endure all things which will come prior to the Second Coming.

To provide an overview of the seven letters, I will analyze the letters from four perspectives, comparing them with each other. The four parts are: 1) *commendation* for faithfulness, 2) *rebukes* for disobedience, 3) *counsel* on what they still have to do, and 4) *blessings* "to him that overcometh."

Remember that a commendation is an acknowledgment for something that someone has done well. The first thing the Lord does in the letters is acknowledge what the people in each area of the Church have done, and then he commends the Saints for their faithful actions. He is aware of the challenges and trials we face and those things are foremost in his mind, but we must also understand that he will also rebuke and counsel where necessary. Christ then ends each letter with blessings for obedience, thereby showing that he is expectant of our repentance and is prepared to bless those who overcome.

It is quite revealing to compare what the Lord knows about each of these cities and the counsel he gives them with what the Lord knows about us today and the counsel he gives to us through the prophets. A great deal of learning can take place if we will apply the lessons of the various cities to areas of similar struggle in our lives. Through the scriptures, we then can receive consolation and blessings or needed correction and reproof.

## REVELATION 2:1–7

1 ¶ Unto the angel of the church of Ephesus write; These things saith he that holdeth the seven stars in his right hand, who walketh in the midst of the seven golden candlesticks;

2 I know thy works, and thy labour, and thy patience, and how thou canst not bear them which are evil: and thou hast tried them which say they are apostles, and are not, and hast found them liars:

3 And hast borne, and hast patience, and for my name's sake hast laboured, and hast not fainted.

4 Nevertheless I have somewhat against thee, because thou hast left thy first love.

5 Remember therefore from whence thou art fallen, and repent, and do the first works; or else I will come unto thee quickly, and will remove thy candlestick out of his place, except thou repent.

6 But this thou hast, that thou hatest the deeds of the Nicolaitans, which I also hate.

7 He that hath an ear, let him hear what the Spirit saith unto the churches; To him that overcometh will I give to eat of the tree of life, which is in the midst of the paradise of God.

## Verse Commentary—the Letter to Ephesus

### Historical

This was the most important city of preconsular Asia and was situated at the mouth of the Cayster River on the gulf of the Aegean Sea. Three great trade routes converged on the city: One route from the Euphrates, another from Galatia through Sardis, and the third from the Maeander Valley to the south and east. These routes would bring a great divergence of people from all different nationalities and beliefs, and the city was the major departure point for trade routes into Asia Minor.

The religious worship had been to Artemis (Diana in Latin) and a great temple was built, which was later considered one of the seven wonders of the ancient world (Fallows, pp. 602–3). Diana was the guardian of springs and streams and the protector of wild animals. She was also believed to be able to grant an easy childbirth to women in her favor (Diana, Microsoft Encarta).

Christianity arrived in Ephesus approximately A.D. 52 with Aquilla and Priscilla. Biblical scholar Robert H. Mounce asserts that in Revelation 2:1 the terms "holdeth and walketh" show that Christ has knowledge and control over what is happening in the city (p. 86). After the fall of Jerusalem in A.D. 70 Ephesus became the center of Christian worship for a period.

Christians in Ephesus faced challenges from Satan as the adversary caused his followers to build false temples of worship, to seek after the monetary things of the world, and to seek after things of a temporary self-satisfying nature. There is a direct correlation between the Saints at Ephesus and the Latter-day Saints, who encounter the same type of challenges and have the agency to choose those things which are eternal in nature and that provide lasting happiness.

### Doctrinal

2:1. Christ holds the **seven stars** in his right hand, meaning that he is in control of all things, and he walks in the midst of the seven golden candlesticks, showing that he is in the presence of the Saints and knows all that is happening.

2:2–3 (*Commendations*). The Lord knows the works of the Saints, their **labour** (actually suffering and weariness in the labor of the ministry), their patience and their faithfulness through trials. He knows also that they have determined who are false apostles among them. The labor of the gospel work is the preeminent focus of their works and faithfulness.

*2:4 (Rebukes).* The Saints had left their first love, the gospel of Jesus Christ (see D&C 4:2), and were seeking after less important things—literally dismissing or setting aside the weightier matters to seek after other gods. Many of us are guilty of the same offense today.

*2:5–6 (Counsel).* Turn back to the truth (repent) and do their first works (those things which brought them the truth in the first place), or they will lose the candlestick (Spirit) and will lose the guidance of the Lord in their trials. The deeds of the Nicolaitans were both idolatrous and immoral, and the Saints were counseled to turn from those deeds. These same sins occur today and some members are guilty of them. Newel K. Whitney was counseled to "be ashamed of the Nicolaitane band and of all their secret abominations, . . . and be a bishop unto my people, . . . not in name but in deed" (D&C 117:11). This reference demonstrates that some people wanted to be called members of the Church but did not want to do the things God required.

*2:6.* "The Nicolaitans taught that, in order to master sensuality, one must know the whole range of it by experience; and that he should therefore abandon himself without reserve to the lusts of the body, since they were only concerned with the body and did not touch the spirit" (Vincent, p. 439). Similar teachings are alive today. Some teach that it is okay to experience the lustful passions of the flesh and enticements of the adversary because that is the only way we can really learn about temptation and repentance. Others teach that it is okay to sin as long as one confesses Christ; the sin is with the body but Christ is with the Spirit. Of such foolish doctrine we should turn and flee (see 2 Ne. 28:7–9).

*2:7 (Blessings for overcoming).* To eat of the **tree of life** in the midst of the **paradise of God**. The first great blessing is to be allowed to partake of the fruit of the tree of life. This fruit is the gospel of Jesus Christ (1 Ne. 11) and comes from the tree of life, which is Christ, and is found in the presence of God. The tree is in the midst of paradise, the Greek *paradĕisōs*, an "Eden" or "place of future happiness" (*Strong's*, Greek Dictionary, p. 54).

## Applicability

The Saints at Ephesus knew what was right and had sent out the liars from among them, but apparently they were also guilty of trying to "sit on the fence" and enjoy the blessings of membership in the Church while simultaneously enjoying the things of the world (see Matt. 6:24). The Lord promises them that they will have eternal fruit and everlasting paradise if they overcome. These things could not be provided by the Greek goddess Diana even though she was the symbol of fertility and childbirth—two things which can potentially provide us with eternal joy and happiness.

The same choices occur in our day with the same consequences. Many desire to be called members and enjoy the blessings of membership, but also desire the things the world has to offer, even though those things may offer only momentary gratification and may take them away from Church responsibilities. As with the Ephesians, we must also overcome in order to receive these first two great promises. It should be our constant desire to eat of the fruit of the tree of life and enjoy the blessings of the paradise of God.

## REVELATION 2:8–11

8 ¶ And unto the angel of the church in Smyrna write; These things saith the first and the last, which was dead, and is alive;

9 I know thy works, and tribulation, and poverty, (but thou art rich) and I know the blasphemy of them which say they are Jews, and are not, but are the synagogue of Satan.

10 Fear none of those things which thou shalt suffer: behold, the devil shall cast some of you into prison, that ye may be tried; and ye shall have tribulation ten days: be thou faithful unto death, and I will give thee a crown of life.

11 He that hath an ear, let him hear what the Spirit saith unto the churches; He that overcometh shall not be hurt of the second death.

### Verse Commentary—the Letter to Smyrna

#### *Historical*

This city was located about thirty-five miles north of Ephesus on the eastern shore of the Aegean Sea, and was second only to Ephesus in exports. Mounce professes that "this strong allegiance to Rome plus a large Jewish population which was actively hostile to Christians made it exceptionally difficult to live as a Christian in Smyrna" (p. 91). This information is extremely important when considering the text of the letter that is sent to the Saints at Smyrna, showing them that the Lord is fully aware of the trials they are facing.

Polycarp, the bishop of Smyrna, was martyred in the city when he refused to deny Christ. He suffered death, being burned at the stake. It is through his sacrifice and those of others that we gain more of an understanding of faithful witnesses. Even Saints in the latter days have endured persecution and death at the hands of the wicked—because they refused to deny their belief in Christ and his restored gospel.

#### *Doctrinal*

2:8. The **first and the last** is Christ. He comes before and after all things. He was dead and is now alive. This information declares his omnipotence and power as our Savior in all things.

2:9 (*Commendations*). Even though the Saints at Smyrna were tried and were in poverty as to worldly things, the Lord declares that they are rich. Why? They are members of his Church and as true believers will receive all things as they become joint-heirs with Christ in our Father's kingdom. The terrible blasphemy of the Jews is that they do not live up to the obligations of whom they truly are, especially in comparison with the Christians at Smyrna.

Notice that there are *no rebukes* to those who are faithful in the face of adversity.

*2:10 (Counsel)*. Satan and his servants can only have temporary physical power. They may have the ability to cast us into
prison, try us, and cause tribulation to come upon us, even unto
death, but Satan cannot destroy us eternally unless we let him.
It is impossible, however, for Satan or his servants to take our
lives until our mortal missions have been completed (see D&C
122:9). Notice also that there is a limit to the amount of time that
Satan will have power to hurt us (**ten days**). The number ten is
used to symbolize the idea that Satan may bring pain upon us
for a rather lengthy period of time, but not for eternity. There
will be an end to our suffering and, if we are faithful, we shall
receive a crown of eternal life.

*2:11 (Blessings for overcoming)*. To **not be hurt of the second
death** means that we will not die a spiritual death (see Rev.
21:8).

## Applicability

The Saints at Smyrna typify those people in life who seem to
be continually faced with challenges and struggles. These challenges range from persecution for beliefs to physical sickness
and death. We must always remember that these things "shall
give [us] experience and shall be for [our] good" (D&C 122:7),
and that the adversary is the one striving to pull us down. This
process of schooling that we call life is our opportunity to grow
and develop our capability to overcome "all things." We have
the assurance that we will be lead "by the hand" and will
receive answers to our prayers (D&C 112:10).

An encouraging aspect of this life is that our Heavenly
Father is aware of each of our individual struggles and difficul-
ties. As Latter-day Saints who are in the same position as the
Saints at Smyrna were, we can be comforted to know that the
Lord is constantly aware of what we face daily. Thankfully, the
sufferings we endure are only temporary (see Rom. 8:18).

Imagine what insight may be gained when we recognize
that we were prepared long ago for the challenges we face
today. If we seek the guidance of the Lord and live worthy of his

promises there is no challenge we may encounter which can defeat us. What a comforting concept to comprehend!

## REVELATION 2:12–17

12 ¶ And to the angel of the church in Pergamos write; These things saith he which hath the sharp sword with two edges;

13 I know thy works, and where thou dwellest, even where Satan's seat is: and thou holdest fast my name, and hast not denied my faith, even in those days wherein Antipas was my faithful martyr, who was slain among you, where Satan dwelleth.

14 But I have a few things against thee, because thou hast there them that hold the doctrine of Balaam, who taught Balac to cast a stumblingblock before the children of Israel, to eat things sacrificed unto idols, and to commit fornication.

15 So hast thou also them that hold the doctrine of the Nicolaitans, which thing I hate.

16 Repent; or else I will come unto thee quickly, and will fight against them with the sword of my mouth.

17 He that hath an ear, let him hear what the Spirit saith unto the churches; To him that overcometh will I give to eat of the hidden manna, and will give him a white stone, and in the stone a new name written, which no man knoweth saving he that receiveth it.

### Verse Commentary—the Letter to Pergamos

#### *Historical*

Pergamos was located about forty miles north and ten miles east of Smyrna. The city's name means citadel in Greek. The city was known specifically for its sacred and royal buildings honoring Zeus and other Greek gods. For this reason, religion flourished in Pergamos. It was the center of worship for four of the most important pagan cults of the day whose gods were 1) Zeus (Jupiter)—god of sky and ruler of the Olympian gods, 2) Athena (Minerva)—goddess of industry, arts, wisdom, and war, 3) Dionysos (Bacchus)—god of wine, and 4) Asklepios—god of healing (see Mounce, pp. 95–97).

Each of these gods was worshipped for particular supernatural qualities. Asklepios, for instance, was worshipped as the god of healing and was symbolically represented by a serpent. A popular Bible encyclopedia observes that, "On the coins struck by the town, Æsculapius [Asklepios] appears with a rod encircled by a serpent (Berger, *Thesaur.*, i. 492)" (Fallows, p. 1309). It is interesting to note how these gods of the cult were very clever counterfeits of the Savior. Nevertheless, each god was only worshipped for a few particular abilities while the Savior is able to do all of these things.

Pergamos was specifically known for three things: 1) It was a major center for emperor worship, 2) it had a library with over 200,000 scrolls, and 3) it was a center for the worship of the Nicolaitan cult which was predominant in the city. Similar conditions are seen in our surroundings today. Emphasis is placed on worldly power, secular knowledge that provides supposed intellectualism but lacks in spiritual understanding, and sensual gratification that seeks after those activities which provide momentary excitement but forget all truth and have nothing to do with eternity. The worship of false gods, whether they be monetary, intellectual, or carnal, is always destructive, misleading us in our search for truth.

### Doctrinal

*2:12.* Elder Bruce R. McConkie writes, "Pergamos was the center of the state religion of Rome, a religion in which the emperor was worshipped, and to which Christians must adhere or suffer death. It was a religion imposed upon them by the sword" (*DNTC*, 3:449–50). The **sharp sword with two edges** is in reference to Jesus Christ and his power to pierce and slay, by his word, those who are wicked.

The sharp two-edged sword is highly symbolic. The sharpness represents exactness or precision and may stab or cut deep below the surface, while the two-edgedness means that it may cut both ways and may be used for blessing and cursing, healing and killing. When compared with the whole armor of God the sword becomes even more significant as the "sword of the Spirit," or in other words, the word of God (Eph. 6:17). It is the word of God which is precise and exact in its judgment, pierces to the very center, and can be used for cursing or blessing the people, dependent on what their actions have been.

*2:13 (Commendations).* Satan's seat was in Pergamos and is in every place where people are required to worship in a certain way. The Saints here were commended for their works and for being faithful in such adverse conditions. The Greek word for seat, *thronos,* has reference to a throne or to one exercising dominion (Vincent, p. 447).

*2:14–15 (Rebukes).* The **doctrine of Balaam** is most easily expressed as priestcrafts. Elder McConkie defines priestcrafts as: "To divine for hire; to give counsel contrary to the divine will; to pervert the right way of the Lord—all with a view to gaining wealth and the honors of men. In effect, to preach for money, or to gain personal power and influence" (*DNTC*, 3:450; see also 2 Ne. 26:29).

The Saints were also guilty of espousing the doctrine of the Nicolaitans, that of immorality, idolatry, and hypocrisy, and the destructive idea that one must experience all sensuality in order to have a correct understanding (see Rev. 2:6).

*2:16 (Counsel).* Repent, turn from your erroneous ways, or else the Lord will come quickly and you will be pierced by the **sword of my mouth,** by the words he speaks and has spoken through the mouths of his prophets (see D&C 1:37–38).

*2:17 (Blessings for overcoming).* To **eat of the hidden manna** is to partake of that spiritual Bread of Life which is the Savior. It is hidden for everyone except those who are prepared to receive it and who will be given their portion. It is also the eternal spiritual "bread" which will cause us to never hunger for the things of the world.

The **white stone** comes from the Greek *psēphŏs* and is a pebble which can mean a ticket for admission or also a voice (see *Strong's,* Greek Dictionary, p. 78), and implies admission into our Father's presence and recognition, in the form of a voice, for the things we speak in heaven.

The **new name** is the name you will receive, and only you know your name. This allows you the opportunity to receive further teachings of truth and light in the paradise of God (see Rev. 2:7). According to Doctrine and Covenants 130:11, "The new name is the key word." Michael (D&C 27:11), Abram (Gen. 17:5), Sarai (Gen. 17:15), and the Anti-Nephi-Lehies (Alma 23:17) all received specific new names, as do we, when we are prepared to receive and make further covenants with the Lord, even to be called Christian and take upon us the name of Christ.

## Applicability

The Saints at Pergamos had the truth but were surrounded by false religion and worship. Many Saints in our day and age feel that they are adults and can handle slight deviations from the truth, whether it is choosing to view inappropriate movies, not living the Word of Wisdom, or choosing not to obey some other counsel given by Church leaders. It is obvious from this example that it is extremely difficult to be surrounded by wickedness and not be affected by it. The doctrine or hypocritical and immoral practice of the Nicolaitans is very close to our doors today as we participate in improper activities when we think "no one will ever know," and that we are an exception to the rule and immune from the destructiveness of these actions.

The blessings available to us for overcoming are added upon as we will have the "bread of life" (hidden manna), and will receive the capability to have a personal Urim and Thummim and our own new name which no other person will know. As you continue to read through the letters to the seven churches take notice how the blessings for overcoming increase and add upon each other until you are granted the right to sit "with [the] Father in his throne" (Rev. 3:21).

## REVELATION 2:18–29

18 ¶ And unto the angel of the church in Thyatira write; These things saith the Son of God, who hath his eyes like unto a flame of fire, and his feet are like fine brass;

19 I know thy works, and charity, and service, and faith, and thy

patience, and thy works; and the last to be more than the first.

20 Notwithstanding I have a few things against thee, because thou sufferest that woman Jezebel, which calleth herself a prophetess, to teach and to seduce my servants to commit fornication, and to eat things sacrificed unto idols.

21 And I gave her space to repent of her fornication; and she repented not.

22 Behold, I will cast her into a bed, and them that commit adultery with her into great tribulation, except they repent of their deeds.

23 And I will kill her children with death; and all the churches shall know that I am he which searcheth the reins and hearts: and I will give unto every one of you according to your works.

24 But unto you I say, and unto the rest in Thyatira, as many as have not this doctrine, and which have not known the depths of Satan, as they speak; I will put upon you none other burden.

25 But that which ye have already hold fast till I come.

26 And he that overcometh, and keepeth my works unto the end, to him will I give power over the nations:

27 And he shall rule them with a rod of iron; as the vessels of a potter shall they be broken to shivers: even as I received of my Father.

28 And I will give him the morning star.

29 He that hath an ear, let him hear what the Spirit saith unto the churches.

## Verse Commentary—the Letter to Thyatira

### Historical

Thyatira was the least known, least important, and least remarkable of the seven cities. It was founded as a military outpost and then under Roman rule it became an outstanding trade and market city. The god of the city was Tyrimnos, the patron of the guilds, and as can be imagined, was worshipped due to the success of the guilds in the city. This will help to explain the association with fine brass and things made with hands (see Mounce, pp. 101–3). Lydia, the seller of purple, was also supposedly from this city (see Acts 16:14).

These people were very similar to those of us today who are concerned with career focus and the everyday routines, cares, and schedule demands associated with making a living. The challenge we face is not to become so caught up in our accomplishments that we forget the power and blessings of the Lord which have given us the ability to do such marvelous things.

### Doctrinal

*2:18*. Jesus Christ is the **Son of God, who hath his eyes like unto a flame of fire.** Fire is used to burn out the dross or impurities, purifying that which is left. Imagine the purifying power of the Son of God for those he comes to look at face to face. The **feet** like unto **fine brass** is actually indicative of whiteness and brilliancy and shows that his appearance will be brighter than all we have seen before. This letter carries special significance for those who work with brass in their crafts and are fully aware of how bright and shiny polished brass can appear.

*2:19 (Commendations)*. The Lord knows thy works, charity, service, faith, and patience, showing that he is aware of all of the good we do and our reasons for doing such.

*2:20–24 (Rebukes)*. The people in Thyatira were allowing Jezebel, someone calling herself a prophetess, to teach, seduce, and lead away the hearts of the members to commit fornication. Fornication is not merely a sexual sin but also involves turning against the very truth one knows to be correct, or in other words, choosing to ignore the laws of God. Specific attention should be given to the word *seduce* which means to draw away carefully (see 2 Ne. 28:20–22).

One who teaches false doctrine almost assuredly knows of the true doctrine, or at least knows that what is being said is *not* true, and it is for this purpose that the Lord allows time to repent. Such were the numerous warnings given to Korihor in his confrontation with Alma (see Alma 30) and those given to Cain prior to his slaying of Abel (see Moses 5). If Jezebel doesn't repent she will be cast into a **bed (JST: hell)**, along with those who commit adultery with her, where they will suffer anguish together for those sins of which they have not repented.

It is important to realize that a change is made in this section from references to fornication to adultery. They are both sexual sins, but also have reference to turning from covenants, thus adultery is more serious because it involves turning from the Lord, who the covenant was made with, along with turning from the covenant made with a spouse.

To **kill her children** means that those who follow after her will also die because they will not follow the truth and will suffer a spiritual death (see *DNTC*, 3:453). The children were not killed because they were born of this relationship, but because after they were born and knew better, they continued to follow in the paths of the parents' sins. The **reins** are from the Greek word *nĕphrŏs* meaning "the inmost mind" (*Strong's*, Greek Dictionary, p. 49). This identifies the fact that the Lord will look upon our thoughts and feelings and will reward us according to our true desires (see Jer. 17:10).

Finally, the Lord tells those who do not know this doctrine that he will not hold them accountable for this as he states, **I will put upon you none other burden.**

*2:25 (Counsel).* Hold fast, remain faithful in what truths you already have, and avoid the pitfalls which cause you to follow after false prophets.

*2:26–28 (Blessing for overcoming).* One must first keep the commandments (see JST v. 26) and shall then be given **power over** many **kingdoms.** Power over kingdoms is the right to rule not just one but many kingdoms.

From the JST we learn that these eternal kingdoms will be ruled by **the word of God** (a rod of iron [KJV]) and shall be **in his hands as the vessels of clay,** implying that those who rule will mold and form their kingdoms according to the manner they desire. They shall **govern them by faith, with equity and justice** in that all judgment will be fair and equitable and all things shall be done in faith. The word for rule or govern refers to the Greek word *poimaino* and is speaking of the manner in which a shepherd would lead his sheep (see *Strong's*, Greek Dictionary, p. 59). A shepherd directs his sheep by leading them on the right path, rather than driving them as a sheepherder does.

The **morning star**, according to Revelation 22:16, is none other than Jesus Christ. To be given the morning star implies that we will have companionship with Jesus Christ. Our companionship with Jesus Christ, our morning star, heralds the dawning of a new day for us.

## Applicability

We identify with the Saints at Thyatira because we live in a day and age when people worship things made with their own hands. The letter applies to each of us who are members of the Church, but who allow false gods or worldly things to draw us away from the Lord. We must remember that these Saints at Thyatira knew who Jezebel was, knew what she did, and could plainly see what she was doing to them, but then allowed their eyes to become blinded. Considering all of the things we encounter on a daily basis, it is easy to realize how many "Jezebels" there are in our own lives and how they attempt to draw us away from the Lord.

We have so many blessings in store for us if we but keep the commandments. The most basic of all truths is that if we keep the commandments the Lord will bless us. "I the Lord am bound when ye do what I say; but when ye do not what I say, ye have no promise" (D&C 82:10). We shall govern. We shall have power to rule over many nations. We shall have the "bright and morning star" (Rev. 22:16) even Jesus Christ, and yet that is not even the culmination of blessings for "[him] that overcometh" (Rev. 2:26). Shouldn't we then do all in our power to overcome all things and lay aside those sins which do so easily beset us? (see 2 Ne. 4:17–36).

# 3

## THE LETTERS TO THE CHURCHES AT SARDIS, PHILADELPHIA, AND LAODICEA

### REVELATION 3:1–6

1 ¶ And unto the angel of the church in Sardis write; These things saith he that hath the seven Spirits of God, and the seven stars; I know thy works, that thou hast a name that thou livest, and art dead.

2 Be watchful, and strengthen the things which remain, that are ready to die: for I have not found thy works perfect before God.

3 Remember therefore how thou hast received and heard, and hold fast, and repent. If therefore thou shalt not watch, I will come on thee as a thief, and thou shalt not know what hour I will come upon thee.

4 Thou hast a few names even in Sardis which have not defiled their garments; and they shall walk with me in white: for they are worthy.

5 He that overcometh, the same shall be clothed in white raiment; and I will not blot out his name out of the book of life, but I will confess his name before my Father, and before his angels.

6 He that hath an ear, let him hear what the Spirit saith unto the churches.

## Verse Commentary—the Letter to Sardis

### Historical

Sardis was located approximately fifty miles east of Ephesus. In the sixth century B.C. it was one of the most powerful cities of the ancient world. By the time Revelation was written it was no longer a "quality" city. The city had a temple dedicated to Artemis (Diana), the patron deity who was possessed with the special power of restoring the dead to life, and also was the goddess of hunting and the moon. It is also interesting to note that "the inhabitants of Sardis bore an ill repute among the ancients for their voluptuous [or lustful] habits of life" (Fallows, p. 1524). This further helps us understand how they have defiled their garments. Once again we find a city worshipping one specific god with supposed specialized powers, but without the actual power of the Son of God (see Mounce, p. 109).

Sardis was very comparable to today's society. Many people succumb to the lustful habits which degrade and destroy and have no lasting eternal value. As they give in to temptations such as pornography, profanity, alcohol, and drugs, the protective garments which shield them from the adversary and from sin become tarnished with the stain of sinful living and lose their value as a protection from Satan. As in the case with the other cities, many Saints in Sardis were tempted by Satan with those things which targeted "specific" weaknesses. The adversary uses the same tactics today, tempting us until he grasps us in his chains and binds us down to an eternal torment (see 2 Ne. 1:13, 23; Alma 5:7).

### Doctrinal

*3:1.* The seven Spirits and the seven stars are once again referred to (see Rev. 2:1). The JST changes this verse, indicating that the seven spirits are seven servants, or leaders, of the Church. The Lord also knows their works, differentiating between their reputation and their deeds. The Saints are told they "have a reputation for righteousness and spiritual strength, but are in fact spiritually dead" (*DNTC*, 3:454). This is even true in our day when people appear to be faithful members of the Church, but their actions disclose where their hearts truly are.

*3:2 (Rebukes).* **Be watchful** for you are **ready to die** means that the people were on the verge of spiritual death. Although the Lord knows the works of the Saints at Sardis, their works were not perfect before God, or in other words, their works were not done with an eye single to the glory of God (see D&C 4).

*3:3 (Counsel).* Remember what you have **received and heard,**

**and hold fast, and repent.** The Saints had been taught the true gospel, now it was up to them to remain faithful to their principles and repent for their lack of obedience. Counsel is also given that if the Saints don't watch, the Lord will come as a thief, at an unknown hour, and they will not be ready to receive him.

*3:4–6 (Blessings for overcoming).* Some of the Saints had not **defiled their garments** and were told that they would **walk** with him **in white,** for they are worthy. The garments represent covenants and promised blessings. When one "defiles their garments," they turn from those covenants made in sacred places and begin to defile themselves with those lustful worldly desires which stain them, thereby causing their garments to lose their brightness and beauty. As the garments are stained with sin, the protection afforded the individual through remembering the associated covenants is lost and the person becomes more susceptible to the temptations of the adversary. Beautiful symbolism is used in the dedication of the Kirtland Temple about wearing pure garments (see D&C 109:76). Imagine the joy of walking with the Savior as you are dressed in white and knowing that you are worthy to be there, that you have remembered the covenants associated with the garments, and that you are prepared to receive the promised blessings.

The blessings for overcoming are being **clothed in white raiment,** being washed and cleansed, and being able to don robes of purity and righteousness, as are found in the temple. Their names will not be blotted out of the book of life, meaning that the righteous will receive eternal life (see D&C 76:68; Rev. 21:27). To have our names **confessed** by the Savior is to have him speak on our behalf, that is, witness to the Father that we are pure and clean of those errors we committed here on the earth.

*3:6.* Once again we see the familiar verse, **he that hath an ear** to hear, **let him hear.**

## Applicability

The Saints at Sardis experienced similar circumstances to those many of us face today. As we live in the world, we may be walking along the precipice as the Sardians did, close to spiritual death, because of the temptations we succumb to. The Lord is well aware of our challenges. He knows our weaknesses. That does not justify our actions in following after those things that we do not believe will kill us, yet have power to bring about a second death. We rarely recognize the spiritual death taking place inside of us as we engage in improper acts which defile our garments. We must remember that the Greek and Roman gods, while appearing to have great power, were simply counterfeits of the true God who has power over all things on the earth and is omnipotent, all powerful.

The Lord's blessings are sure. We have the assurance that we will be clothed in white. We can even enjoy these blessings in the temple today. We must avoid the pitfalls, watch and strengthen ourselves, and continue to stay worthy in order to have our names confessed by the Savior. As verse 2 counsels, some are "ready to die." It is hoped that those who have embraced sin will see the error of their ways and correct them before it is too late (see Alma 34:32–34).

## REVELATION 3:7–13

7 ¶ And to the angel of the church in Philadelphia write; These things saith he that is holy, he that is true, he that hath the key of David, he that openeth, and no man shutteth; and shutteth, and no man openeth;

8 I know thy works: behold, I have set before thee an open door, and no man can shut it: for thou hast a little strength, and hast kept my word, and hast not denied my name.

9 Behold, I will make them of the synagogue of Satan, which say they are Jews, and are not, but do lie; behold, I will make them to come and worship before thy feet,

and to know that I have loved thee.

10 Because thou hast kept the word of my patience, I also will keep thee from the hour of temptation, which shall come upon all the world, to try them that dwell upon the earth.

11 Behold, I come quickly: hold that fast which thou hast, that no man take thy crown.

12 Him that overcometh will I make a pillar in the temple of my God, and he shall go no more out: and I will write upon him the name of my God, and the name of the city of my God, which is new Jerusalem, which cometh down

out of heaven from my God: and I will write upon him my new name.

13 He that hath an ear, let him hear what the Spirit saith unto the churches.

## Verse Commentary—the Letter to Philadelphia

### Historical

Philadelphia was about thirty miles northwest of Sardis. It was considered the gateway to the East and was a city of commercial importance. The economy was based on agriculture and industry and was very prosperous. One major drawback was that it was subject to severe earthquakes. The city was also very well-known for its many temples and religious festivals, with the chief pagan cult worshipping Dionysus (see Mounce, p. 115). One interesting ruin that still remains includes four strong marble pillars which once supported the dome of a church. Perhaps reflecting ancient architecture, the promise of Revelation to the Saints who overcome is that they are to be made pillars in the temple of God.

Latter-day Saints should strive to understand the symbolism of being a pillar in the temple of God. We should be pillars, being faithful and stalwart members of the Church, in these perilous times. While the earth is shaking all around us with the upheavals of sin and wickedness, we must remain strong and true to the covenants entered into in the house of the Lord.

### Doctrinal

3:7. The Savior is holy, true, holds the key of David, openeth and shutteth, and no man has power to undo what the Savior has done. David was a type of Christ. "The house of David is the typical designation of the kingdom of Jesus Christ (Ps. 122:5). The holding of the keys, the symbols of power, thus belongs to Christ as Lord of the kingdom and Church of God" (Vincent, p. 464). The Lord is in complete control of all things. Keys, tools that provide access to something that is locked, have always symbolized power and authority, and are the rights of presidency. In comparison with Isaiah 22:22, "the key of David is the absolute power resident in Christ whereby his will is expressed in all things both temporal and spiritual" (*MD*, p. 409).

*3:8 (Commendations).* The Lord knows their works and has set open his door. We are free to come in to him whenever we desire, but we must enter. Even if the Saints are cast out of the synagogue they are still able to enter his door and stay with him eternally. The statement that thou **hast kept my word, and hast not denied my name** acknowledges that the Saints have been faithful, even in their lack of strength (notice the comparison of pillars where strength is concerned), and have not denied their membership in Christ's Church. Some scholars specifically note that the letters to both Smyrna and Philadelphia are "designed to strengthen the faithful and, in fact, point by point cover the same ground" (Mounce, p. 116).

*3:9.* The **synagogue of Satan** is the church of the devil, including those groups who persecute the righteous. One of the worst forms of hypocrisy is the outward expression or statement that one is a believer while actually denying the Lord. The synagogue was the center of Jewish society and the place where the law of Moses was read, studied, and learned. The implication of the synagogue of Satan would denote that the law is apostate and is based upon covenants and directions from Satan, not the Lord. "To come and worship is simply an Oriental metaphor that in this context involves no more than the acknowledgment that the church is the object of Christ's love and that with his return their faith in him will be vindicated" (Mounce, p. 119).

*3:10.* The promises are from the Lord. Because the Church was patient and stood by the Lord in his hour of trial, he will do the same for us. The **hour of temptation** is the time when great testing and trials will come upon the earth and the wicked will suffer for their rejection of the Lord and his saving power.

*Rebukes.* The letter to Philadelphia is the same as the letter to Smyrna in that there are no rebukes to those who are faithful in the face of adversity and trial.

*3:12 (Blessings for overcoming).* First we will be made **pillar[s] in the temple,** which connotes stability, strength, and permanence in the presence of our God, in his dwelling place. A dual implication is made in the phrase to **go no more out** and means that once we have entered into an exalted state we will never have to leave, and all tests and trials are finished. It also may be in reference to the numerous times that the Saints at Philadelphia had to flee for their lives in the midst of devastating earthquakes (see Mounce, p. 121).

The Lord then writes three names upon the person who overcomes: 1) **The name of my God,** 2) **the name of the city of my God—new Jerusalem,** and 3) **my (Christ's) new name.** Another phrase which implies having a name written is to be sealed on one's forehead as found in Revelation 7:3. "To have his name written on a person is to identify that person as a god. How can it be said more plainly?" (*DNTC,* 3:458). To have the name of the city indicates that we are considered citizens of the heavenly city where our God will dwell and are called by his name. Finally, to have the Savior write upon us his new name implies that he will reveal all things to us and we will dwell with him in that city.

*3:13.* He that hath an ear . . . (see Rev. 2:7, 11, 17, 29; 3:6, 22).

## Applicability

There are so many times in life when we can relate to the Saints at Philadelphia because of the challenges and struggles we face, particularly in the manner in which we are shunned or ostracized for our beliefs. We may dwell in what appears to be the center of the synagogue of Satan. The Prophet Joseph Smith proclaimed, "Persecutions may rage, mobs may combine, armies may assemble, calumny may defame, but the truth of God will go forth boldly" (*HC,* 4:540). Do we believe that the Lord will deliver us? Do we have the necessary faith to overcome and receive the promised blessings of dwelling in his city, with his name and the name of our Savior written upon us? Can we even imagine any trial worthy of being compared with the glory which awaits us for faithfulness? (see Rom. 8:16–18).

The promise in verse 10 is sure. The Lord will not leave us comfortless but will provide a way for us to escape the temptation in the very hour we need him (see 1 Cor. 10:13). In an eternal perspective, the Lord will come quickly, but maybe not in our expectation; nonetheless, he will come and deliver those who have been faithful and they will receive their crown. Remember, some already have the crown (v. 11) because of their faithfulness, and must now watch so that no one can come in and take it from them for lack of patience, or in other words, for not enduring to the end.

## REVELATION 3:14–22

14 ¶ And unto the angel of the church of the Laodiceans write; These things saith the Amen, the faithful and true witness, the beginning of the creation of God;

15 I know thy works, that thou art neither cold nor hot: I would thou wert cold or hot.

16 So then because thou art lukewarm, and neither cold nor hot, I will spue thee out of my mouth.

17 Because thou sayest, I am rich, and increased with goods, and have need of nothing; and knowest not that thou art wretched, and miserable, and poor, and blind, and naked:

18 I counsel thee to buy of me gold tried in the fire, that thou mayest be rich; and white raiment, that thou mayest be clothed, and that the shame of thy nakedness do not appear; and anoint thine eyes with eyesalve, that thou mayest see.

19 As many as I love, I rebuke and chasten: be zealous therefore, and repent.

20 Behold, I stand at the door, and knock: if any man hear my voice, and open the door, I will come in to him, and will sup with him, and he with me.

21 To him that overcometh will I grant to sit with me in my throne, even as I also overcame, and am set down with my Father in his throne.

22 He that hath an ear, let him hear what the Spirit saith unto the churches.

### Verse Commentary—the Letter to Laodicea

#### *Historical*

Laodicea was located in the Lycus Valley at the juncture of two trade routes, one coming from Pergamos and the other from Ephesus. The city occupied a nearly-square plateau and was named by Antiochus after his wife Laodice. In Roman times it was one of the wealthiest cities, but after a devastating earthquake of A.D. 60 the city was rebuilt without the help of Rome. "Laodicea's major weakness was its lack of an adequate and convenient source for water" (Mounce, p. 123).

Here you will notice that the references in the letter deal with water and the value it has in everyday life. When water first enters a pipe it may be very hot, yet by the time it reaches its destination it may become lukewarm and be of no real value to the recipients. An interesting analogy takes place when we compare our zeal for the gospel with the water at Laodicea. Are we hot when we first accept the fulness of the gospel, but as we continue down the path do we become complacent, and then by the time we join with the rest of the Saints in the gospel city have we lost our zeal and are neither "hot nor cold, but are lukewarm"? Is it not true that we determine the temperature of our spiritual water?

#### *Doctrinal*

*3:14.* The Lord provides us with three titles for himself. He is the **Amen, the faithful and true witness,** and **the beginning of the creation of God.** The "Amen" is "a title given to show that it is in and through him that the seal of divine affirmation is placed on all the promises of the Father" (*MD*, p. 32). "The faithful and true witness" is the same as expressed earlier and is one who has sealed his testimony with his blood. "The beginning of the creation of God" is a marvelous affirmation that the Firstborn is a creation of our Father, and is the Creator, having divine investiture of authority from the Father.

*3:15–17 (Rebukes).* This is one of the most severe of all of the letters to the seven churches. Thou art neither **cold nor hot**, but are **lukewarm.** One interpretation that has been offered is that the church in Laodicea "was providing neither refreshment for the spiritually weary, nor healing for the spiritually sick. It was totally ineffective, and thus distasteful to its Lord (p. 178)" (M. J. S. Rudwick and E. M. B. Green as quoted in Mounce, p. 125). Other scholars feel that some members of the Church were neither fully committed to, nor rejectful of, their Church membership, but essentially were "fence-sitters," those who remain faithful when things are good and withdraw when challenges arise.

Because they have the material things of the world, these Saints don't concern themselves with the spiritual things of God. Hence, they are neither hot (spiritually on fire) or cold (spiritually disinterested) and seem to say, "All is well in Zion; yea, Zion prospereth" (2 Ne. 28:21), because they have their material things and have no need of the spiritual. The Lord will **spue** them out of his mouth—he will reject the unrighteous.

*3:18–20 (Counsel).* Buy **gold tried in the fire**. This is an appeal to the wealth that comes from spiritual faithfulness. Jacob counsels us, in the Book of Mormon, to seek first the kingdom of God, and then riches shall be added unto us (see Jacob 2:18–19). The kingdom of God is where we will be rich, both materially and spiritually, if our hearts are in the right place. **White raiment** is the clothing the Lord places on us, clothing that we cannot buy with money, and it applies to the garments we receive in the temple as we covenant with the Lord.

To **anoint thy eyes with eyesalve** is, Elder McConkie suggests in his rephrasing of the verse, to "receive the companionship of the Holy Spirit so that your spiritual eyes shall be opened and your whole body filled with light" (*DNTC*, 3:461; see also Matt. 6:22). An eyesalve was often used to heal blindness, and after washing the eyes, the afflicted was generally able to see more clearly. The application here is that the Holy Ghost can enable the Saints to see how they are afflicted spiritually and will chasten them to seek repentance. The Lord anoints their eyes with salve because he is desirous that they change their ways and return to him.

As he clothed the ancient Saints, the Lord clothes us physically in white raiment and clothes us spiritually with the blessings and companionship of the Holy Ghost in order to provide us with a complete protective covering against the powers of the adversary.

Verse 20 expresses the Lord's love for us and describes his long-suffering. How oft he must **stand at the door, and knock;** he will not force his way in. This verse is so beautiful if we truly strive to understand his message. He knocks, if we **hear [his] voice, and open the door, [he] will come in to [us], and will sup with [us], and [we] with [him].** The Savior desires to be with us, in our presence, but is bound by his own laws, and must await our invitation. Think of how glorious a moment it would be to sit with the Savior, even as Mary and Martha, and sup (both spiritually and physically) with him who has the gift of eternal sustenance, the bread of life.

*3:21 (Blessings for overcoming).* We will **sit with [Christ] in [his] throne . . . even as [he] overcame, and [sits with the Father] in his throne.** We will be gods! Is there any more glorious promise than that? Can we even comprehend the glory which awaits us if we but overcome? Abraham, Isaac, and Jacob have attained this glory. They have overcome all things through their obedience, and "are not angels, but are gods" (D&C 132:37). The Prophet Joseph Smith gives us a wonderful understanding of this blessing of sitting with the Father in his throne when he states: "What is it? To inherit the same power, the same glory and the same exaltation, until you arrive at the station of a God, and ascend the throne of eternal power, the same as those who have gone before. What did Jesus do? Why; I do the things I saw my Father do when worlds came rolling into existence. My Father worked out his kingdom with fear and trembling, and I must do the same; and when I get my kingdom, I shall present it to my Father, so that he may obtain kingdom upon kingdom, and it will exalt him in glory. He will then take a higher exaltation, and I will take his place, and thereby become exalted myself. So that Jesus treads in the tracks of his Father, and inherits what God did before; and God is thus glorified and exalted in the salvation and exaltation of all his children. It is plain beyond disputation, and you thus learn some of the first principles of the gospel" (*TPJS*, pp. 347–48).

3:22. In this verse we see the final admonition to listen to the Lord. These letters, although to each church in particular, are also applicable to various situations that each of the churches will encounter at some time. **He that hath an ear, let him hear what the Spirit saith unto the churches.**

## Applicability

The letter to Laodicea admonishes us to consider where our hearts truly are. Are they on the things of the world? Do we place too much emphasis on the fact that we are members of the Lord's Church, and yet set aside the things of God? Alma 5 encourages us to evaluate our own standing before the Lord and to determine whether or not we are one that the Lord would spue out of his mouth.

We must also remember that he has given us time to repent, but we must do so quickly. As in the case of the Laodicean Saints, we are almost to the point of receiving our thrones, kingdoms, and glories, of dwelling with the Savior and our Father in their kingdom. Can there possibly be promised a more glorious blessing than this? "Who's on the Lord's side? Who? Now is the time to show. We ask it fearlessly: Who's on the Lord's side? Who?" (*Hymns*, no. 260). The purpose of the letters to the seven churches is not to discourage. They are to be used when reprimand, counsel, and chastening at the hand of the Lord will benefit and protect the Saints from the deceptions of the adversary.

## SUMMARY

Note that every one of the churches is known by the Lord for its works. The Lord acknowledges the works of the seven churches and gives commendations and rebukes as necessary.

The Saints are commended for their successes and rebuked for their excesses. Two congregations, the Saints at Smyrna and Philadelphia, were not rebuked because they were living as faithful Christians despite being persecuted for their beliefs. No matter what world environment you may find yourself in, the Lord knows your works and is aware of your level of faithfulness through your actions.

One of the greatest challenges the ancient Saints were facing was that of allowing false doctrines to creep in among them. Some of the Saints were even fully aware of the false doctrines, knew that the doctrines were incorrect, and *still* allowed them to exist or be taught among them. How many of us would allow a cancer to coexist with us if we knew there was a way we could rid ourselves of this destructive disease? How many of us, today, are aware of the destructiveness of R-rated (and many other) movies, pornography, violence, and inappropriate music but still consume such influences? Is it even remotely possible that we can fool the Great Judge?

The counsel of the Lord is to watch and be ready because he "will come on thee as a thief" (Rev. 3:3). The Savior compares his coming to that of a thief; he will come when the world least expects it, the slothful and unrighteous will be caught unprepared. As Latter-day Saints we must be watchful and prepared—both temporally and spiritually—for his coming.

The Lord loves us, and chastens or rebukes us in order to counsel us about how we can better ourselves. His counsel helps us prepare to overcome the temptations and ways of the world. In each of the letters the Saints are commanded, "he that hath an ear, let him hear" (Rev. 3:22). Realizing that all have ears, the Lord is thereby telling us to understand, not just physically hear, all that he is saying through the prophets. There is much of this counsel which applies to each of us individually as well as to the whole Church. If we will read the counsel the Lord gives and then change our lives in the areas where we need to improve, we will then be prepared to receive the blessings promised in the letters.

We should focus our earthly desires on the blessings

promised to "him that overcometh" (Rev. 2:7; see also 2:11, 17, 26; 3:5, 12, 21). By overcoming persecution, temptation, and doubt, and by enduring to the end these blessings will be ours.

As the promises continue, greater blessings seem to be evident, until at last, one is allowed to receive a position of godhood beside the Savior and his Father. The Lord promises us that we will receive "line upon line" (2 Ne. 28:30) until we come to a knowledge of the truth. This same principle holds true as we clarify the promises of the letters to the seven churches.

"To eat of the tree of life" (Rev. 2:7) is the very thing which man has desired from the time that Adam and Eve were cast out of the Garden. Nephi tells us that the tree of life is Christ (see 1 Ne. 11:9–27). It represents the love of God in sending his Son here to the earth to die for us. The tree of life is just as it implies, a tree of life, and to him that partakes of the tree's fruit is given eternal life. As Lehi partook of the tree in his dream he was "desirous that [his] family should partake of it also" (1 Ne. 8:12), and the fruit of the tree is the gospel. The first step we have to do then is to receive the basic ordinances of the gospel.

"The paradise of God" (Rev. 2:7) is, according to Elder Bruce R. McConkie, "that part of the spirit world inhabited by the righteous as they await the day of a glorious resurrection in which they shall inherit eternal life" (*DNTC*, 3:447). Paradise here on earth is found in the temple.

To "not be hurt of the second death" (Rev. 2:11) is to not be affected by spiritual death and receive ordinances of eternal life in the temple.

"The hidden manna" (Rev. 2:17) is "the bread of life, the good word of God, the doctrines of Him who is the Bread of Life—all of which is hidden from the carnal mind" (*DNTC*, 3:451). As we enter the temple that which is hidden from the world is ours to partake of.

"The white stone . . . [and] a new name" (Rev. 2:17) are speaking of the time when this earth becomes a celestial sphere. The Lord told Joseph Smith that, "the white stone mentioned in Revelation 2:17, will become a Urim and Thummim to each individual who receives one, whereby things pertaining to a higher order of kingdoms will be made known; And a white stone is given to each of those who come into the celestial kingdom, whereon is a new name written, which no man knoweth save he that receiveth it. The new name is the key word" (D&C 130:10–11).

"Power over many kingdoms; . . . ruled by the word of God; . . . as the vessels of clay . . . govern them by faith, with equity, and justice" (JST Rev. 2:26–27) refers not only to earthly power but eternal power patterned after the kingdom of our Father. We will rule through God's power and will mold worlds through the faith, equity, and justice we have learned by observing the Father and the Son.

"Clothed in white raiment" (Rev. 3:5), Elder McConkie says, symbolizes the "temple garments [see v. 4], garments of the holy priesthood, symbolical of the robes of righteousness with which the Saints must clothe themselves if they are to gain eternal life" (*DNTC*, 3:454). The dedicatory prayer of the Kirtland Temple also provides us with some insight to being clothed in white: "That our garments may be pure, that we may be clothed upon with robes of righteousness, with palms in our hands, and crowns of glory upon our heads, and reap eternal joy for all our sufferings" (D&C 109:76). Notice how much symbolism is used in the dedicatory prayer!

"The book of life" (Rev. 3:5) is the record kept in heaven which contains the names of the faithful along with an account of their righteous covenants. Not to be blotted out means that our names will remain intact on that record of faithful Saints (see D&C 128:6–7; Rev. 3:5; 21:27). Joseph Smith and the Apostle Paul both taught that the names of faithful Saints are recorded in the book of life while they are yet in mortality (see *TPJS*, p. 9; Philip. 4:3). All necessary ordinances which must be performed while here on the earth are recorded in the book of life, and will allow us to pass through the veil as we are presented before the Lord.

"I will confess his name before my Father" (Rev. 3:5) means

that if we have repented and confessed his name the Savior will plead our case before the Father by showing that he (Christ) has paid the price of all our sins and we are thereby washed pure through his blood to enter into the Father's presence. He judges us and allows us into his presence and declares that we are worthy to enter the presence of the Father.

Being made "a pillar in the temple" (Rev. 3:12) symbolically refers to "those who overcome," meaning that the righteous will serve as firm supports of the temple on high.

When we "go no more out" (Rev. 3:12) we will be eternally in an exalted state and will not fall, but will dwell forever in our Father's presence. Elder McConkie writes, "Their inheritance is in that realm from which no friend departs and into which no enemy enters. They are as God, and God is as he is from everlasting to everlasting" (*DNTC*, 3:458). Acceptance into the celestial kingdom is assured.

"I will write upon him the name of God" (Rev. 3:12) means that we are to be identified as gods and will be called gods. "Then shall they be gods, because they have no end; therefore shall they be from everlasting to everlasting, because they continue; then shall they be above all, because all things are subject unto them. Then shall they be gods, because they have all power, and the angels are subject unto them" (D&C 132:20).

"The name of the city of my God" (Rev. 3:12) is New Jerusalem and will be the holy city where all of the righteous Saints through all the ages will dwell for all eternity. To have the city's name written upon us means that we are residents of the holy city and dwell there eternally.

The Savior will write upon us his "new name" (Rev. 3:12) showing that he will share all things in common with us. Of this, Elder McConkie writes, "Thus, Christ's 'new name' shall be written upon all those who are joint-heirs with him (Rev. 3:12), and shall signify that they have become even as he is and he is even as the Father (3 Ne. 28:10)" (*DNTC*, 3:567).

To be granted "to sit with me [the Savior] in my throne," even as the Savior sits down with his Father in his throne (Rev.

3:21) is the culminating experience of all mortality and the temple. As we pass through the veil after having proven ourselves in *all* things, we are then found worthy to receive all that the Father has (see D&C 84:33–38). Eternal life is "to inherit the same power, the same glory and the same exaltation, until you arrive at the station of a God, and ascend the throne of eternal power, the same as those who have gone before" (*TPJS*, p. 347). These last four promises deal with being in the presence of the Father and the Son and knowing that we have been invited to be there. What greater blessing can we ever possibly hope for?

## SUMMARY

Though the seven letters were written almost 1,900 years ago, they are specifically for us. There were no printing presses as we know them today. The word was not copied for every member of the Church to have, as we find in the magazines of the Church today. Each of us can sit down, study the scriptures—especially the letters to the seven churches—and realize their relevancy for our day. It is clear what must be done to inherit all things in order to sit with the Savior and his Father in a celestial inheritance.

Robert Mounce recorded the following summary of the seven letters: "[John F.] Walvoord calls it a 'comprehensive warning' in which the dangers of losing our first love (Ephesus), fear of suffering (Smyrna), doctrinal compromise (Pergamum), moral compromise (Thyatira), spiritual deadness (Sardis), failure to hold fast (Philadelphia), and lukewarmness (Laodicea) are brought home with amazing relevance for the contemporary church" (p. 130).

The message is the same today as anciently. The Lord knows our works! He commends us for the actions we have already taken to prove our faithfulness. Like a loving Father he corrects, chastens, and rebukes us when we fall into error, allowing sin to creep in among us. Like a loving Father he counsels us in ways that we can better ourselves. Finally, as our Eternal Father, he promises us blessings which he is bound to give (see D&C 82:10) and which increase line upon line, precept upon precept, until we have received a fulness of joy in his kingdom, to go no more out. Can we even comprehend the great joy which awaits us? The great plan of happiness? (see Rom. 8:35–39; D&C 78:17).

# 4

## Descriptions of the Heavenly Throne

Chapter 4 of Revelation brings about significant changes. Previously John saw those things occurring on the earth, but now he is provided with a vista of heaven. As his view of the heavenly realm is brought to pass, he is able to leave the multitude of problems facing the earthly Church behind and focus on the heavenly glories. The opportunity to gaze into the expanses of eternity provides John with a view that few people have been allowed to enjoy.

The following chapters, encompassing Revelation 4–22, will teach us what will happen after John's time. The number seven comes into full discourse at this time. "The Hebrew name for the number 7, *sheva*, comes from the root meaning 'fulness' or 'perfection' " (*New Testament Seminary Teacher Outline*, p. 431). The number seven is used in conjunction with six specific areas in the book of Revelation, namely: churches, seals, trumpets, persons, vials, and judgments on the harlot. Note that the Savior also had seven wounds on his body when he was crucified (hands, wrists, feet, and side).

### REVELATION 4:1–3

1 ¶ AFTER this I looked, and, behold, a door was opened in heaven: and the first voice which I heard was as it were of a trumpet talking with me; which said, Come up hither, and I will shew thee things which must be hereafter.

2 And immediately I was in the spirit: and, behold, a throne was set in heaven, and one sat on the throne.

3 And he that sat was to look upon like a jasper and a sardine stone: and there was a rainbow round about the throne, in sight like unto an emerald.

**Verse Commentary**

4:1–3. The door is now opened for John to gaze into heaven and he sees the Father sitting on his throne. Here, the imagery of the rainbow and its transcendent beauty in an apparent half circle exemplify the beauties of heaven. In actuality the rainbow is a full circle and we only see the half above the horizon. From a plane one can see the full circle of light, very similar to John's position of seeing things from a totally new perspective. The things John will now see are those things to come, the hereafter, and will pertain to all things—past, present, and future—for all things are present before the Lord (see *TPJS*, p. 220).

4:3. The sardine stone (more popularly known as sard) is blood red. "The name jasper was given to a number of stones mostly green in color, though there was a red and yellow variety" (Draper, p. 45, n. 7). John combines the colors symbolizing life and death and has them radiating from the one who is the God of both. Even though numerous judgments will be poured out upon the earth, the rainbow is a symbol of one of God's covenants—he will not forget his people.

**Applicability**

John is allowed to see into heaven and we may be inclined to feel that he is experiencing things we can't even begin to imagine. But he has written this record to show unto us the mysteries revealed to him. Verse 2 records spiritual experiences which greatly strengthen our faith. Despite this example, often we don't record our experiences for future generations to read. We may not see into heaven as John did, but our spiritual experiences are of great enough importance that the Lord saw fit to give them to us. Adam and Eve kept a record of their experiences with the Lord, a "book of remembrance," and from that record they taught their children how to read and write (see Moses 6:5–6). What a great example for us to follow!

## REVELATION 4:4–11

4 And round about the throne were four and twenty seats: and upon the seats I saw four and twenty elders sitting, clothed in white raiment; and they had on their heads crowns of gold.

5 And out of the throne proceeded lightnings and thunderings and voices: and there were seven lamps of fire burning before the throne, which are the seven Spirits of God.

6 And before the throne there was a sea of glass like unto crystal: and in the midst of the throne, and round about the throne, were four beasts full of eyes before and behind.

7 And the first beast was like a lion, and the second beast like a calf, and the third beast had a face as a man, and the fourth beast was like a flying eagle.

8 ¶ And the four beasts had each of them six wings about him; and they were full of eyes within: and they rest not day and night, saying, Holy, holy, holy, Lord God Almighty, which was, and is, and is to come.

9 And when those beasts give glory and honour and thanks to him that sat on the throne, who liveth for ever and ever,

10 The four and twenty elders fall down before him that sat on the throne, and worship him that liveth for ever and ever, and cast their crowns before the throne, saying,

11 Thou art worthy, O Lord, to receive glory and honour and power: for thou hast created all things, and for thy pleasure they are and were created.

## Verse Commentary

4:4. John sees **round about the throne . . . four and twenty seats and . . . four and twenty elders . . . clothed in white raiment** and wearing **crowns of gold.** Latter-day revelation indicates that these elders would seem to be leaders of the Church in the dispensation of the meridian of time who have proven their faithfulness and are given power and authority, as spoken of in Revelation 2–3, to rule in our Father's presence. Through inspiration, the Prophet Joseph Smith received the following explanation, "We are to understand that these elders whom John saw, were elders who had been faithful in the work of the ministry and were dead; who belonged to the seven churches, and were then in the paradise of God" (D&C 77:5).

The number *twelve* represents priesthood. Here its multiple
(24) is used to suggest fulness. There were twenty-four priestly
courses and Levitical orders among the Jews, whose heads were
also called Elders (see 1 Chr. 24:7–18; 25:9–31). "According to
Homer Hailey, 'the number twenty-four suggests a combination
of the twelve patriarchs of the twelve tribes of Israel and the
twelve apostles, thus representing the redeemed of both
covenants now united through Christ' " (Draper, p. 46). In Revelation 21:12, 14 the names of the twelve Apostles are placed on
the foundation stones and the twelve Patriarchs are inscribed
over the gates. The priesthood office of these men is that of an
Elder, they are judges over Israel, they have received the oath
and covenant of the Father, and all that the Father has shall be
theirs (see D&C 84:33–40).

4:5. John describes the powerful forces of nature, which
majesty causes one to wonder at the glory, power, and majesty
of him who rules the heavens, and proclaims his messages to all
the earth by utilizing these forces. **Seven lamps** again refers us
to the lampstand from whence the light shines forth through the
Holy Spirit.

4:6. The **sea of glass** "is the earth, in its sanctified, immortal,
and eternal state" (D&C 77:1). The beast, **full of eyes before and
behind**, has the capability of seeing things to come (before), and
things which have passed (behind). The four beasts are
explained concisely in the following verses: "Q. What are we to
understand by the four beasts, spoken of in the same verse?

"A. They are figurative expressions, used by the Revelator,
John, in describing heaven, the paradise of God, the happiness
of man, and of beasts, and of creeping things, and of the fowls
of the air; that which is spiritual being in the likeness of that
which is temporal; and that which is temporal in the likeness of
that which is spiritual; the spirit of man in the likeness of his
person, as also the spirit of the beast, and every other creature
which God has created.

"Q. Are the four beasts limited to individual beasts, or do
they represent classes or orders?

"A. They are limited to four individual beasts, which were

shown to John, to represent the glory of the classes of beings in their destined order or sphere of creation, in the enjoyment of their eternal felicity" (D&C 77:2–3).

Note what the Prophet Joseph Smith said about the beasts: "The prophets do not declare that they saw a beast or beasts, but that they saw the *image* or *figure* of a beast. Daniel did not see an actual bear or a lion, but the images or figures of those beasts. The translation should have been rendered 'image' instead of 'beast,' in every instance where beasts are mentioned by the prophets. But John saw the actual beast in heaven, showing to John that beasts did actually exist there, and not to represent figures of things on the earth. When the prophets speak of seeing beasts in their visions, they mean that they saw the images, they being types to represent certain things. At the same time they received the interpretation as to what those images or types were designed to represent" (*TPJS*, p. 291).

4:6 9. The **four beasts** represent each of the classes of living beings on the earth and in the heavens, namely: lion—wild creatures, calf—domestic creatures, man—children of God, eagle—creatures in the skies. Notice that they are praising and thanking the Lord and **rest not day and night,** or in other words, continually praising the Lord for what he has done. Each of the beasts had **six wings,** representing power to move and to act. They were **full of eyes,** representing light and knowledge. In other words, the living beasts are full of light and knowledge and have the ability to act and move quickly (see D&C 77:4).

John uses the Greek word *zōon,* meaning living being, to describe the beasts, but later uses *thēriŏn* to describe the wild beasts, or associates of Satan, who use entrapment to snare their prize.

4:10–11. The **four and twenty elders** respond to God the same as the beasts; they **fall down before him that sat on the throne, and worship him.** All things are in subjection to the Lord and they praise him for his works. They **cast their crowns before the throne.** They realize and acknowledge him who is King of Kings and Lord of Lords, having all prestige, authority, power, and dominion over all those who dwell upon the earth.

They are in subjection to their king and cast their crowns before him as a symbol of their honor and respect of his authority. Joseph Smith, being directed by the Lord, expounds: "We are to understand that these elders whom John saw, were elders who had been faithful in the work of the ministry and were dead; who belonged to the seven churches, and were then in the paradise of God" (D&C 77:5).

The time will come that all things which have been created will bow down and give praise and glory to the Savior and his Father.

## Applicability

Those beings and beasts standing before and around the throne are not singing praises because they are required to by their King. They are singing the praises of the person who has delivered them from the adversary. Many religions in the world today falsely assume that when we die and return to that God who gave us life we will simply praise him all day long for his glory. God does not create things simply for the gratification of having praises sung to him forevermore. Obviously, God does not need us to sing praises to him, rather, we will sing as a sincere expression of our love and gratitude for what we have become through his assistance.

## SUMMARY

The fulness of the Savior's glory is realized as all creation express their love and gratitude and praise for the King of Kings and Lord of Lords. All things are in subjection to the Lord and they shall worship him continually, for ever and ever, eternally. Our love and gratitude for the sacrifice of the Savior will always be manifest in our expressions of praise and honor for him as our Lord and King. As is evidenced by this chapter, all life flows from him, and those who are exalted shall return to him and praise him forever.

# 5

## THE LAMB WHO IS WORTHY
## TO OPEN THE SEALS

We continue to learn more about the greatness, glory, and power of the Savior. A book is seen containing "the revealed will, mysteries, and the works of God" (D&C 77:6) but which no man can open because of unworthiness. Here, unworthiness represents lack of authority, and only Christ has overcome all things and is worthy to open the sealed pages of the book. This chapter will provide us with more evidence of the power the Savior has, through his obedience and faithfulness, and the truths which are provided for our understanding because of his sacrifice.

All things are present before God. He has established the plan of salvation from the beginning of time but one must come forth who has proven himself worthy in all things, and that one is Christ. At the time that the Lord opens the book it is full of the events to take place here on the earth. There is nothing in God's plan he doesn't know, otherwise he would cease to be God.

A seal is symbolic of authority from the one who has sealed the object, and only one with proper authority is allowed to break the seal. Until the seal was broken, by the proper authority, the contents were considered authentic and all things included therein were unknown to the world and would remain as such until they were carried out.

### REVELATION 5:1–7

1 ¶ And I saw in the right hand of him that sat on the throne a book written within and on the back-side, sealed with seven seals.

2 And I saw a strong angel proclaiming with a loud voice, Who is

worthy to open the book, and to loose the seals thereof?

3 And no man in heaven, nor in earth, neither under the earth, was able to open the book, neither to look thereon.

4 And I wept much, because no man was found worthy to open and to read the book, neither to look thereon.

5 And one of the elders saith unto me, Weep not: behold, the Lion of the tribe of Juda, the Root of David, hath prevailed to open the book, and to loose the seven seals thereof.

6 ¶ And I beheld, and, lo, in the midst of the throne and of the four beasts, and in the midst of the elders, stood a Lamb as it had been slain, having seven horns and seven eyes, which are the seven Spirits of God sent forth into all the earth.

7 And he came and took the book out of the right hand of him that sat upon the throne.

## Verse Commentary

*5:1.* He **that sat on the throne** with the book in his right hand is the Father, Elohim. We understand that the book with the seven seals "contains the revealed will, mysteries, and the works of God; the hidden things of his economy concerning this earth during the seven thousand years of its continuance, or its temporal existence" (D&C 77:6). We also understand that the seven seals are composed of each thousand-year period of the earth's existence, thus "the first seal contains the things of the first thousand years, and the second also of the second thousand years, and so on until the seventh" (D&C 77:7).

*5:2.* The **strong angel** would seem to be one of the noble and great ones (see Abr. 3:22–23) who has proven his faithfulness, but is not **worthy**. The Greek *axios* means "deserving," and would indicate that none is qualified or has accomplished the necessary requirements to open the book (*Strong's*, Greek Dictionary, p. 13).

*5:3–5.* No one is found worthy to open the book! The truths of God would not be revealed unless one is found. Even John states that he **wept much** because no one was found. One of the elders declares who has the power—the **Lion of the tribe of Juda, the Root of David** (Christ), has prevailed and is deserving to open the book and loose the seals. Christ is the Root of David.

Elder Bruce R. McConkie declares that, "this designation signifies that he who was the Son of David was also before David [the root], was pre-eminent above him, and was the root or source from which the great king in Israel gained his kingdom and power" (*MD*, p. 657).

Although man has prevailed over many things, Christ is the only one who has prevailed over all things, thereby giving him the power to break the seals and reveal the will of God regarding all eternal things.

5:6. The **Lamb** is the Savior, slain from the foundation of the world. He stands in the midst of the throne and the assembly of elders and beasts, as the eternal center focus. He was foreordained in the premortal life to be the Savior and Redeemer of mankind. From the days of Adam down to Jesus Christ, a lamb without blemish, unspotted, was offered in similitude of the sacrifice of the Only Begotten of the Father (see 1 Pet. 1:19; Moses 5:6–7). It is through the blood of the Lamb that, "though [our] sins be as scarlet, they shall be as white as snow" (Isa. 1:18). John sees a lamb, even though the Savior has also just been spoken of as a lion (v. 5). This beautiful comparison shows both the power (lion) and humility or meekness (lamb) of our Lord and Savior.

The **twelve horns ... twelve eyes ... twelve servants** (JST) are clearly priesthood holders with special power (horns) and gifts of seership (eyes) (see Symbols Guide). The Greek word *apŏstĕllō* is translated as "set apart" and **sent forth** (*Strong's, Greek Dictionary*, p. 15), and represents the Apostles (servants) who were sent forth unto all the world by Christ.

5:7. The Lamb takes the book **out of the right hand** (the covenant hand), of the Father. It is the responsibility of the Lamb to see that the things recorded in the book are fulfilled. The Father has committed all things unto the Son, and for this reason the Son is the one who has the authority to take the book out of the covenant hand of the Father and fulfill his promises.

## Applicability

Only Christ the Lord has the authority to open the seven

seals which have been sealed by the hand of God. He is the center of the plan of salvation and is the one who broke the bands of death, in the same way that he broke the seven seals of the book. Through him all things are possible. Through Christ, the trials, difficulties, and challenges we face are not impossible to overcome.

## REVELATION 5:8–14

8 And when he had taken the book, the four beasts and four and twenty elders fell down before the Lamb, having every one of them harps, and golden vials full of odours, which are the prayers of saints.

9 And they sung a new song, saying, Thou art worthy to take the book, and to open the seals thereof: for thou wast slain, and hast redeemed us to God by thy blood out of every kindred, and tongue, and people, and nation;

10 And hast made us unto our God kings and priests: and we shall reign on the earth.

11 And I beheld, and I heard the voice of many angels round about the throne and the beasts and the elders: and the number of them was ten thousand times ten thousand, and thousands of thousands;

12 Saying with a loud voice, Worthy is the Lamb that was slain to receive power, and riches, and wisdom, and strength, and honour, and glory, and blessing.

13 And every creature which is in heaven, and on the earth, and under the earth, and such as are in the sea, and all that are in them, heard I saying, Blessing, and honour, and glory, and power, be unto him that sitteth upon the throne, and unto the Lamb for ever and ever.

14 And the four beasts said, Amen. And the four and twenty elders fell down and worshipped him that liveth for ever and ever.

## Verse Commentary

*5:8–10.* As the Savior takes the book, the four beasts and twenty-four elders take the opportunity to sing a song of praise and gratitude for the Savior. He is worthy! The book can be opened and the mysteries of God can be unfolded. The Savior was slain, and **he hast redeemed us!** It is important that we comprehend the term *redemption.* In *Mormon Doctrine,* Elder McConkie draws from President Joseph Fielding Smith to provide a definition. "*Redemption* is of two kinds: conditional and unconditional. *Conditional redemption* is synonymous with exaltation or eternal life. It comes by the grace of God coupled with good works and includes redemption from the effects of both the temporal and spiritual fall. Those so redeemed become sons and daughters in the Lord's kingdom and inherit all things. And this is the chief sense in which the term *redemption* is used in the scriptures (*Doctrines of Salvation*, vol. 2, pp. 9–13.)" (p. 623).

Each of the groups breaks forth and sings a new song. Notice the words of the song which the beasts and the elders sing. "Thou art worthy to take the book, and to open the seals thereof: for thou wast slain, and hast redeemed us to God by thy blood out of every kindred, and tongue, and people, and nation; And hast made us unto our God kings and priests: and we shall reign on earth" (Rev. 5:9–10).

What a glorious and beautiful song! Consider the doctrinal teachings in each line of the song, along with the testimony of the plan of salvation brought about through Jesus Christ. He is worthy to take the book and reveal the eternal truths therein. He was slain, and by his sacrifice, has provided us with the opportunity to be redeemed and to return to our Father's presence. Finally, he has shared all of the rights, powers, and privileges of exaltation with us as we are made kings and priests in the kingdom of his Father. Imagine our feelings if we could witness and participate in such an event!

*5:11–12.* An army of angels surrounds the throne. **Ten thousand times ten thousand and thousands of thousands**. That sum is one hundred million—and more! This grand assembly of exalted beings now joins in singing the second anthem of the new song which is: "Worthy is the Lamb that was slain to receive power, and riches, and wisdom, and strength, and honour, and glory, and blessing" (Rev. 5:12).

All of the attributes of the Savior are praised by this vast army of angels with each of the attributes revealing an omnipotent aspect of him, all of which he receives because he was slain and is worthy of these things.

*5:13–14.* All beings now fall down and worship the Savior.

All of creation now joins together in singing the final anthem of the song and expressing our gratitude for him, King and Lord. "Blessing, and honour, and glory, and power, be unto him that sitteth upon the throne, and unto the Lamb for ever and ever" (Rev. 5:13).

## Applicability

Those who have experienced the blessings of forgiveness and who have been able to overcome some temptation, look forward to the day when they, through the assistance of the Savior, can stand before him and sing praises of glory to him. Redeemed! To redeem is to pay a price for someone when it is impossible for them to pay the price. Because of the sacrifice of Jesus Christ, we have been redeemed and are made kings and priests to our God. It is up to each of us to take advantage of this redemption and enjoy the blessings and the joys of repentance in our lives, and gain full appreciation for the remission of our sins.

## SUMMARY

The greatness and glory of the Son of God, the Savior of the World is declared once again. Could we ever possibly express too much recognition for our Redeemer? Can we fully comprehend what he has done for us? He was able to open the book. He was slain, has redeemed us by his blood, and has made us kings and priests, queens and priestesses unto our God! He has saved us, and exalted us. No one is excluded from these opportunities except by rejecting the Savior. All kindreds, tongues, peoples, and nations have this opportunity before them and it is theirs to accept or reject. The Son of God, a God himself, gave himself as a sacrifice, or ransom, for his brothers and sisters, all of our Father's children, so that we could return to live with him again. What a *great* plan of happiness!

# 6

# THE SIX SEALS

The Savior will now begin to do what no other being could do, and so one by one he breaks each of the seven seals. Each seal corresponds to a set portion of the earth's history: "The first seal contains the things of the first thousand years, and the second also of the second thousand years, and so on until the seventh" (D&C 77:7). Although each seal is broken, the scroll (of which the exact meaning is unknown) will not open until the seventh seal has been broken. A brief explanation of the opening of the seals is found in Doctrine and Covenants 88:108–10 which says, "Then shall the first angel sound his trump in the ears of all living, and reveal the secret acts of men, and the mighty works of God in the first thousand years. And then shall the second angel sound his trump, and reveal the secret acts of men, and the thoughts and intents of their hearts, and the mighty works of God in the second thousand years—and so on, until the seventh angel shall sound his trump; and he shall stand forth upon the land and upon the sea, and swear in the name of him who sitteth upon the throne, that there shall be time no longer; and Satan shall be bound."

The Symbols Guide will help to distinguish what the colors of the horses represent in this chapter. The horse symbolizes battle, therefore chapter 6 will describe battles between the forces of good and evil, and will prepare us for the eventual overcoming of all things by the Lord.

## REVELATION 6:1–11

1 ¶ AND I saw when the Lamb opened one of the seals, and I heard, as it were the noise of thunder, one of the four beasts saying, Come and see.

2 And I saw, and behold a white horse: and he that sat on him had a bow; and a crown was given unto him: and he went forth conquering, and to conquer.

3 ¶ And when he had opened the second seal, I heard the second beast say, Come and see.

4 And there went out another horse that was red: and power was given to him that sat thereon to take peace from the earth, and that they should kill one another: and there was given unto him a great sword.

5 And when he had opened the third seal, I heard the third beast say, Come and see. And I beheld, and lo a black horse; and he that sat on him had a pair of balances in his hand.

6 And I heard a voice in the midst of the four beasts say, A measure of wheat for a penny, and three measures of barley for a penny; and see thou hurt not the oil and the wine.

7 And when he had opened the fourth seal, I heard the voice of the fourth beast say, Come and see.

8 And I looked, and behold a pale horse: and his name that sat on him was Death, and Hell followed with him. And power was given unto them over the fourth part of the earth, to kill with sword, and with hunger, and with death, and with the beasts of the earth.

9 ¶ And when he had opened the fifth seal, I saw under the altar the souls of them that were slain for the word of God, and for the testimony which they held:

10 And they cried with a loud voice, saying, How long, O Lord, holy and true, dost thou not judge and avenge our blood on them that dwell on the earth?

11 And white robes were given unto every one of them; and it was said unto them, that they should rest yet for a little season, until their fellowservants also and their brethren, that should be killed as they were, should be fulfilled.

## Verse Commentary

*6:1–2.* The first thousand years, approximately 4000 B.C. to 3000 B.C., extends from "the fall of Adam . . . to shortly after the translation of Enoch and his city in 3017 B.C." (*DNTC*, 3:476).

The **white horse** is symbolic of purity and victory in battle. The **bow** is a weapon of war, and he who sat on the horse wore a **crown**, the emblem of victory. He went forth **conquering, and**

**to conquer**. Nothing can stand in his path. His righteousness overcomes all evil. There is one who stands firmly in this position in this time frame and that is Enoch. Notice the parallels with what we read in the book of Moses: "And so great was the faith of Enoch that he led the people of God, and their enemies came to battle against them; and he spake the word of the Lord, and the earth trembled, and the mountains fled, even according to his command; and the rivers of water were turned out of their course; and the roar of the lions was heard out of the wilderness; and all nations feared greatly, so powerful was the word of Enoch, and so great was the power of language which God had given him. . . . And from that time forth there were wars and bloodshed among them; but the Lord came and dwelt with his people, and they dwelt in righteousness. The fear of the Lord was upon all nations, so great was the glory of the Lord, which was upon his people" (7:13, 17).

The battle does not speak specifically of bows and swords but quite often references the power and word of the Lord. It is comparable to our fighting the servants of Satan when we must use priesthood power to destroy them. "Pray always, that you may come off conqueror; yea, that you may conquer Satan, and that you may escape the hands of the servants of Satan that do uphold his work" (D&C 10:5).

6:3–4. The second thousand years, approximately 3000 B.C. to 2000 B.C., depicts the **horse that was red** as a symbol of war and bloodshed. The dragon in chapter 12 is the same color as this horse and is representative of Satan. Men became so wicked during this period of time that peace was taken from the earth; death was prevalent everywhere. The **great sword** is from the Greek word *machaira*, symbolizing "war" and "judicial punishment" (*Strong's*, Greek Dictionary, p. 46). The earth received judicial punishment in 2348 B.C. when it was cleansed by water and of all wickedness during the time of Noah, the second millennial prophet.

6:5–6. The third thousand years, approximately 2000 B.C. to 1000 B.C., shows the **black horse** representing death by hunger. "As famine follows the sword, so the pangs of hunger gnawed in the bellies of the Lord's people during the third seal" (*DNTC*, 3:479).

The third thousand-year period was represented by Abraham and his challenges with famine and drought, which took the life of his brother, Haran. Famine continued into the days of Jacob and Joseph, when Joseph saved the life of his family. After being delivered from the Pharaoh, the children of Israel were preserved from the famine and death, being fed by manna from heaven during their forty years in the wilderness.

The **pair of balances** represents judgment and is figurative of man's tribulation (see *Strong's*, Greek Dictionary, p. 26). God's judgment is balanced and although he will bring famine upon the earth because of the wickedness of men, he will also remember his covenants and will provide a way for his promises to the righteous to be fulfilled. Famine also represents scarcity (whether of food and sustenance or of the word of God) and the use of balances insures complete equity in all of the dealings between men and God.

Both of the measures (**a measure of wheat . . . and three measures of barley for a penny**) represent a payment for what a man would receive for one day's wages (a penny). The barley was the cheaper and less nutritious of the two grains, and would be bought by him who could not buy enough wheat for his family with his day's wages.

To **hurt not the oil and the wine** refers to providing enough resources so that man would not perish. "[Oil and wine] were closely associated with the burnt offerings of the temple in which they acted as sacrificial elements along with the animal. . . . The Seer [John] may have been suggesting that God's house would survive the famine" (Draper, p. 66). One must also consider that when the Lord requires an offering, the individual making the offering will have sufficient for the sacrifice and for his needs.

6:7–8. The fourth thousand years, approximately 1000 B.C. to the coming of the Messiah, exhibits a pale horse. Some translations, the New Revised Standard Version for example, describe the fourth horse as "pale green." The Greek original uses *chlōrŏs* to identify the color of Death's horse. *Chlōrŏs*, according to *The New Strong's Exhaustive Concordance of the Bible*, can be translated as "green" or "pale" (Greek Dictionary, p. 78). If we consider green to be the color of life, the pale coloring of the horse could be interpreted as a counterfeit of true green—the horse's color identifies the rider, Death. **Death, and Hell,** the two forms opposite of life (see 2 Ne. 9:10–12), both physical and spiritual, are continually present during this period of time. Great battles took place during this period and death was preeminent as thousands of lives were lost on the battlefield and kingdoms were divided and overrun.

From 1095 B.C. when Saul assumed power in Israel continuing with David's slaying of Goliath in 1063 B.C. and even up through the Assyrian attack of 760 B.C., it seems that Israel was constantly engaged in some type of war. This continued during the Babylonian era of 605 to 538 B.C., including the destruction of Jerusalem in 586 B.C. The citizens of Jerusalem also endured the Medo-Persian empire from 538–333 B.C., Alexander the Great's conquest of Persia in 332 B.C., and finally Julius Caesar's world domination in 60 B.C. (see *DNTC*, 3:481).

**Power was given unto them over the fourth part of the earth.** It is impossible for Satan to have any power to tempt or afflict man unless it is given to him, but the opportunity to tempt must be given to him to *allow* for our agency, an integral part of the whole plan of salvation. To be given power over the fourth part (a portion of the whole) means that his power was restricted to just a portion of the earth; this is significant in that Satan's influences are always partially restricted.

We must understand the manner in which Death (physical) will be allowed to carry on his wicked desires, by **sword, hunger, death** (plagues and diseases), and **the beasts of the earth.** To kill with death is "to slay with pestilence" (*DNTC*, 3:482). Once again the use of four things (sword, hunger, death, beasts) is representative of geographic fulness. The whole world is subject to these horrors, brought about through the evil designs of men seeking after power.

*6:9–11.* The fifth thousand-year period, approximately A.D. 0

to A.D. 1000, is described without any horses being ridden. The form of battle has changed as the adversary attempts to eradicate the followers of Christ by destroying their testimonies or inflicting pain or suffering upon the righteous, even unto death, in his feeble attempt to nullify the cause of Christ. The battlegrounds are centered in the following periods: 1) the birth of Jesus Christ, his ministry, his atoning sacrifice in Gethsemane, and the crucifixion on Golgotha, 2) the organization and spread of Christianity, and 3) the complete apostasy of the Church from truth.

The **altar** suggests sacrifice. Those men and women that John saw in vision and who had died for the word's sake were, in reality, sacrificing their lives on the altar of God. "Their position **under the altar** suggests that they were martyrs, their souls resting there only because their lives had been offered, as it were, upon it. During sacrificial rites the blood of the victim, symbolic of its life, was poured out at the altar's base, seeping beneath it (see Lev. 4:7; 17:11). . . . What made their lives a sacrifice for righteousness was not in dying for the faith, but in living for it" (Draper, p. 69, emphasis added; see also Rom. 12:1).

Those who are the martyrs then cry out to the Lord, **How long, O Lord, holy and true, dost thou not judge and avenge our blood on them that dwell on the earth?** They plead with him to avenge their blood by pouring out his judgments upon the wicked.

*6:11.* The **white robes** are given to the pure and victorious. Those who were martyrs will yet receive glories beyond comprehension for their sacrifices. They are told to rest, until all those who would be slain, for the same beliefs, had been slain and all things were fulfilled. Apostles, prophets, saints, missionaries, and pioneers who have given their lives in proclamation of the gospel of Jesus Christ, are martyrs for the cause of Christ, and they will receive their white robes (see Matt. 23:29–33; Luke 11:47–51; Acts 7; 22:20; Hel. 13:24–28; D&C 135).

## Applicability

Many times we pass over the first five-thousand-year period of the earth's existence and act as though it doesn't really apply to us. In reality, there are many great things to learn from the history of this period. Whenever the people were righteous they were abundantly blessed, and whenever they began to forget the Lord and to worship the creations of their own hands, they turned from the Lord and brought judgment upon themselves. It is no different in this day and age. We see the plagues, pestilences, and diseases that are prevalent upon the earth and they are often upon those who have not hearkened to the counsels of the Lord. The plagues are not necessarily vindictive punishment unleashed on the wicked, but are consequences directly resulting from unrighteous behavior.

It is also important to remember that the Lord allows righteous people to suffer at the hands of the wicked as a testimony against the wicked at the last day. Those who suffer in such a manner have the assurance of the Lord that they will receive glory in our Father's presence.

## REVELATION 6:12–17

12 And I beheld when he had opened the sixth seal, and, lo, there was a great earthquake; and the sun became black as sackcloth of hair, and the moon became as blood;

13 And the stars of heaven fell unto the earth, even as a fig tree casteth her untimely figs, when she is shaken of a mighty wind.

14 And the heaven departed as a scroll when it is rolled together; and every mountain and island were moved out of their places.

15 And the kings of the earth, and the great men, and the rich men, and the chief captains, and the mighty men, and every bondman, and every free man, hid themselves in the dens and in the rocks of the mountains;

16 And said to the mountains and rocks, Fall on us, and hide us from the face of him that sitteth on the throne, and from the wrath of the Lamb:

17 For the great day of his wrath is come; and who shall be able to stand?

**Verse Commentary** *

*6:12.* The **sixth seal** now opens. The sixth thousand-year period, approximately A.D. 1000 to A.D. 2000, is typified by much unrest occurring upon the earth, both temporally and among mankind. The Greek word for **earthquake**, *sĕismŏs*, represents a "commotion" or "tempest," either figurative or literal, and can imply any experience that causes one to fear and tremble (*Strong's*, Greek Dictionary, p. 64). Verses 12–17 are all indicative of the last days leading up to the opening of the seventh seal and the return of the Savior to the earth. The wicked will have cause to fear and tremble when the judgments of the Lord come down upon them to cleanse the earth.

*6:12–14.* On December 27, 1832, the Lord revealed to Joseph Smith the following: "Not many days hence and the earth shall tremble and reel to and fro as a drunken man; and the sun shall hide his face, and shall refuse to give light; and the moon shall be bathed in blood; and the stars shall become exceedingly angry, and shall cast themselves down as a fig that falleth from off a fig-tree" (D&C 88:87; see also D&C 29:14; 133:49).

*6:14.* The **heavens opened as a scroll is opened** (JST) seems to indicate that a new heaven and new earth will be brought about when the Lord comes again (see *DNTC*, 3:487). One is also left to consider that the book (scroll) of life of the heavens and earth is now about to be seen and experienced by all people on the earth and in heaven.

*6:15.* The earthquake will cause such commotion on the earth that all men, except for those who know the signs of the times and place their faith in God and Christ, will be fleeing for their lives. They will flee because they know that their works have been works of darkness and that they are fully accountable before the Lord. The day of their reckoning has arrived. No one will escape the judgments to be poured out upon the earth.

Mindful that the Hebrew number seven connoted completeness, Richard Draper writes, "The Seer notes seven consequences to the wickedness of mankind: (1) the earthquake, (2) the darkened sun, (3) the reddening of the moon, (4) the stars falling, (5) the heavens rolling up, (6) the mountains and islands moving out of their places, and (7) the universal consternation of mankind. Further, he notes seven classes of men who will be affected: (1) kings, (2) great men, (3) rich men, (4) chief captains, (5) mighty men, (6) bondmen, and (7) free men" (p. 73).

No one will be able to hide from the consequences poured out upon the earth. At this point in the Revelation, the Lord has done all things possible to entice men on earth to take advantage of the things of God. Their time is now past.

*6:16.* The men of the earth will plead for the chance to hide from the face and wrath of the Lamb and will even plead to the mountains, **Fall on us, and hide us from the face of him that sitteth on the throne, and from the wrath of the Lamb.** All things will now be subdued under his feet, and judgment will begin to be sent forth upon the earth.

"Hearken, O ye nations of the earth, and hear the words of that God who made you. O, ye nations of the earth, how often would I have gathered you together as a hen gathereth her chickens under her wings, but ye would not! How oft have I called upon you by the mouth of my servants, and by the ministering of angels, and by mine own voice, and by the voice of thunderings, and by the voice of lightnings, and by the voice of tempests, and by the voice of earthquakes, and great hailstorms, and by the voice of famines and pestilences of every kind, and by the great sound of a trump, and by the voice of judgment, and by the voice of mercy all the day long, and by the voice of glory and honor and the riches of eternal life, and would have saved you with an everlasting salvation, but ye would not! Behold, the day has come, when the cup of the wrath of mine indignation is full" (D&C 43:23–26).

Can we even comprehend any greater statement from the Lord as to his feelings? No mere mortal could have possibly penned such a great declaration of judgment as this! Anyone living a telestial law will be destroyed at his coming and will not endure his presence. How many times has the Lord given some type of sign or warning to those upon the earth? How many ways has he attempted to turn his people to him, and they would not? Therefore, those who have not heeded the warning voice of God must now endure his wrath.

6:17. The **great day of his wrath** is now descending upon the earth and all those who have mocked God, or his servants, will receive the judgments that are theirs. It is not because he is vindictive and wants to pour out judgments upon the wicked, but, the law and the consequences of wickedness must be paid by the unrepentant. Who shall stand? The answer will begin to come forward in chapter seven.

## Applicability

There can be no one who says that they were never warned or told of the judgments to come upon those who reject the Lord or his servants. There are some in the world today who think that their wealth and precious things, or their position and power, or their honors of men will save them. They think that they are impervious to the destructions to come upon the earth, but this is not the case. Wealth, in and of itself, is not bad, but "the *love of money* is the root of all evil" (1 Tim. 6:10, emphasis added). In many ways, the wealth one has is measured by his testimony of and faith in Jesus Christ. When destructions come upon the earth, in the form of earthquakes, floods, fire, and so forth, no one is exempt. If this is truly the case, wouldn't it be wise for us to purchase that which is not for sale in monetary aspects, but requires a broken heart and contrite spirit?

## SUMMARY

John is allowed to see the great consequences which will be poured out upon the wicked and to see what they will do to flee from the Lord. Before these judgments can be poured out, the gospel and its fulness must be upon the earth. In 1830, as the sixth seal progressed to its close, the gospel was restored. Some have been fooled into thinking that because the Restoration was over 160 years ago everything is now past. However, if some of the things spoken of in chapter 6 have now taken place, how much closer can the other things be?

Whenever the Lord has uttered his promises of things to come to pass, whether by his voice, or that of his servants, it will come to pass (see D&C 1:37–38). This glorious promise should provide comfort to the faithful Saints, and should cause fear to come upon the wicked. The righteous have no need to fear, for they will be caught up to meet him.

# THE 144,000 AND THE SEAL OF THE LIVING GOD

Chapter 6 ended with many people fleeing from the wrath of God. One would expect the next chapter to entail the plagues and destructions which will come upon those people, but suddenly the vision changes. Those individuals who would be righteous and abide the Lord's coming are now given comfort and encouragement for the things to come. Before the Lord sends forth his angels with power over all things on the earth, he will comfort those who have had to face such adversity in their time here, and he will restore the fulness of the gospel to the earth.

Those who are, or truly consider themselves, faithful should read chapter 7 with the understanding that the Lord will, and does, fulfill his promises (see D&C 82:10; 130:20–21). This whole chapter is one of promised blessings for the faithful who overcome. The seventh seal will be opened and with it will come judgments the world has never known, but the Lord will also bless and prosper his people. He will gather them in and will protect them from the judgments to be poured out upon the wicked. All who read these things should truly desire to be counted with the faithful when the Lord gathers his people home.

## REVELATION 7:1–8

1 ¶ And after these things I saw four angels standing on the four corners of the earth, holding the four winds of the earth, that the wind should not blow on the earth, nor on the sea, nor on any tree.

2 And I saw another angel

ascending from the east, having the seal of the living God: and he cried with a loud voice to the four angels, to whom it was given to hurt the earth and the sea,

3 Saying, Hurt not the earth, neither the sea, nor the trees, till we have sealed the servants of our God in their foreheads.

4 And I heard the number of them which were sealed: and there were sealed an hundred and forty and four thousand of all the tribes of the children of Israel.

5 Of the tribe of Juda were sealed twelve thousand. Of the tribe of Reuben were sealed twelve thousand. Of the tribe of Gad were sealed twelve thousand.

6 Of the tribe of Aser were sealed twelve thousand. Of the tribe of Nepthalim were sealed twelve thousand. Of the tribe of Manasses were sealed twelve thousand.

7 Of the tribe of Simeon were sealed twelve thousand. Of the tribe of Levi were sealed twelve thousand. Of the tribe of Issachar were sealed twelve thousand.

8 Of the tribe of Zabulon were sealed twelve thousand. Of the tribe of Joseph were sealed twelve thousand. Of the tribe of Benjamin were sealed twelve thousand.

## Verse Commentary

*7:1.* The **four angels** are sent forth from God. The number four represents geographical fulness, meaning that the whole earth will be involved. The Doctrine and Covenants further states, "Q. What are we to understand by the four angels, spoken of in the 7th chapter and 1st verse of Revelation?

"A. We are to understand that they are four angels sent forth from God, to whom is given power over the four parts of the earth, to save life and to destroy; these are they who have the everlasting gospel to commit to every nation, kindred, tongue, and people; having power to shut up the heavens, to seal up unto life, or to cast down to the regions of darkness. . . .

"Q. What time are the things spoken of in this chapter to be accomplished?

"A. They are to be accomplished in the sixth thousand years, or the opening of the sixth seal" (D&C 77:8, 10).

The four angels are holding in the winds, powers so devastating that people in biblical times viewed these winds as evidence of divine wrath. "The mention of sun and withering heat in verse sixteen suggests that John had in mind a sirocco, a scorching wind that burnt up vegetation and left the land dust dry" (Draper, p. 77). As the winds are unleashed they will bring forth a destructive power which will cover the face of the earth, as represented by the use of four angels, but the winds are not released upon the earth—yet.

7:2. The angel **ascending from the east** and **having the seal of the living God** is explained as follows: "Q. What are we to understand by the angel ascending from the east, Revelation 7th chapter and 2nd verse?

"A. We are to understand that the angel ascending from the east is he to whom is given the seal of the living God over the twelve tribes of Israel; wherefore, he crieth unto the four angels having the everlasting gospel, saying: Hurt not the earth, neither the sea, nor the trees, till we have sealed the servants of our God in their foreheads. And, if you will receive it, this is Elias which was to come to gather together the tribes of Israel and restore all things" (D&C 77:9).

Any messenger coming from the presence of the Lord, with a revelation or message for his people can be considered an Elias. We are told that Christ is the Elias who was to restore all things (see JST John 1:21–28). We also know of other individuals who have the title of Elias, such as the angel Gabriel, otherwise known as Noah (see *TPJS*, p. 157; D&C 27:6–7; Luke 1:11–19), along with the promised Elias being named as John the Revelator (see D&C 77:9, 14).

All of the messengers who would qualify as an Elias—Moroni, John the Baptist, Peter, James, John, Moses, Elijah, Elias, Gabriel, and Michael (see *DS*, 1:170–74)—have returned to the earth in the latter days, as testified by Joseph Smith. Each brought the keys of their dispensation back to the earth and bestowed those privileges upon the head of this dispensation, namely Joseph Smith.

The phrase **hurt not** (v. 3) indicates that the angels will not bring justice upon the people at this time, but they will be allowed to do so in the future. Speaking to a group of temple workers assembled in Brigham City, Utah's Box Elder Stake

Tabernacle, President Wilford Woodruff said, "Can you tell me where the people are who will be shielded and protected from these calamities and judgments which are even now at our doors? I'll tell you. The priesthood of God who honor their priesthood, and who are worthy of their blessings are the only ones who shall have this safety and protection. They are the only mortal beings. No other people have a right to be shielded from these judgments. They are at our very doors; not even this people will escape them entirely. They will come down like the judgments of Sodom and Gomorrah. And none but the priesthood will be safe from their fury. God has held the angels of destruction for many years, lest they should reap down the wheat with the tares. But I want to tell you now, that those angels have left the portals of heaven, and they stand over this people and this nation now, and are hovering over the earth waiting to pour out the judgments. And from this very day they shall be poured out. Calamities and troubles are increasing in the earth, and there is a meaning to these things. Remember this, and reflect upon these matters. If you do your duty, and I do my duty, we'll have protection, and shall pass through the afflictions in peace and in safety. Read the scriptures and the revelations. They will tell you about these things" (*The Young Woman's Journal* 5, 11:512–13).

7:3. The angels will not be loosed until the **servants of our God** have been **sealed . . . in their foreheads.** According to Joseph Smith this sealing "signifies sealing the blessing upon their heads, meaning the everlasting covenant, thereby making their calling and election sure. When a seal is put upon the father and mother, it secures their posterity, so that they cannot be lost, but will be saved by virtue of the covenant of their father and mother" (*TPJS*, p. 321).

Oftentimes the people in John's day would mark their foreheads with the sign or symbol of whomever they desired to follow, especially as it related to the god they worshipped. To have his name "sealed . . . in [our] foreheads" (Rev. 7:3) is to be designated as a true and faithful servant of the Lord.

7:4–8. The number sealed were **an hundred and forty and four thousand of all the tribes of the children of Israel.** Two important things are to be considered about this number. First, this number is representative of a great priesthood body representing each of the twelve tribes and being sent forth to the nations of the earth. The Doctrine and Covenants fully explains what is meant as follows: "Q. What are we to understand by sealing the one hundred and forty-four thousand, out of all the tribes of Israel—twelve thousand out of every tribe?

"A. We are to understand that those who are sealed are high priests, ordained unto the holy order of God, to administer the everlasting gospel; for they are they who are ordained out of every nation, kindred, tongue, and people, by the angels to whom is given power over the nations of the earth, to bring as many as will come to the church of the Firstborn" (D&C 77:11).

It is interesting to note that the priesthood quorums of the Church are organized in multiples of twelve. First, the deacons are a body of 12 members, teachers are of 24, priests are of 48, and elders are of 96. The first quorum, that of the deacons, is complete when the membership reaches the basic priesthood number of twelve (see Symbols Guide). Then, as the powers and responsibilities increase through the priesthood offices, the number of priesthood holders needed to fill each successive quorum increases. It is also interesting to consider that when one takes the 48 members, the fulness of the priests quorum (representing the Aaronic Priesthood), and adds them to the 96 members of the elders quorum (representing the Melchizedek Priesthood), the number of 144 is achieved. Not only would the 144,000 represent 12,000 from every tribe of Israel but it would symbolize a fulness and unity of both the Aaronic and Melchizedek priesthoods.

Second, the number 144,000 is a symbolic series of multiples. As shown in the Symbols Guide, the number 12 represents priesthood, it is then multiplied by itself to come up with 144, symbolizing an even greater priesthood power and magnitude, and finally it is multiplied by 1,000 signifying multitudes, which expresses the idea that this power which the 144,000 possess is an overwhelming priesthood power. The reference in the Doctrine and Covenants also discusses a "power over the nations of the earth" (77:11). John uses the same idea when talking about the beasts full of wings and full of eyes, an expression of magnitude of power (see Rev. 4:6; D&C 77:4). Anytime multiples of a number are used in the Revelation it is to symbolically expand the powers and strength of the things being described, whether they are beasts, armies, or servants of God.

Concerning these verses Elder McConkie observes that, "John here sees 144,000 of these kings and priests, 12,000 from each tribe, converted, baptized, endowed, married for eternity, and finally sealed up unto eternal life, having their calling and election made sure" (*DNTC*, 3:491). The twelve tribes are the twelve sons of Israel (Jacob), and each received a promised blessing from their father. "The tribes listed by John include Levi, count Ephraim (Joseph) and Manasseh separately, and omit Dan. Why Dan should lose his inheritance is not clear" (*DNTC*, 3:494).

## Applicability

There is a way we can receive the guarantee of protection in the latter days, and that is being sealed in the temple. Those who are sealed "in their foreheads," both literally and figuratively, know that they have received the necessary ordinances performed through the endowment and sealing, and are sealed as a part of Heavenly Father's family forever. This does not mean that the sealed can rest on their accomplishments or that "all is well in Zion" (2 Ne. 28:21), but it does mean that if they continue true and faithful, and consecrate their lives in building up the kingdom of God, they will be numbered with those of the first resurrection (see Rev. 20). In fact, many have received the reassurance of these blessings by words spoken in their patriarchal blessings. The promises are secured through faithfulness and righteousness. If one performs the saving ordinances and is faithful, it is guaranteed that that person will be numbered with the righteous.

## REVELATION 7:9–17

9 After this I beheld, and, lo, a great multitude, which no man could number, of all nations, and kindreds, and people, and tongues, stood before the throne, and before the Lamb, clothed with white robes, and palms in their hands;

10 And cried with a loud voice, saying, Salvation to our God which sitteth upon the throne, and unto the Lamb.

11 And all the angels stood round about the throne, and about the elders and the four beasts, and fell before the throne on their faces, and worshipped God,

12 Saying, Amen: Blessing, and glory, and wisdom, and thanksgiving, and honour, and power, and might, be unto our God for ever and ever. Amen.

13 ¶ And one of the elders answered, saying unto me, What are these which are arrayed in white robes? and whence came they?

14 And I said unto him, Sir, thou knowest. And he said to me, These are they which came out of great tribulation, and have washed their robes, and made them white in the blood of the Lamb.

15 Therefore are they before the throne of God, and serve him day and night in his temple: and he that sitteth on the throne shall dwell among them.

16 They shall hunger no more, neither thirst any more; neither shall the sun light on them, nor any heat.

17 For the Lamb which is in the midst of the throne shall feed them, and shall lead them unto living fountains of waters: and God shall wipe away all tears from their eyes.

## Verse Commentary

*7:9–10.* **I beheld ... a great multitude ... clothed with white robes, and palms in their hands.** An innumerable company of righteous Saints from all over the world stand **before the throne** (God's seat) and **before the Lamb** (Christ's seat, recognizing that both the Father and the Son are separate and distinct) and are dressed in the white robes of the temple. The robes are white signifying purity and are given to the righteous for their faithfulness. The palms are waved as a token of victory, as palms were strewn in the road when Christ rode into Jerusalem in his final triumphal entry (see Matt. 21:8; John 12:13). Thus, the robes and palms together are a double token of victory, indicating those who have overcome all things and are in the presence of

God. An innumerable company of spirits will be before the throne of God clothed in white robes and waving their palm fronds symbolizing the dual victory of Christ over death and hell.

This great multitude then cry, **Salvation to our God which sitteth upon the throne, and unto the Lamb.** Both the Father and the Son are recognized and praised for the salvation they have provided; the Father for allowing his Son to come here to the earth as a ransom for his children, and the Son for his sacrifice in coming down from his throne on high as the infinite sacrifice. This is part of the explanation of the condescension of God as Nephi learned in his vision of the tree of life (see 1 Ne. 11:9–26).

Of those who would stand before God, President Joseph Fielding Smith said, "All mortals shall be resurrected, but only those who merit celestial glory shall stand before the throne of God" (*ACQ*, 3:187).

7:11–12. All the angels now stand round about the throne, fall on their faces and worship God saying, **Amen: Blessing, and glory, and wisdom, and thanksgiving, and honour, and power, and might, be unto our God for ever and ever. Amen.** This song of praise is similar to the songs of praise which the elders and beasts sang to the Lord God in their recognition of what he had accomplished (see Rev. 4:9–11). We assume that among these angels are the ones to whom the power will be given to inflict all things upon the face of the earth, including the judgments. All fall down and worship God for his goodness. Note the use of seven characteristics proclaimed to the Lord, indicating that the angels are praising him eternally with all glory.

7:13–17. The question is now posed, by one of the elders, **What are these which are arrayed in white robes? and whence came they?** Concerning the white robes, Joseph Fielding McConkie says, "All who are to feast in the heavenly kingdom must be properly clothed. They must be wearing the garments of purity and holiness, garments made white through '**the blood of the Lamb'** " (*Gospel Symbolism*, p. 133). The Saints will pass through a period of great tribulation which is in reference

to the woes that the "angels are about to loose upon the world"
(Draper, p. 85). Our robes are made white, or in other words,
clean and pure, through the blood which Christ shed for us.
Because of Christ's sacrifice, we are able to wash our robes **in
the blood of the Lamb.**

The people are serving the Lord **day and night in his
temple,** which should be self-explanatory. Only those who are
righteous and deserving are allowed to enter the house of the
Lord. The promises of the righteous dwelling with the Lord are
eloquently expressed in verses 15–17. He shall **dwell among
them,** they shall **hunger no more, neither thirst any more**
(remember, Christ is the Bread of Life and the living water). Neither shall the **sun light on them, nor any heat.** Why the
grandeur of all these things? Because Christ is the Light, we will
be in his presence and will feel the warmth of his light shining
upon us (see also Rev. 22:5).

**The Lamb . . . shall feed them, and shall lead them unto
living fountains of waters: and God shall wipe away all tears
from their eyes.** What a glorious moment! We shall be in the
presence of the Father and the Son, will have overcome all
things, and shall be able to dwell with our heavenly parents, our
Savior, and the righteous for all eternity. All of the pains, sor-
rows, and tears of this life will be wiped away and we will experience an inexpressible joy as we receive all that our Father hath
(see Rom. 8:18, 38–39). A great expression of where these tears
come from is as follows: "And God shall wipe away all tears
from their eyes; and there shall be no more death, neither sorrow, nor crying, neither shall there be any more pain: for the former things are passed away" (Rev. 21:4).

## Applicability

Who shall stand before the throne of God clothed in robes of
white? clothed with glory and immortality and eternal life?
Why, those who have performed the necessary ordinances to do
so! One of the greatest, and yet most challenging, principles of
the gospel of Jesus Christ is that we have our agency to choose.

It is great because we individually decide if we desire to be numbered with those who have been faithful, and as a result, receive all that the Father has; but oftentimes this opportunity of choice, or agency, can become extremely challenging because the temporary things of the world seem so enticing.

I know the feeling of being in the presence of the prophet of God and how comforting it felt to shake his hand. Confirming witnesses came to my mind and heart that he was a prophet. Can we even begin to comprehend the feelings of love that would emanate from being in the presence of the Savior and feeling the calm reassurance that all of our tears shall be wiped away? The joys expressed in these previous verses can be ours, if we are willing to forsake the world and seek after those things which provide eternal joy and happiness.

## SUMMARY

Chapter 7 has been a comforting catalog of the promised blessings of the Father to his children. It is imperative that we always keep focused on what is in store for the faithful Saints, because we have also been told that we will not be exempt from the plagues, pestilences, and destructions which will afflict the earth (see IIel. 5:12). The respite of the righteous will be glorious, but they must first overcome the tribulation which awaits them. The angels are ready and simply waiting for the command of the Lord to cleanse the earth.

The greatest comfort to each of us should be that we can be numbered with the innumerable company of Saints who are praising the Lord. Either we can choose to kneel down before the Savior and confess his name, or we can be compelled to do so (see D&C 58:26). It is left up to us to decide. Hopefully, each of us will desire the aforementioned blessings and seek no other thing but to dwell with our Father forever, and to be provided for throughout all eternity by his Son.

# 8

## THE OPENING OF THE
## SEVENTH SEAL AND THE
## DESTRUCTIONS TO FOLLOW

After promising blessings to those who overcome, the Lord continues to give the rest of the vision. The Saints have been prepared to endure all things and now those who have fought against and killed the prophets shall receive their reward. Prophesied destructions will come upon the wicked of the earth. The angels are now given the authority to release their destructions upon the inhabitants of the earth. In every age of the earth's existence the Lord has sent prophets to allow the people to repent and turn to their God. It is no different as the sixth seal ends and the seventh seal is now opened. Righteous Saints are watching for the signs of the times and the prophecies of the Lord's servants (see D&C 1:37–38). All of his children have been given every opportunity to repent.

Every seal represents a thousand-year period of the earth's existence, and now the seventh (complete) seal is opened. It is the dawning of the millennium, but first the earth must be cleansed of the wickedness upon its face. The first seven chapters dealt with the first six thousand years since the Fall, and now the earth will be renewed, Christ will reign personally upon it, and it will receive its paradisiacal glory (see A of F 1:10). The angels will carry out the responsibility the Lord has placed on their shoulders and will prepare a place for the Savior of the world to come and dwell.

As the last seal is opened, the earth will be subjected to some fantastic forces. In the Doctrine and Covenants, the Prophet Joseph Smith recorded some of the events that will occur prior to the Second Coming. "For not many days hence and the earth shall tremble and reel to and fro as a drunken man; and the sun shall hide his face, and shall refuse to give light; and the moon shall be bathed in blood; and the stars shall become exceedingly angry, and shall cast themselves down as a fig that falleth from off a fig-tree. And after your testimony cometh the testimony of earthquakes, that shall cause groanings in the midst of her, and men shall fall upon the ground and shall not be able to stand. And also cometh the testimony of the voice of thunderings, and the voice of lightnings, and the voice of tempests, and the voice of the waves of the sea heaving themselves beyond their bounds. And all things shall be in commotion; and surely, men's hearts shall fail them; for fear shall come upon all people. And angels shall fly through the midst of heaven, crying with a loud voice, sounding the trump of God, saying: Prepare ye, prepare ye, O inhabitants of the earth; for the judgment of our God is come. Behold, and lo, the Bridegroom cometh; go ye out to meet him" (88:87–92).

## REVELATION 8:1–5

1 ¶ AND when he had opened the seventh seal, there was silence in heaven about the space of half an hour.

2 And I saw the seven angels which stood before God; and to them were given seven trumpets.

3 And another angel came and stood at the altar, having a golden censer; and there was given unto him much incense, that he should offer it with the prayers of all saints upon the golden altar which was before the throne.

4 And the smoke of the incense, which came with the prayers of the saints, ascended up before God out of the angel's hand.

5 And the angel took the censer, and filled it with fire of the altar, and cast it into the earth: and there were voices, and thunderings, and lightnings, and an earthquake.

## Verse Commentary

*8:1.* The **seventh seal** is now opened, but instead of immediate destruction there is **silence** for **the space of half an hour.** Nothing has yet been revealed concerning what the silence

represents or regarding the unit of time. The most important
thing to consider about this silence is that the heavens are silent.
There is no noise coming to the earth from the heavens for the
space of half an hour. It can either be in the Lord's time, where
one day equals 1,000 earth years, or in other words, approximately twenty-one years (time enough for a generation to grow
up without hearing the word of the Lord), or it can be in earth
time and simply be silence of some type for thirty minutes. All
we know is that there is silence. A similar period of silence took
place prior to the advent of the Savior to the Americas, following his death in Jerusalem and the corresponding destructions
in the Americas (see 3 Ne. 10:1–2).

8:2. **Seven angels** now stand before God and each is given a
**trumpet**. The angels are God's messengers and servants, and he
has now given them the work to carry forth. The trumpet is used
in heralding the coming of an event. We read the following
description from Doctrine and Covenants: "Q. What are we to
understand by the sounding of the trumpets, mentioned in the
8th chapter of Revelation?

"A. We are to understand that as God made the world in six
days, and on the seventh day he finished his work, and sanctified it, and also formed man out of the dust of the earth, even so,
in the beginning of the seventh thousand years will the Lord
God sanctify the earth, and complete the salvation of man, and
judge all things, and shall redeem all things, except that which
he hath not put into his power, when he shall have sealed all
things, unto the end of all things; and the sounding of the trumpets of the seven angels are the preparing and finishing his
work, in the beginning of the seventh thousand years—the
preparing of the way before the time of his coming" (77:12).

The Lord will not return to the earth at the commencement
of the seventh thousand years. The cleansing will take place
prior to his second coming (see D&C 77:13). Doctrine and
Covenants section 88 tells us that there shall be "a great sign in
heaven" (v. 93), following which will be the destruction of the
great and abominable church (v. 94), and then "There shall be
silence in heaven for the space of half an hour; and immediately

after shall the curtain of heaven be unfolded, as a scroll is unfolded after it is rolled up, and the face of the Lord shall be unveiled; And the Saints that are upon the earth, who are alive, shall be quickened and be caught up to meet him" (88:95–96).

It specifies those Saints who are upon the earth, and *alive*, meaning that some righteous Saints will die during these destructions. Comfort comes from the Doctrine and Covenants which says that "death shall be sweet to them" (42:46).

*8:3–4.* Can we even begin to comprehend the joy the righteous will experience? Immediately following the silence the veil will be unfolded, unrolled as a scroll, and we shall see the Lord, being quickened to endure his presence and caught up to meet him. The **prayers of the saints** will rise up to the Lord. Elder McConkie says, "The Saints on earth pray, while the angels burn incense on a golden altar before the throne of God, an act of devotion patterned after similar rites in ancient Israel" (*DNTC*, 3:498).

Faithful Saints will not be surprised with the ensuing destructions. "The coming of the Lord draweth nigh, and it overtaketh the world as a thief in the night—Therefore, gird up your loins, that you may be the children of light, and that day shall not overtake you as a thief" (D&C 106:4–5).

*8:5.* The angel now takes the censer (which is carried in his hand) and fills it with the **fire of the altar.** In Old Testament times, "The officiating priest in the tabernacle or temple took the fire for his censer from the brazen altar, and then offered the incense upon the golden altar" (Vincent, p. 505). Our prayers are comparable to the smoke from the fire. As our prayers are offered, they rise toward the heavens like the smoke from the altar. The Holy Ghost assists in this process by conversing with our spirits and carrying the thoughts and intents of the heart before the Father. Paul said, "Likewise the Spirit also helpeth our infirmities: for we know not what we should pray for as we ought: but the Spirit itself maketh intercession for us with groanings which cannot be uttered" (Rom. 8:26).

It is obvious that the fire of the altar is that which burns, cleanses, and purifies and it will begin to do so as it is cast to the earth. The **voices, and thunderings, and lightnings, and an earthquake** all represent ways in which the power of God is manifest and how that power brings people into subjection to him. Each of these natural phenomena proclaim the fact that there is a power above that of the earth which we cannot control, and these phenomena will focus all of our attention on the events taking place.

## Applicability

With the opening of the seventh seal comes a time when our prayers will be indicative of the faith we have in the Savior. How can we ever invoke the blessings of the Lord upon us if we are not offering our prayers morning and night and praying for the constant protection of the Lord in such trying circumstances as we find today? Calamities can come upon the earth at any time and if we don't take the time to pray to the Lord, what does that indicate about the time we allot for him? We cannot fool ourselves into thinking that our prayers will be heard, or that we will even know how to pray, if we never pray until the destructions come. We have already been warned that destructions will come upon the earth.

## REVELATION 8:6–13

6 And the seven angels which had the seven trumpets prepared themselves to sound.

7 ¶ The first angel sounded, and there followed hail and fire mingled with blood, and they were cast upon the earth: and the third part of trees was burnt up, and all green grass was burnt up.

8 And the second angel sounded, and as it were a great mountain burning with fire was cast into the sea: and the third part of the sea became blood;

9 And the third part of the creatures which were in the sea, and had life, died; and the third part of the ships were destroyed.

10 And the third angel sounded, and there fell a great star from heaven, burning as it were a lamp, and it fell upon the third part of the rivers, and upon the fountains of waters;

11 And the name of the star is called Wormwood: and the third

part of the waters became worm-wood; and many men died of the waters, because they were made bitter.

12 And the fourth angel sounded, and the third part of the sun was smitten, and the third part of the moon, and the third part of the stars; so as the third part of them was darkened, and the day shone not for a third part of it, and the night likewise.

13 And I beheld, and heard an angel flying through the midst of heaven, saying with a loud voice, Woe, woe, woe, to the inhabiters of the earth by reason of the other voices of the trumpet of the three angels, which are yet to sound!

**Verse Commentary**

*8:6–13.* The **seven angels which had the seven trumpets** now begin to sound. The destructions are unimaginable. First, we encounter **hail and fire mingled with blood,** resulting in the third part of the trees being burnt up, along with all the green grass. Some of the beauty of the earth is now being destroyed as the trees and grass are burnt. Wickedness is being cast off and the earth is in its final stages as it prepares to be renewed and receive its paradisiacal glory (see A of F 1:10). Just as the Holy Ghost cleanses the soul of the repentant through the burning of the spirit, the earth is cleansed as fire sweeps down upon it. This completes the earth's baptism. The earth was baptized of water in the days of Noah, and now it is baptized of fire.

The **second angel** sounds and **a great mountain burning with fire** is cast into the sea, resulting in a **third part of the sea** becoming blood. Blood holds a dual symbolism in representing death (from a loss of blood), but also representing life (in the blood of the Savior which was shed for us). **The third part of the creatures which were in the sea, and had life, died; and the third part of the ships were destroyed.** It is interesting to note the similarity of plagues in comparing Moses' time with the occurrences at the opening of the seventh seal. All things are in similitude of His coming.

Only the third part of the things on the earth are affected. This appears to have a possible correlation to the third part of those who followed after Satan in the premortal life. This number then may seem to indicate that although the destructions will be widespread, they will specifically affect those who are unrepentant or do not exhibit faith in Christ and who incur the Lord's wrath because of their unbelief. Their unbelief is part of the reason for their lack of repentance.

*8:10–11.* The **third angel** sounds and a **great star** falls from heaven, **burning as it were a lamp, and it fell upon the third part of the rivers, and upon the fountains of waters; And the name of the star is called Wormwood: and the third part of the waters become wormwood. And many men died of the waters, because they were made bitter.** Wormwood, a strong herb of the Middle East, can make water unfit for drinking. The third angel unleashes a plague that causes an actual physical phenomenon: a poisoning of the earth's fountains.

Just as a substance such as wormwood can adversely affect us physically, Satan's influence can be destructive to us spiritually. While still in our Father's presence, Lucifer, a star of the morning, poisoned one-third of the host of heaven with his seditious rhetoric spoken in opposition to the plan of salvation. Cast out from heaven, Satan strives to corrupt mankind. Consider the following from the Book of Mormon: "Wherefore, the Lord God gave unto man that he should act for himself. Wherefore, man could not act for himself save it should be that he was enticed by the one or the other. And I, Lehi, according to the things which I have read, must needs suppose that an angel of God, according to that which is written, had fallen from heaven; wherefore, he became a devil, having sought that which was evil before God. And because he had fallen from heaven, and had become miserable forever, he sought also the misery of all mankind. Wherefore, he said unto Eve, yea, even that old serpent, who is the devil, who is the father of all lies, wherefore he said: Partake of the forbidden fruit, and ye shall not die, but ye shall be as God, knowing good and evil. And after Adam and Eve had partaken of the forbidden fruit they were driven out of the garden of Eden, to till the earth" (2 Ne. 2:16–19).

Opposition allows for God's children to experience agency. We have the opportunity to choose for ourselves whom we will follow. "Wherefore, men are free according to the flesh; and all things are given them which are expedient unto man. And they are free to choose liberty and eternal life, through the great Mediator of all men, or to choose captivity and death, according to the captivity and power of the devil; for he seeketh that all men might be miserable like unto himself" (2 Ne. 2:27). Satan cannot force us to partake of his wickedness; we can choose for ourselves. But if we do submit to the adversary's temptations it is as if we have drunk the poisonous waters that John saw.

*8:12–13.* As the **fourth** angel sounds, the **third part of the sun . . . moon . . . and stars** are darkened and do not give off their light. A portion of our Father's creations have lost the light that made them shine in the first place and now they must endure the consequences. It is vital to remember that although these destructions will encompass the whole earth, those who are righteous will be spared. Listen to the words provided to the faithful Saints as found in 1 Nephi concerning these latter days: "For the time soon cometh that the fulness of the wrath of God shall be poured out upon all the children of men; for he will not suffer that the wicked shall destroy the righteous. Wherefore, *he will preserve the righteous by his power,* even if it so be that the fulness of his wrath must come, and the righteous be preserved, *even unto the destruction of their enemies by fire.* Wherefore, *the righteous need not fear;* for thus saith the prophet, *they shall be saved, even if* it so be as *by fire.* Behold, my brethren, I say unto you, that these things must shortly come; yea, even blood, and fire, and vapor of smoke must come; and it must needs be upon the face of this earth; and it cometh unto men according to the flesh if it so be that they will harden their hearts against the Holy One of Israel" (22:16–18, emphasis added).

*8:13.* The four angels have sounded their trumps and the destructions are raining over the entire earth, but these are just a preview of what will take place as the remaining three angels unleash their devastations. After what would seem to be more than enough destruction rained down upon the earth, consider the cry of the angel as he flies over the earth, **Woe, woe, woe, to the inhabiters of the earth by reason of the other voices of the trumpet of the three angels, which are yet to sound!**

## Applicability

These aforementioned destructions are a part of the signs of the times which have been spoken of by the prophets ever since the fall of man. If I know what the signs are, and am faithful, I should realize that the coming of the Lord is at the door and I will endure whatever comes upon the earth. The Lord does not tell us these things to create fear in our hearts! He tells us what will come upon the earth so that we will see the signs of his coming and recognize that he is cleansing the earth of wickedness. These destructions are a direct result of disobedience, on the part of the wicked, to his law. Consider for a moment what forces would have to be unleashed today to get rid of all drugs, pornography, alcohol, and every other evil which permeates our society. Can we even begin to imagine the destructions and powers to be released to compel men to repent from their sins and turn to that God who gave them life? The choice is truly ours. We must keep in mind throughout these judgments that the protecting arm of the Lord is always upon his people. Even if the time comes that I die, if I am faithful, I die unto the Lord.

### SUMMARY

We have now seen the process the Lord will use to cleanse the earth as he prepares to return. The importance of the continual use of one-third part is that the destructions will be detrimental to those who continue to mock, and refuse to hearken to the counsels to repent, but will not "hurt" those who are righteous. We must have faith in the Lord and know that through this faith we will be protected. Remember the words of counsel found in Revelation, "Fear none of those things which thou shalt suffer" (2:10) along with the words of Paul to the Romans, "For I am persuaded, that neither death, nor life, nor angels, nor principalities, nor powers, nor things present, nor things to come, Nor height, nor depth, nor any other creature, shall be able to separate us from the love of God, which is in Christ Jesus our Lord" (8:38–39).

Sufficient time has been allowed for all who desire to repent. The ensuing forces to be hurled upon the earth are a direct result of promised destructions awaiting those who fail to heed the counsels of the Lord. He is bound by his own law to cleanse the earth and his fury will sweep off the wicked. Those who do not obey his law cannot endure his presence and so it becomes imperative that those who are wicked be removed from his dwelling place prior to his return. Chapter 8 has given us some idea of the destructions which await those who choose not to repent.

# 9

## THE BOTTOMLESS PIT
## AND THE FORCES OF THE
## ADVERSARY

We have learned to this point that each of the seven seals is representative of a thousand-year period of time in the history of the earth. We have also learned that those who choose to remain wicked will have to encounter the judgments of God brought down upon them by his servants, the angels. Those who are righteous need not fear, but we must also keep in mind that these continuing destructions will be far greater than anything we have ever before encountered.

Throughout all of these destructions we must always keep in mind that the Lord uses his powerful forces of nature and judgment for two reasons. First, as in the case of taking the life of Laban, "Behold the Lord slayeth the wicked to bring forth his righteous purposes. It is better that one man should perish than that a nation should dwindle and perish in unbelief" (1 Ne. 4:13). There are times when the life of a person or people must be taken to allow for the righteous to be preserved. Secondly, as in the case with the people at the time of Noah, God cleansed the earth because of the people's wickedness (see Gen. 6:6–7). These people are still his children, the Savior suffered for their sins if they would repent (see D&C 19:16–19). His arm is stretched out still, but they do not respond, and so he is required by his own law to bring upon them the judgments for failure to obey his law. We now continue to see what his judgments will be for those who have failed to hearken to his voice.

The Doctrine and Covenants also gives particular insight into the time frame of chapter 9 of Revelation with the following verse: "Q. When are things to be accomplished, which are written in the 9th chapter of Revelation?

"A. They are to be accomplished after the opening of the seventh seal, before the coming of Christ" (77:13).

### REVELATION 9:1–11

1 ¶ AND the fifth angel sounded, and I saw a star fall from heaven unto the earth: and to him was given the key of the bottomless pit.

2 And he opened the bottomless pit; and there arose a smoke out of the pit, as the smoke of a great furnace; and the sun and the air were darkened by reason of the smoke of the pit.

3 And there came out of the smoke locusts upon the earth. and unto them was given power, as the scorpions of the earth have power.

4 And it was commanded them that they should not hurt the grass of the earth, neither any green thing, neither any tree; but only those men which have not the seal of God in their foreheads.

5 And to them it was given that they should not kill them, but that they should be tormented five months: and their torment was as the torment of a scorpion, when he striketh a man.

6 And in those days shall men seek death, and shall not find it; and shall desire to die, and death shall flee from them.

7 And the shapes of the locusts were like unto horses prepared unto battle; and on their heads were as it were crowns like gold, and their faces were as the faces of men.

8 And they had hair as the hair of women, and their teeth were as the teeth of lions.

9 And they had breastplates, as it were breastplates of iron; and the sound of their wings was as the sound of chariots of many horses running to battle.

10 And they had tails like unto scorpions, and there were stings in their tails: and their power was to hurt men five months.

11 And they had a king over them, which is the angel of the bottomless pit, whose name in the Hebrew tongue is Abaddon, but in the Greek tongue hath his name Apollyon

## Verse Commentary

*9:1–2.* As the **fifth angel** sounds, we see **a star fall from heaven** (see Rev. 8:10–11) and he is given the **key to the bottomless pit.** The key is Satan's to use, but the Savior is the one who had rightful ownership of the key, and once the time is past, Satan must return it. In this pre-millennial time we can be assured that Satan will now unleash his forces in one final attempt to draw down and destroy. During the previous six thousand years, the Lord had power over the key and controlled, so to speak, the powers of the adversary, but now it is in possession of the Destroyer and he will do all he can to afflict and torment man, as we shall see. "For I [God] am no respecter of persons, and will that all men shall know that the day speedily cometh; the hour is not yet, but is nigh at hand, when peace shall be taken from the earth, and the devil shall have power over his own dominion" (D&C 1:35).

The smoke arose **as the smoke of a great furnace** showing that in the same way that prayers of the Saints arose, representing their desires, the smoke (desires) of those who were cast off with Satan now comes out of the pit and sweeps forward to cover the earth. The sole desire of the things to come forth from the pit will be to afflict, torment, and destroy all they can here upon the earth.

9:3–5. The **locusts** come up out of the smoke and are compared to the scorpions of the earth, which have power to sting men—generally their sting is not deadly, but it is extremely painful. They do not have power to kill nor to hurt anything that has **the seal of God in their foreheads.** The forehead is the center of thought, or where ideas enter into the mind, and those who are sealed will know within their mind or forehead that they are sealed to the Lord. They will know by the works which have sealed them to the Lord and by the power of the Holy Ghost (the sealing of the Holy Spirit of Promise). They will also know the tokens they have been given and will know the truth when it is presented to them.

It is at this point that we must remember those who followed after Satan as he was cast down from premortality (see Jude 1:6). Those who followed Satan were not locusts but were spirit children just like ourselves. At this point in the history of the earth and eternity they have been bound in prison for many millennia and are now loosed to carry forth their destructive work upon those who are not protected under the wings of the

Father. Verses 6–11 will make it apparent that those who are carrying on this destruction and affliction are servants of Satan who are arrayed in all their "glory" as they go forth into battle like the righteous went into battle earlier riding upon their horses (see Rev. 6:1–8).

The best comparison John can portray in describing this terrible scene is that of locusts as they swarm over the fields of the earth. A swarm of locusts often cause darkness, but these do not cause it, they come from it! Their torment is only **five months.** It is not indefinite and the pain will be comparable to the pain inflicted by the sting of a scorpion. Clearly, these "locusts" we are reading about are servants of Satan who are taking commands from their king. Of the locusts, Draper says "These insect demons were often associated with darkness. This was not accidental. The cloud they form is often so compact that it obscures the light of the sun. However, John's monsters do not cause the darkness; they result from it. They are men, blinded by the lack of light due to sin and corruption. According to the Doctrine and Covenants 93:39, 'that wicked one cometh and taketh away light and truth, through disobedience, from the children of men.' The result is a frenzy of evil not unlike the feeding frenzy of the locusts" (p. 103).

9:6. According to Revelation men shall **seek death, and shall not find it.** This explains the agony of the condemnation these men are experiencing. Not only are they being tormented "not unto death," but they are so miserable that they would rather pass through death than experience what is taking place in their lives. It is a sad commentary on their lives that at the moment when they are surrounded by wickedness and tribulation, rather than turn to their Lord and repent, they would prefer to seek death.

9:7–11. The followers of Satan are now aptly described by John with human characteristics and battle armament. It is interesting to note that their shape is **like unto horses prepared unto battle,** especially in view that this is very similar to Revelation 6:1–8 and the riders which rode their various horses into battle. All of the descriptions are those of mankind and characteristics that followers of Satan would desire to have and were without, physically, in view that they never received bodies of flesh and blood.

*9:7–8.* They wore **crowns *like* gold** which means that these were not true crowns of gold like the twenty-four elders had, but false crowns lacking any kind of authority. Their **faces were as the faces of men. . . . They had hair as the hair of women, and their teeth as the teeth of lions.** These followers of Satan, were cast down to the earth and are now intent on destroying all that they have power to destroy. They will afflict any who are not protected by the seal, and will torment as they have been tormented. They have been loosed on earth and are prepared to do battle, and the noise and devastation they will unleash upon the earth is the final opportunity they have to make all men miserable like unto themselves. Commenting on John's description of the locusts, Draper says, "Whatever his purpose, he does continue to finish the fearful portrait of the monsters. Breastplates of iron make them nearly impregnable, wings give them great mobility, but the scorpions' tails hold the greatest fear. The Seer uses the threat of the poisonous sting as the symbol of that which causes men to be in torment" (p. 106).

It is also very possible that John is seeing things which are commonplace in our day, but which he has never seen. The armament, noise, sting in the tail, and destruction rained upon the earth is very similar to what we find in modern day weapons and warfare. Elder McConkie indicates that "It is not improbable that these ancient prophets were seeing such things as men wearing or protected by strong armor; as troops of calvary and companies of tanks and flame throwers; as airplanes and airborn missiles which explode, fire shells and drop bombs; and even other weapons yet to be devised in an age when warfare is the desire and love of wicked men" (*DNTC,* 3:503).

*9:11.* The **king,** the **angel of the bottomless pit,** is **Abaddon.** His name is symbolic of one who was capable of producing fruit and life, yet because of his overwhelming desire to control or rule over things, he lost that which had been given him. **Apollyon,** *Apŏlluōn* in the Greek, is "a destroyer," or one who destroys fully (*Strong's*, Greek Dictionary, p. 14). He has gone from one who bears the light and has life to one whose sole intent is to destroy. Notice how similar he was to the Son of God, but how drastic the differences have become since he rebelled against the Father (see D&C 76:25–29). He is the king of the bottomless pit and is not the creator of anything, but is the destroyer and imitator of everything!

## Applicability

It is essential that we realize some of the powers of the adversary, and know that he has a tremendous force that follows after him. There is a very powerful assurance in verse 4, and it is that the locusts, or servants of Satan, shall have no power to hurt those men who are protected by the seal of the living God. Once again we see the shield offered to us through the temple blessings and sealing power. How often must the Lord tell us of the blessings of the temple? There is no question that one of the most important weapons of the armor of God is the shield of faith because it is this shield that will preserve us against the power of the adversary. Satan cannot break the seal of our God, and therein lies the beauty of the refuge we find in being faithful, endowed members of the Church.

## REVELATION 9:12–21

12 One woe is past; and, behold, there come two woes more hereafter.

13 ¶ And the sixth angel sounded, and I heard a voice from the four horns of the golden altar which is before God,

14 Saying to the sixth angel which had the trumpet, Loose the four angels which are bound in the great river Euphrates.

15 And the four angels were loosed, which were prepared for an hour, and a day, and a month, and a year, for to slay the third part of men.

16 And the number of the army of the horsemen were two hundred thousand thousand: and I heard the number of them.

17 And thus I saw the horses in the vision, and them that sat on them, having breastplates of fire, and of jacinth, and brimstone: and the heads of the horses were as the heads of lions; and out of their

mouths issued fire and smoke and brimstone.

18 By these three was the third part of men killed, by the fire, and by the smoke, and by the brimstone, which issued out of their mouths.

19 For their power is in their mouth, and in their tails: for their tails were like unto serpents, and had heads, and with them they do hurt.

20 And the rest of the men which were not killed by these plagues yet repented not of the works of their hands, that they should not worship devils, and idols of gold, and silver, and brass, and stone, and of wood: which neither can see, nor hear, nor walk:

21 Neither repented they of their murders, nor of their sorceries, nor of their fornication, nor of their thefts.

## Verse Commentary

*9:12.* Woes are expressions of grief. In this case **one woe is past,** with all of the destructions it brought with it, and two are still to come. It is sad commentary that even after this much pain and suffering there are still many who will not repent. Joel says, "For the day of the Lord cometh, for it is nigh at hand; A day of darkness and of gloominess, a day of clouds and of thick darkness, as the morning spread upon the mountains: a great people and a strong; there hath not been ever the like, neither shall be any more after it, even to the years of many generations. A fire devoureth before them; and behind them a flame burneth: the land is as the garden of Eden before them, and behind them a desolate wilderness; yea, and nothing shall escape them. The appearance of them is as the appearance of horses; and as horsemen, so shall they run. Like the noise of chariots on the tops of mountains shall they leap, like the noise of a flame of fire that devoureth the stubble, as a strong people set in battle array. Before their face the people shall be much pained: all faces shall gather blackness. They shall run like mighty men; they shall climb the wall like men of war; and they shall march every one on his ways, and they shall not break their ranks: Neither shall one thrust another; they shall walk every one in his path: and when they fall upon the sword, they shall not be wounded. They shall run to and fro in the city; they shall run upon the wall, they shall climb up upon the houses; they shall enter in at the windows like a thief. The earth shall quake before them; the heavens shall tremble: the sun and the moon shall be dark, and the stars shall withdraw their shining: And the Lord shall utter his voice before his army: for his camp is very great: for he is strong that executeth his word: for the day of the Lord is great and very terrible; and who can abide it?" (2:1–11).

*9:13–14.* The **sixth angel** sounds, and a voice comes from the **four horns of the golden altar** before God. The four horns are representative of the power encompassing the whole earth. The altar is God's (as represented by the golden color), and the earth is present before the altar where all eternal offerings are made. The voice says to the angel, **Loose the four angels which are bound in the great river Euphrates.** The four angels do not have power to loose themselves, the sixth angel must do it thereby signifying that these four angels are bound in the "bottomless pit" (JST Rev. 9:14), and due to the nature of four being represented, their destructions will cover the earth. "To the prophets the **Euphrates** was the symbol of all that was disastrous in the divine judgments" (Vincent, p. 511).

These four angels are loosed from the bottomless pit and will bring suffering upon those who are not protected by the power of God. It is often the wicked who the Lord uses to punish the wicked. Nephi is told that his seed will be blessed upon the promised land, but also that Laman and Lemuel's seed will be preserved and will be a "scourge unto thy seed, to stir them up in the ways of remembrance" if Nephi's people rebel (see 1 Ne. 2:21–24). We find a similar situation in the book of Mormon, "But, behold, the judgments of God will overtake the wicked; and it is by the wicked that the wicked are punished; for it is the wicked that stir up the hearts of the children of men unto bloodshed" (4:5; see also D&C 63:32–33).

*9:15.* The four angels are loosed, having been **prepared** by none other than their master, Satan, to **slay the third part of men.** The army has been prepared for that hour, which is not a literal time, but the hour appointed by God in its day, month, and year.

*9:16.* **Two hundred thousand thousand.** The word for

thousand is actually *murias* in the Greek and represents a myriad (an innumerable host) of horsemen coming forth to do battle. John **heard the number of them** which is indicative of the multitude of armies coming to do battle (but see JST—"saw").

*9:17–18.* The riders who sit on the horses wear fiery breastplates whose coloring represent fire and burning. **Jacinth** is often red and the **brimstone,** or sulphur, is a yellowish color. **The horses heads were as the heads of lions** and out of their mouths came forth those things representing everlasting burnings: fire, smoke, and brimstone. The torment being issued forth is indicative of all that the riders of the horses have endured from the time they chose to follow their new king. Then, by the fire, smoke, and brimstone, **the third part of men** are killed. Consider the similarity of one-third part in comparison with those who were cast down. All who follow after Satan will reap the consequences of their choices, if they do not repent (see D&C 19:16–19).

*9:19–21.* As these beasts inflict their punishments upon the wicked, not all of the men are killed. **The rest of the men which were not killed** still fail to repent or turn from the works of their hands, those things which have not power to save, preserve, or protect. In fact, the wickedness of the men being tormented is so great and they are so far past feeling that they do not repent of any of their wickedness. They are worshipping false gods and are breaking many of the Lord's commandments—incurring the torment of damned souls upon them—yet even this does not bring about their repentance.

The power of the beasts to afflict and torment man is **in their mouth and in their tails.** Consider the snake, it was a serpent that deceived Adam and Eve and that can also strike and kill a man with its bite (mouth), or twist around its prey using its tail until there is no escaping its embrace.

The serpent is a perfect complement of Satan. It lies in wait, content to allow the unsuspecting victim to move close enough until it can strike. Once the victim is grasped, either with the tail or mouth, the end is near and death is usually imminent. Such is the lot of those who follow after the evil enticements of the adversary and become entangled in the chains of Satan's influence!

Observe Nephi's description of the evil one: "For behold, at that day shall he rage in the hearts of the children of men, and stir them up to anger against that which is good. And others will he pacify, and lull them away into carnal security, that they will say: All is well in Zion; yea, Zion prospereth, all is well—and thus the devil cheateth their souls, and leadeth them away carefully down to hell. And behold, others he flattereth away, and telleth them there is no hell; and he saith unto them: I am no devil, for there is none—and thus he whispereth in their ears, until he grasps them with his awful chains, from whence there is no deliverance" (2 Ne. 28:20–22).

## Applicability

Destructions will come upon the earth in ways that we have never before seen and can't even comprehend. These events will occur in their set time. They will come when all of the words of the prophets are fulfilled and man has had sufficient time to repent of his iniquities. Only those who have not repented will incur these judgments upon them. Once again, as constantly as can be expressed, we see that the blessings of the Lord are continually over those who keep the commandments and remember the covenants they have made with their Protector.

## SUMMARY

All of these events are occuring at the opening of the seventh seal, and prior to the second coming of the Savior. Wickedness will be so pervasive upon the earth that only those who have the seal of God in their foreheads will be preserved from the wrath to come. Even though nothing is expressly stated, it is still possible for those who have been wicked to repent of their wickedness, if they choose to do so, but our Heavenly Father will not force them.

The destructions will be poured out and the forces of evil

will be loosed in all of their power and supposed glory. They will unleash a destructive force upon the earth which we have never before seen, but will have no power over us if we are righteous. The greatest principle of salvation taught in these verses is that the Lord will protect his people from the forces of the adversary and all who desire may have those protective influences. The Savior is in control of the key of the bottomless pit and once Satan has completed his destruction, the earth will then be completely prepared to be cleansed.

# 10

## THE SCROLL AND THE
## RESTORATION OF ALL THINGS

A brief interlude occurs in this chapter as we see John understand the great role which he will play in the telling of this vision and in the restoration of all things. He will partake of the book so that it becomes a part of him and will experience both the joy (sweetness) of the things he has seen and will see, and the sorrow (bitterness) of the destructive forces and wickedness which will abound upon the earth.

An interesting parallel can be made regarding the sacrament. We are allowed to partake of the sacrament weekly and may enjoy the blessings of sanctification as we eat of the bread and drink the water, thereby enjoying the sweetness of the blessings of the Atonement; while simultaneously remembering the bitterness of the sins we may have committed and that we must be cleansed of.

### REVELATION 10:1–7

1 ¶ AND I saw another mighty angel come down from heaven, clothed with a cloud: and a rainbow was upon his head, and his face was as it were the sun, and his feet as pillars of fire:

2 And he had in his hand a little book open: and he set his right foot upon the sea, and his left foot on the earth,

3 And cried with a loud voice, as when a lion roareth: and when he had cried, seven thunders uttered their voices.

4 And when the seven thunders had uttered their voices, I was about to write: and I heard a voice from heaven saying unto me, Seal up those things which the seven thunders uttered, and write them not.

5 And the angel which I saw stand upon the sea and upon the earth lifted up his hand to heaven,

6 And sware by him that liveth for ever and ever, who created heaven, and the things that therein are, and the earth, and the things that therein are, and the sea, and the things which are therein, that there should be time no longer:

7 But in the days of the voice of the seventh angel, when he shall begin to sound, the mystery of God should be finished, as he hath declared to his servants the prophets.

**Verse Commentary**

*10:1–2.* John sees **another mighty angel . . . clothed with a cloud** who Elder McConkie says is "one like unto the Son of Man" (*DNTC*, 3:505). The rainbow, face, and feet describe the appearance of the celestial being. He sets his **right foot upon the sea and his left foot on the earth.** As he comes here upon the earth, one foot is in the sea and the other is on the earth, symbolically representing that he is over all things. Note the differences between the star we encountered in the previous chapter that was cast out of heaven and fell to the earth, and the mighty angel here who stands as **pillars of fire.** All of the descriptors regarding this angel are of glory, light, and radiance as opposed to the darkness of the star that lost its light, or brightness.

In his hand he is holding **a little book.** The book he now holds open is different from the book of chapter 5. Ezekiel saw a similar book during his ministry. "And when I looked, behold, an hand was sent unto me; and, lo, a roll of a book was therein; And he spread it before me; and it was written within and without: and there was written therein lamentations, and mourning, and woe" (Ezek. 2:9–10).

*10:3–4.* The **angel crie[s] out with a loud voice** that is heard over all things, yet we do not know what is cried, nor what the seven thunders utter, because John is told to seal up the things which the thunders uttered. All of these things are in preparation for the events which will usher in the Savior's coming.

*10:5–6.* The angel now lifts up his right hand (see New International Version Rev. 10:5) and swears by the heavens that **there should be time no longer.** There will be time no longer for men to delay their repentance, the time of judgment is now and the time for them is past. This does not mean that time will no longer be measured but rather that the earth is now prepared for the Second Coming.

The following verses shed light on what has been discussed so far in this chapter and the insights as to what was uttered by the angels: "And then shall the first angel again sound his trump in the ears of all living, and reveal the secret acts of men, and the mighty works of God in the first thousand years. And then shall the second angel sound his trump, and reveal the secret acts of men, and the thoughts and intents of their hearts, and the mighty works of God in the second thousand years— And so on, until the seventh angel shall sound his trump; and he shall stand forth upon the land and upon the sea, and swear in the name of him who sitteth upon the throne, that there shall be time no longer; and Satan shall be bound, that old serpent, who is called the devil, and shall not be loosed for the space of a thousand years" (D&C 88:108–10; see also Dan 12:1–7).

10:7. The **mystery of God should be finished** as the seventh angel sounds his trump. We then ask what is the mystery of God? A thing is only a mystery to those who don't understand it, or have not been taught by those who do know the truth of the facts associated with the mystery. As W. E. Vine explains: Our word *mystery* comes from the Greek *mūsteriŏn* and is "primarily that which is known to the *mustēs*, the initiated. . . . In the N[ew] T[estament] it denotes, not the mysterious (as with the Eng. word), but that which, being outside the range of unassisted natural apprehension, can be made known only by Divine revelation, and is made known in a manner and at a time appointed by God, and to those only who are illumined by His Spirit. In the ordinary sense a mystery implies knowledge withheld; its Scriptural significance is truth revealed" (*Expository Dictionary*, sv. "mystery").

We encounter the same situation in the temple, not that the things therein are secret or mysterious, but that they are made known by the initiated to those desirous to become initiated and taught by the Spirit. Without question, the Spirit is the guide in the temple.

## Applicability

Angels are now coming to the earth to deliver their messages and to declare the day of the Lord. As we read through these verses we saw that John was forbidden to write some of the experiences he had and they were to be sealed up. Why? Because the earth was not yet prepared to receive them. At times we face the same situation when we begin to share a spiritual experience with someone and feel inclined to stop. There are some spiritual experiences which are too sacred to share and the Spirit prompts us to cease from what we were saying. To some people in the world it is impossible to understand the mysteries of God and when they hear something so sacred they begin to treat it with contempt or derision. Such was the case with many neighbors of Joseph Smith when he related the First Vision. Many other faithful Saints have also been treated poorly because of the testimonies they bore of the truth.

## REVELATION 10:8–11

8 ¶ And the voice which I heard from heaven spake unto me again, and said, Go and take the little book which is open in the hand of the angel which standeth upon the sea and upon the earth.

9 And I went unto the angel, and said unto him, Give me the little book. And he said unto me, Take it, and eat it up; and it shall make thy belly bitter, but it shall be in thy mouth sweet as honey.

10 And I took the little book out of the angel's hand, and ate it up; and it was in my mouth sweet as honey: and as soon as I had eaten it, my belly was bitter.

11 And he said unto me, Thou must prophesy again before many peoples, and nations, and tongues, and kings.

## Verse Commentary

*10:8–11.* John is now commanded to **go and take the little book,** and then **eat it up.** It will now become a part of him and will be sweet to taste but will be bitter in his belly. "Q. What are we to understand by the little book which was eaten by John, as mentioned in the 10th chapter of Revelation?

"A. We are to understand that it was a mission, and an ordinance, for him to gather the tribes of Israel; behold, this is Elias, who, as it is written, must come and restore all things" (D&C 77:14).

A major part of John's mission here was to receive the Revelation and then to impart it to the house of Israel as they are scattered upon the earth. Further insight is gained by reading from the Book of Mormon: "And it came to pass that the angel spake unto me, saying: Look! And I looked and beheld a man, and he was dressed in a white robe. And the angel said unto me: Behold one of the twelve apostles of the Lamb. Behold, he shall see and write the remainder of these things; yea, and also many of the things which have been. And he shall also write concerning the end of the world. . . . But the things which thou shalt see hereafter thou shalt not write; for the Lord God hath ordained the apostle of the Lamb of God that he should write them. And also others who have been, to them hath he shown all things, and they have written them; and they are sealed up to come forth in their purity, according to the truth which is in the Lamb, in the own due time of the Lord, unto the house of Israel. And I, Nephi, heard and bear record, that the name of the apostle of the Lamb was John, according to the word of the angel" (1 Ne. 14:18–22, 25–27). This helps us to understand why it is important that John was able to remain here, as a translated being, so that he could fulfill his mission of taking these truths found in Revelation to Israel. The Prophet Joseph Smith verified the truth of John's mission with the following: "John the Revelator was then among the Ten Tribes of Israel who had been led away by Shalmaneser, king of Assyria, to prepare them for their return from their long dispersion, to again possess the land of their fathers" (*HC*, 1:176n).

It will be sweet to his taste because it will show him that the Lord is in control of all things and will overcome the adversary in the end, but it will be bitter because of the destructions facing the wicked.

*10:11.* John is again told of the mission he has to perform, that of proclaiming this message to all of the earth: **Thou must**

**prophesy again before many peoples, and nations, and tongues, and kings.** The charge to John to prophesy is also recorded by Joseph Smith: "Thou [John] shalt tarry until I come in my glory, and shalt prophesy before nations, kindreds, tongues, and people. . . . I will make him as flaming fire and a ministering angel; he shall minister for those who shall be heirs of salvation who dwell on earth" (D&C 7:3–6).

It is obvious that John has already participated in some of the restoration of all things as he came to Joseph Smith and Oliver Cowdery and, in union with Peter and James, conferred the keys of the Holy Melchizedek Priesthood upon their heads.

## Applicability

There is no question that the book of Revelation is a book that is either sweet or bitter to those who read it. If people are wicked, and all they read about are the destructions to come upon the unrighteous, then it will be extremely bitter and it is doubtful they will want to continue to read about the calamities they will face. For the righteous the book is truly sweet because it is a continual message of hope and of victory over the adversary. Our Father has given us agency to choose which path we will follow. Our Father is not trying to condemn or destroy us, but is attempting to help us see the benefits of repentance. There will be destructions, of that we are assured; but that doesn't have to mean that the judgments of God will be bitter for us, if we are true and faithful. They were bitter for John because he saw the judgments inflicted upon the wicked and the resultant sorrow and suffering.

### SUMMARY

Chapter 10 has provided us with great insight into the experiences John had in learning about his own responsibilities regarding the book of Revelation. It must have been an awe-inspiring feeling to know that he was allowed to see things which only a select few before and after would see. Imagine the joy he felt as he was able to see with his own eyes, in vision, the eventual victory of the Savior over all things, and also the sorrow he felt and experienced for those who would not repent.

The Three Nephites experienced much the same promise as they were told, "And again, ye shall not have pain while ye shall dwell in the flesh, neither sorrow save it be for the sins of the world" (3 Ne. 28:9). We have been allowed to share in a brief picture of John's calling and responsibility to carry the message of Revelation to the nations of the earth, inclusive of the house of Israel who have been scattered. There will be no further delay in the unfolding of the rest of the history of the earth and the second coming of the Lord. Now that John has eaten the book, it becomes a part of him and he now becomes an active participant in the rest of the events to unfold.

# 11

## THE TWO PROPHETS,
## THE SEVENTH TRUMPET,
## AND THE REIGN OF CHRIST

Now that John has received his commission to prophesy before all the earth, along with the knowledge that his will be a ministry which will last until the Savior comes again, John is prepared to fulfill his responsibilities. He will now actively participate in the earth's final days and will take on certain tasks to prepare the temple and make it ready for the coming of the Lord. It is important to realize that he is not to concern himself with the area outside the temple itself, that is "given to the Gentiles," but is to concern himself solely with the temple's interior.

John is now to strengthen those who worship in the Church, especially during the time when the two prophets will be slain in Jerusalem and the "holy city" is under siege for a period of forty-two months. As the prophets are on the earth and prophesying in Jerusalem there is no one who can hurt them, but the time will come when they will have completed their mission and Satan will be allowed to take their lives. They will become faithful witnesses as they give their lives for the testimony they bear. Wickedness will be so prevalent upon the earth that the people will rejoice when the prophets are killed and will give gifts to one another, but will flee upon their resurrection. All of these events signal the coming of the Lord as the four and twenty elders fall down before the Lord and worship him as the heavenly temple is revealed and power comes forth from it.

## REVELATION 11:1–14

1 ¶ And there was given me a reed like unto a rod: and the angel stood, saying, Rise, and measure the temple of God, and the altar, and them that worship therein.

2 But the court which is without the temple leave out, and measure it not; for it is given unto the Gentiles: and the holy city shall they tread under foot forty and two months.

3 ¶ And I will give power unto my two witnesses, and they shall prophesy a thousand two hundred and threescore days, clothed in sackcloth.

4 These are the two olive trees, and the two candlesticks standing before the God of the earth.

5 And if any man will hurt them, fire proceedeth out of their mouth, and devoureth their enemies: and if any man will hurt them, he must in this manner be killed.

6 These have power to shut heaven, that it rain not in the days of their prophecy: and have power over waters to turn them to blood, and to smite the earth with all plagues, as often as they will.

7 And when they shall have finished their testimony, the beast that ascendeth out of the bottomless pit shall make war against them, and shall overcome them, and kill them.

8 And their dead bodies shall lie in the street of the great city, which spiritually is called Sodom and Egypt, where also our Lord was crucified.

9 And they of the people and kindreds and tongues and nations shall see their dead bodies three days and an half, and shall not suffer their dead bodies to be put in graves.

10 And they that dwell upon the earth shall rejoice over them, and make merry, and shall send gifts one to another; because these two prophets tormented them that dwelt on the earth.

11 And after three days and an half the Spirit of life from God entered into them, and they stood upon their feet; and great fear fell upon them which saw them.

12 And they heard a great voice from heaven saying unto them, Come up hither. And they ascended up to heaven in a cloud; and their enemies beheld them.

13 And the same hour was there a great earthquake, and the tenth part of the city fell, and in the earthquake were slain of men seven thousand: and the remnant were affrighted, and gave glory to the God of heaven.

14 ¶ The second woe is past; and, behold, the third woe cometh quickly.

## Verse Commentary

*11:1–2.* John is given the divine commission to **measure the**

**temple of God, and the altar, and them that worship therein.**
He is only to concern himself with the Saints and the temple.
The rest of the courtyard and that area outside the temple is left
to the Gentiles, those who do not belong in the temple. The holy
city is plundered for **forty and two months.** We find the period
of forty and two months in "three forms in the Apocalypse:
*forty-two months* (13:5); *twelve-hundred and sixty days* (v. 3; 12:6); *a
time, times and half a time,* or three years and a half (12:14, compare Dan. 7:25; 12:7)" (Vincent, p. 517).

Draper says, "It may be best not to take John too literally
here. The message probably lies behind the symbol. Three and
one-half, half of seven (see Rev. 11:9, 11), denotes what is
arrested midway in its normal course. The apocalyptic usage of
this number goes back to Daniel 7:25 (cf. 9:27; 12:7). . . . The
number six also connotes deficit, a failure to attain the completeness of seven, while eight designates superabundance.
Symbolically forty-two is pejorative, since, as one scholar has
pointed out, 'it is the result of six multiplied by seven, i.e. "perfection missing the mark" ' " (p. 121).

As of this day nothing specific has been revealed concerning
the forty-two months or when they will begin.

*11:3–12.* We now find **two witnesses** who have been given
power to prophesy for twelve hundred and sixty days who will
be **clothed in sackcloth.** First, "in the mouth of two or three witnesses shall every word be established" (2 Cor. 13:1). These two
witnesses are wearing sackcloth, the symbol of repentance and
are therefore declaring repentance to the inhabitants of the city.
They will preach repentance for roughly the same amount of
time that the Savior bore witness in Jerusalem, and as in the case
of the Savior, their lives will also be offered up as testimony
against the inhabitants.

More information on these two prophets has been revealed
in the latter days as we read the following: "Q. What is to be
understood by the two witnesses, in the eleventh chapter of
Revelation?

"A. They are two prophets that are to be raised up to the
Jewish nation in the last days, at the time of the restoration, and

to prophesy to the Jews after they are gathered and have built the city of Jerusalem in the land of their fathers" (D&C 77:15).

*11:4.* The **two olive trees, and the two candlesticks** are symbols of the olive tree (one literal—the olive trees, one figurative—the candlesticks), and as such they represent the cleansing power associated with the olive oil, along with the olive oil representing the Holy Ghost. President Joseph Fielding Smith said, "So we find through all the prophetic writings that olive trees and olive oil are emblems of sacredness and purity. . . . No other kind of oil will do in anointing. It is very apparent that the oil from animal flesh would never do, and there is no other kind of oil that is held so sacredly and is more suited to the anointing than the oil of olive; moreover, the Lord has placed his stamp of approval on it" (*AGQ*, 1:152–53).

The candlesticks (or lampstands) carry the light from within to share with all who would desire to receive it in the holy city. Once again we see the opportunities for repentance which our Father allows his children prior to the time that he inflicts judgment upon them. The candlesticks represent two servants of the Lord who carry the gospel light to those who are without and allow those people the opportunity of receiving the blessings of the gospel if they would repent.

Of the two servants, Elder McConkie writes, "And these two shall be followers of that humble man, Joseph Smith, through whom the Lord of Heaven restored the fulness of his everlasting gospel in this final dispensation of grace. No doubt they will be members of the Council of the Twelve or of the First Presidency of the Church" (*DNTC*, 3:509).

*11:5–6.* **No man can hurt them.** They are prophets of God sent forth to the holy city and any man who tries to stop their progress will be burnt by the fire (power) coming from their mouths. They will be similar to Elijah as they can call down fire from heaven by the word of their mouth (see 2 Kgs. 1:10), and will be like Moses as they call down plagues, and turn the water to blood (see Ex. 7:19), along with shutting up the heavens that they will not give forth rain (see 1 Kgs. 17:1).

*11:7.* Once they have **finished their testimony,** in similar fashion to Abinadi (see Mosiah 13:1–3; 17:20), the beast from the bottomless pit (Satan) **shall make war with them and shall overcome them, and kill them,** but only as to the body and only temporarily. The beast will use whatever servants he has to physically take their lives, in the same manner that he has always used those (with their physical bodies) who follow him here on the earth to do his will. They have killed the Lord, and have killed his prophets throughout all ages.

*11:8–9.* Although many people consider **the great city** to be Jerusalem, it **spiritually is called Sodom and Egypt** and has reference to any city that casts out the prophets and the Lord and rebels against their message. Sodom represents all lustful desires, Egypt signifies that which was forbidden (see Abr. 1:23). They thereby allude to all those things which are in direct opposition to the things of God. The two prophets' bodies lay in the street; there are none who come to give them a decent burial, but they are left in the street for all the people to look upon and rejoice over.

*11:9–10.* The wicked people of the earth will now **rejoice . . . and make merry,** even to the point of sending **gifts one to another** to celebrate the demise of these two men who bore witness of the wickedness of the people. The king whom they choose to follow has temporarily overcome and killed the servants of God, and now the people stand and rejoice in wickedness. Once again we see the similitude of the Savior as the people rejoice over the persecution and death of the righteous.

*11:11–12.* Imagine the feeling of those who have been persecuting these prophets and celebrating their murders, when all of a sudden those two men rise from the dead in front of all of the celebrants. Not only are they resurrected, but a voice calls out from heaven commanding them to **come up hither** and they ascend **in a cloud.** In place of exultation and unrighteous celebration the people now experience great fear as a realization of what has just happened comes upon them. These two men were truly prophets of God and the people have rejected the prophets which means that they will incur the vengeance of a just God upon them.

*11:13.* God has now taken control. As the prophets ascend up to heaven a **great earthquake** causes a **tenth part** of the city to fall killing seven thousand men. The tenth is representative of the Lord's portion, his tithe. It appears that only those who rejoiced at the death of the prophets are slain here. The number seven thousand can also be used figuratively to denote a complete multitude of people who were slain and therein may refer to all those who directly opposed the prophetic messages.

According to Bible scholar Marvin R. Vincent, "The phrase [gave glory to the God of heaven] signifies not conversion, nor repentance, nor thanksgiving, but *recognition,* which is its usual sense in scripture. Compare Josh. 7:19 (Sept.). John 9:24; Acts 12:23; Rom. 4:20" (p. 520).

Although the remainder of the people give glory to the God of heaven, they do not fall down and worship him, nor do they repent of their sins. All that is evident here is that they have recognized a power far greater than their own which has caused this destruction to come upon the city and take the lives of so many people.

*11:14.* **The second woe is past.** The first woe was the destructive warfare preceding the final great battle (see Rev. 9:1–12). The second woe has just concluded and includes all of the various battles and destructions in which one-third of the hosts of men were slain (see Rev. 9:12–21; 10; 11:1–14). Now comes the **third woe,** one of such magnitude and destruction that all who are wicked will be swept from off the face of the earth. The great and dreadful day of the Lord is come! It is great for the righteous and dreadful for the wicked. All of the righteous who have waited for millennia will now see the dawning of the Lord when he rises from the East in power and great glory. The wicked shall flee from before his face.

## Applicability

Righteous men will go forth upon the earth proclaiming that the day of the Lord is at hand and that the world must repent of her iniquities. Because of these cries, the wicked of the earth will raise their voices against the righteous. They will call good evil and evil good. It does not take us too long to consider who is on the Lord's side in this day and age. Many of the people producing movies, television, and music, are serving the adversary. They sell those things that provide momentary and fleeting satisfaction and entice the lusts of the flesh. Their grasp is as evident as the burning of a dying ember, and they feed upon the desires of the natural man. They create the desires for more sensual gratification and heap upon their subjects a continual flood of subtle destruction. They are not foolish. As a great shark, they will not release their prey until it is dead. Is there any wonder why so much emphasis is placed on advertising and the responsiveness of viewers?

## REVELATION 11:15–19

15 And the seventh angel sounded; and there were great voices in heaven, saying, The kingdoms of this world are become the kingdoms of our Lord, and of his Christ; and he shall reign for ever and ever.

16 And the four and twenty elders, which sat before God on their seats, fell upon their faces, and worshipped God,

17 Saying, We give thee thanks, O Lord God Almighty, which art, and wast, and art to come; because thou hast taken to thee thy great power, and hast reigned.

18 And the nations were angry, and thy wrath is come, and the time of the dead, that they should be judged, and that thou shouldest give reward unto thy servants the prophets, and to the saints, and them that fear thy name, small and great; and shouldest destroy them which destroy the earth.

19 And the temple of God was opened in heaven, and there was seen in his temple the ark of his testament: and there were lightnings, and voices, and thunderings, and an earthquake, and great hail.

## Verse Commentary

*11:15.* The **seventh angel sound[s]** and great voices now proclaim, **The kingdoms of this world are become the kingdoms of our Lord, and of his Christ; and he shall reign for ever and ever.** What a glorious moment! All of the earthly kingdoms and their apostate leaders are now done away and the true King has taken his rightly place as king over the whole earth. He shall reign for ever. The seventh angel indicates all things are completed at this point and now the Savior's reign here on earth will occur. The earth has been prepared to receive the personal reign of the Lord and the righteous have been awaiting this heralded day since the beginning of time.

Speaking prophetically, Daniel says, "I beheld till the thrones were cast down, and the Ancient of days did sit, whose garment was white as snow, and the hair of his head like the pure wool: his throne was like the fiery flame, and his wheels as burning fire. A fiery stream issued and came forth from before him: thousand thousands ministered unto him, and ten thousand times ten thousand stood before him: the judgment was set, and the books were opened. . . . And there was given him dominion, and glory, and a kingdom, that all people, nations, and languages, should serve him: his dominion is an everlasting dominion, which shall not pass away, and his kingdom that which shall not be destroyed" (Dan. 7:9–10, 14).

*11:16–19.* At the very moment all these things take place, the twenty-four elders fall before the Lord and worship him saying, **We give thee thanks, O Lord God Almighty, . . . because thou hast taken to thee thy great power, and hast reigned.** The elders recognize and worship the rightful king and praise him for what has just been accomplished. All things will now be subdued. Those who have chosen wickedness over righteousness shall be destroyed because of the law, God's law, which he must fulfill (see D&C 1:37–38). The righteous need not fear, but the wicked will be full of fear and trembling.

"For the day cometh that the Lord shall utter his voice out of heaven; the heavens shall shake and the earth shall tremble, and the trump of God shall sound both long and loud, and shall say to the sleeping nations: Ye saints arise and live; ye sinners stay and sleep until I shall call again" (D&C 43:18). Another warning also comes from the Doctrine and Covenants: "And every corruptible thing, both of man, or of the beasts of the field, or of the fowls of the heavens, or of the fish of the sea, that dwells upon all the face of the earth, shall be consumed" (101:24).

*11:19.* In almost an anticlimatic moment, the temple of God is **opened in heaven** and the **ark of his testament,** or covenant, is seen. Anciently the ark carried the tablets of the covenant and served as a constant reminder that God would remember and keep his covenants. We now see the ark again and are shown that God has remembered his covenants! Keep in mind, though, that there is no temple in heaven, but heaven itself is a temple and "the Lord God Almighty and the Lamb are the temple of it" (Rev. 21:22). To dwell with the Father and the Son is to dwell in the temple of God because we are in their presence.

He will now fulfill one of the great covenants—to change this earth to its paradisiacal state on which all of the righteous will dwell for a thousand years. In order to do so, he must wipe off those wicked people who still have not repented of their sins, and therefore must die in them. As a final notification of what is about to happen, the Lord sends forth **lightnings, and voices, and thunderings, and an earthquake, and great hail.** Each of these things represent the power of God over the elements of the earth. He commands and they must obey (see Hel. 12:8–17). This will be a destruction the world has never known as all of God's fury is unleashed against the wicked. No longer will the wicked persecute the wicked—all judgment is left to God!

## Applicability

The Lord will return to the earth and reward his Saints with blessings. He will be our king and we will rejoice to serve under such an honorable and faithful sovereign. We will dwell in his presence. How does that relate to now? We can choose to be in subjection to the King as we dwell in our own homes. Do we keep his commandments in the hope that we will prosper in the land? Do we honor our fathers and our mothers that our days may be long upon the land which the Lord our God gave us? Do we remember the Sabbath day to keep it holy? Do we pay an honest tithe? Do we love the Lord our God with all our heart, might, mind, and strength? Do we love our neighbor? The list goes on and on, but if we will do the things he has commanded we will see that his promises are sure and we will be blessed. If we are choosing the right, the transition to his reign will be very tranquil and familiar.

We have the opportunity to attend the temple which prepares us for the promises of heaven and for dwelling in the presence of God. Our desire to be in the temple reflects our desire to be with God. If we feel peace and tranquility in the temple we will also feel the same in our heavenly home.

## SUMMARY

We have now seen many of the servants of the Lord, John included, as they have performed their earthly responsibilities in preparation for the Lord's coming. John has performed his works in the temple and has taken his message to the nations of the earth, and the two prophets have been the final witnesses, sealing their testimonies with their blood. It is now left up to the Lord to fight the final battle and to subdue all enemies under his feet.

This is a time for the righteous to sing out. Yes, the wicked still remain, but their day is now at hand and they will be cleansed from the earth. We will rejoice in righteousness. We will not be boastful, counting ourselves better than others, but we will be overjoyed that the Lord finds us worthy to be called his people.

The sorrow we will feel is like that of John and the Three Nephites, grieving for the wicked, for those who will not repent of their sins. The Lord will never force his people to follow him. The wicked, as well as the righteous, have agency and it is this agency that has lead them to the kingdom they desire to receive (see D&C 88:32). Nephi teaches that, "Wherefore, men are free according to the flesh; and all things are given them which are expedient unto man. And they are free to choose liberty and eternal life, through the great Mediator of all men, or to choose captivity and death, according to the captivity and power of the devil; for he seeketh that all men might be miserable like unto himself" (2 Ne. 2:27).

It is truly our choice and we can be guaranteed that the Lord will give to his children just what they desire to receive. There will be very few wicked left to destroy, but those of the wicked who remain will be swept off by the righteousness of the people who follow the Savior. Not only will the battle be won by the Savior and his hosts in heaven, but the forces for good here upon the earth will also join in the battle and will be victorious.

# 12

## THE WAR IN HEAVEN AND ON EARTH BETWEEN THE DRAGON, THE WOMAN, AND THE CHILD

One would expect the angelic trumpeting to continue at this point as the second woe is past and the third is about to begin, but all of a sudden we have a change in the vision as the woes are left behind and we begin anew with another wonder in heaven.

This new part of the vision begins by showing the premortal existence when the dragon (Satan) was cast out of heaven and drew the third part of the hosts of heaven with him. The moment Satan is cast out he begins a war with all who come to the earth—his sole intent being to destroy the souls of those who come. When the dragon fails to destroy the seed of the woman, John sees that Satan then makes war with all of her seed.

Chapter 12 provides a wonderful tool to help us understand much of what happened in the pre-earth life, along with assisting us in realizing that Satan was indeed one of our Heavenly Father's sons. The reason Satan was cast out in the beginning is that he turned to wickedness and rebelled against the Father. It is for this purpose that the serpent uses hatred to sway the hearts of the wicked to make war with the righteous.

### REVELATION 12:1–5

1 ¶ AND there appeared a great wonder in heaven; a woman clothed with the sun, and the moon under her feet, and upon her head a crown of twelve stars:

2 And she being with child cried, travailing in birth, and pained to be delivered.

3 And there appeared another wonder in heaven; and behold a great red dragon, having seven heads and ten horns, and seven crowns upon his heads.

4 And his tail drew the third part of the stars of heaven, and did cast them to the earth: and the dragon stood before the woman which was ready to be delivered, for to devour her child as soon as it was born.

5 And she brought forth a man child, who was to rule all nations with a rod of iron: and her child was caught up unto God, and to his throne.

## Verse Commentary

*12:1–3.* **And there appeared a great wonder in heaven.** The great wonder is more aptly described as a "sign" (JST Rev. 12:1; see also New International Version Rev. 12:1). This sign is not something one wonders about, but, more important, one understands that it signifies an event which is about to occur. In view that this sign is in "the likeness of things on the earth" (JST Rev. 12:1), there is no question that it is applicable to things on the earth at the specific reference point of this part of the vision.

The **woman** represents the "church of God" in heaven (see JST Rev. 12:7) and she is preparing to be delivered of a **man child** who represents "the kingdom of God and his Christ" (see JST Rev. 12:7). The woman represents both the kingdom of God in heaven and on earth, because it is at this point that she is joining the two together. She is to be delivered of a man child thereby bringing the kingdom of God in heaven to the earth as the Son will now bring the kingdom to the earth.

The religion course manual *The Life and Teachings of Jesus and His Apostles* helps clarify the passage: "Though at first it may seem confusing to speak of the Church and the kingdom as separate entities, the one giving birth to the other, this in fact is the condition to exist in the Millennium. The Church is a spiritual organization governed by priesthood and revelation. Only those who have covenanted with Christ in the waters of baptism hold membership therein. The kingdom of God is a product of the Church. It is a political organization in which all men who live in the millennial era will belong" (p. 462).

President Joseph Fielding Smith said, "After Christ comes, all the peoples of the earth will be subject to him, but there will be multitudes of people on the face of the earth who will not be members of the Church; yet all will have to be obedient to the laws of the kingdom of God, for it will have dominion upon the whole face of the earth. These people will be subject to *the political government*, even though they are not members of *the ecclesiastical kingdom which is the Church. This government which embraces all the peoples of the earth, both in and out of the Church, is also sometimes spoken of as the kingdom of God*, because the people are subject to the kingdom of God which Christ will set up" (*DS*, 1:229).

Although some would suppose that the man child is the Savior, this cannot be because the Savior is the one who brings about the Church, and not the other way around. As this portion of the vision continues, it will be obvious to see that the man child is the Church because of the way Satan is set to devour the man child when born. It is impossible for Satan to devour Christ, even when he (Christ) was here in mortality, because Satan has no power over the Savior.

The woman is **clothed with the sun,** symbolic of the glory of the celestial worlds, **the moon is under her feet,** representative of the glory and light which reflects to those below, or in other words, at her feet, and she is **pained to be delivered.** The deliverance of her child can no longer be delayed, it is time, and the Son of God will bring forth the kingdom of heaven on earth, in fulfillment of prophetic utterances.

The **crown of twelve stars** may represent the Twelve Apostles who stand at the head of the Church and direct its affairs through what is revealed by its head, Jesus Christ

Joseph Fielding McConkie describes some symbolism related with stars: "(1) Christ is the 'bright and morning star' (Rev. 22:16). (2) Pre-earth spirits are frequently referred to as stars (Job 38:7; Rev. 12:4; Abr. 3). (3) Those obtaining the celestial kingdom are also called stars (Dan. 12:3; Rev. 12:1). (4) By way of contrast with the sun and the moon the stars are used to represent the glory of the telestial kingdom (D&C 76:98)" (*Gospel Symbolism*, p. 272).

The man child will rule all nations with the rod of iron. Marvin R. Vincent says that "The correct reading [of man child] is *arsen*, the neuter, not agreeing with the masculine individual (*uiov son*) but with the neuter of the genus. The object is to emphasize, not *the sex*, but *the peculiar qualities of masculinity*—power and vigor" (pp. 522–23). This man child, as now explained and understood is not speaking of a literal man, as in the case of Christ, but with a nonhuman thing (the Church) which will have power to lift people to a higher plane, as a man could do.

The **rod of iron** (see Rev. 2:27) is the word of God (see 1 Ne. 11:25). It is the word that is used to shepherd the Father's children into the protection of the covenant.

*12:3–5.* **And there appeared another wonder in heaven.** The **great red dragon, having seven heads** and **ten horns, and seven crowns upon its heads.** In direct contrast to a beautiful woman clothed with glory we now see a red dragon, with red symbolizing blood and the word *dragon* representing Satan. The Greek word *drakōn*, refers to "a fabulous kind of serpent" (*Strong's*, Greek Dictionary, p. 24). The number seven represents completeness, ten is a complete part but not the whole, and a head is representative of power or control, horns represent power, and crowns symbolize royalty or rule (political authority) (see Symbols Guide). This dragon has power and authority to rule over his kingdom but none else, and will cause war and bloodshed in order to secure further power. The dragon's sole desire is to make war with the woman, her man child, and then her remnants, or in other words, those who follow the gospel covenants in future dispensations. Note that the Lamb of Revelation 5:6 is depicted with seven horns, and even though it *appears* to have less horns than the dragon, the number seven symbolizes the complete power, control, and authority over all kingdoms which it possesses.

The dragon draws the **third part of the stars of heaven** (see Jude 1:6) with him and they are cast to the earth. All those who chose to follow Satan were cast from heaven to the earth, where ever since a constant battle has raged between the forces of

Satan and those of the Lord's host. We must remember that this battle being raged is just a continuation of the War in Heaven and, although Satan was cast out and figuratively lost that battle, he still desires to win the war.

The dragon stands ready to devour the woman's child after it is born, but the **woman fled into the wilderness, and her child is caught up unto God and to his throne.** The woman (the kingdom of God) is taken from the earth, and the child (the kingdom of God on earth) flees the earth as it is caught up to God and his throne. This was the time of the Apostasy. The battle was so fierce here upon the earth that the new "man child" could not remain without being devoured and so it was removed. This was the Church in its infant state, and as history has shown, the persecutions were so great that by the time that John was on the isle of Patmos most of the Apostles and Church leaders had been killed for their belief in Christ. The leaders passed on and the Church was taken up. It was returned, however, via the Restoration of 1830 through Joseph Smith.

The woman fled into the wilderness to be fed a **thousand two hundred and three score years** (JST Rev. 12:5). Although the King James Version uses the word *days* instead of *years*, various sources, including Strong's Concordance (Greek Dictionary, p. 35), agree the word *hemera* is a period of time that can be translated as years.

An article in the Church newspaper at Nauvoo, Illinois, states: "We are informed by the renowned historian, Whelpley, as also in the Revolutions of Europe, that the church of Jesus Christ was overrun, and driven into the wilderness, A.D. 570, and John the Revelator informs us it must remain there 1260 years, which makes exactly the time, the year 1830, that the Church of Jesus Christ of Latter-day Saints was organized, with the gifts and blessings" (*Times and Seasons*, 5:732).

The dates fit perfectly to herald the restoration of the true Church of Jesus Christ to the earth. It is not just coincidental that the dates came about in this manner, nor is it very likely that Joseph Smith was well-versed enough to decide that 1830 would be the perfect year for the Restoration. Without direction from on high, how would the Prophet know that such things corresponding to the scriptures would be brought to pass?

## Applicability

The glory of the Church is described in poetic beauty in these verses, but it must be remembered that "the Church" is not describing the members, it is describing the sacred covenants of salvation and organization used to save the children of God on earth. The Church of Jesus Christ of Latter-day Saints is the true vehicular organization through which the eternal covenants of the Lord are administered to the Father's children here upon the earth. The Church is true and the organization is intended to perfect the Saints, redeem the dead, and proclaim the gospel (see Eph. 4:11–14). Much too often we invite the dragon into our Church relationships as we backbite, gossip, and take offense where none is intended, and then either fall away into forbidden paths or fail to return to partake of sacred covenants.

When we were baptized we made a covenant with Christ to stand as "witnesses of God at all times and in all things, in all places that ye may be in, even until death" (Mosiah 18:9). The covenant was not made with anyone but Christ and it is our personal obligation to live up to the responsibilities of that covenant. We have the glorious opportunity to have the fulness of the gospel upon the earth in this dispensation, unlike those who lived in the dark ages when the organization of truth fled from the earth.

## REVELATION 12:6–12

6 And the woman fled into the wilderness, where she hath a place prepared of God, that they should feed her there a thousand two hundred and threescore days.

7 And there was war in heaven: Michael and his angels fought against the dragon; and the dragon fought and his angels,

8 And prevailed not; neither was their place found any more in heaven.

9 And the great dragon was cast out, that old serpent, called the

Devil, and Satan, which deceiveth the whole world: he was cast out into the earth, and his angels were cast out with him.

10 And I heard a loud voice saying in heaven, Now is come salvation, and strength, and the kingdom of our God, and the power of his Christ: for the accuser of our brethren is cast down, which accused them before our God day and night.

11 And they overcame him by the blood of the Lamb, and by the word of their testimony; and they loved not their lives unto the death.

12 ¶ Therefore rejoice, ye heavens, and ye that dwell in them. Woe to the inhabiters of the earth and of the sea! for the devil is come down unto you, having great wrath, because he knoweth that he hath but a short time.

## Verse Commentary

*12:6–8.* In the great war in heaven, **Michael** (Adam) **and his angels fought against the dragon** (Satan) and his angels; and the dragon could not prevail against Michael, the child, or the woman. Read and understand this phrase. Satan cannot prevail over us at any time! With the power and ability we have, both as believers and as holders of the priesthood, the adversary cannot win. The whole message of the book of Revelation is expressly written in these verses. When he could not prevail against them in the premortal existence, he was cast out, and his angels with him. He lost but will not accept defeat! Now all he has to hope for is the opportunity to make others as miserable as he is.

The great war continues. Satan could not prevail in the premortal life and so he continued his battle against the woman and man child, along with her remnants, and the war still remains. It is a spiritual war we are fighting, a war with both physical and eternal consequences. We must realize that Satan's only hope is to corrupt us in the short time of our mortal lives. If we can resist his influence, he has lost the chance to drag us down. If we will but endure to the end, and overcome all things, we will be victorious (see D&C 14:7). Consider the inspiring words of Paul in his second epistle to Timothy: "For I am now ready to be offered, and the time of my departure is at hand. I have fought a good fight, I have finished my course, I have kept the faith: Henceforth there is laid up for me a crown of righteousness, which the Lord, the righteous judge, shall give me at that day: and not to me only, but unto all them also that love his appearing" (4:6–8).

The war on earth began in heaven and was carried to the earth by Satan and his forces. Any who followed Satan were as the "stars" of heaven who were cast down and lost the opportunity to receive physical bodies. Periodically, throughout history, Satan has prevailed momentarily over the forces for good. In the meridian of times we find this evident as the universal apostasy came to pass, and those who followed the adversary *appeared* to have triumphed as the Church fled from the earth. This was not the case though, as the woman was taken and fed for a period of time so that when she returned there would be no stopping her from establishing truth and righteousness upon the earth forever.

The prophet Daniel foretold the coming of the Lord's kingdom. "And in the days of these kings shall the God of heaven set up a kingdom, which shall never be destroyed: and the kingdom shall not be left to other people, but it shall break in pieces and consume all these kingdoms, and it shall stand for ever. Forasmuch as thou sawest that the stone was cut out of the mountain without hands, and that it brake in pieces the iron, the brass, the clay, the silver, and the gold; the great God hath made known to the king what shall come to pass hereafter: and the dream is certain, and the interpretation thereof sure" (Dan. 2:44–45).

Although it sometimes appears that wickedness is becoming more prevalent upon the face of the earth, causing our hearts to fear, we, the righteous, are also becoming more numerous. The Lord has reserved us for these days. There is no question that it is the Lord's work which is going forth here upon the earth, it is not ours, nor Joseph Smith's, nor any other prophet's, it is the Lord's. Joseph Smith testified as to the source of the work in the so-called Wentworth Letter. "The Standard of Truth has been erected; no unhallowed hand can stop the work from progressing; persecutions may rage, mobs may combine, armies may assemble, calumny may defame, but the truth of God will go forth boldly, nobly, and independent, till it has penetrated every continent, visited every clime, swept every country, and sounded in every ear, till the purposes of God shall be accomplished, and the Great Jehovah shall say the work is done" (*HC*, 4:450).

*12:9–10.* **The accuser of our brethren is cast down.** Here we find another descriptor for Satan. Along with Lucifer, Perdition, a son of the morning, that old serpent, the devil, the dragon, and the father of lies, we now find the word *accuser,* the direct opposite of advocate which refers to Jesus Christ. Accuser, from the Greek *katēgŏrĕō,* is "to charge with some offence." (*Strong's,* Greek Dictionary, p. 41). Satan has brought an offense upon others and accuses them of it, whereas the Lord takes our offenses upon himself and pays the price for them.

Joseph Fielding McConkie writes, "Every Old Testament reference to Satan is in the context of an adversary bringing an accusation (see Job 2; Zechariah 3). The rest of the standard works use the name more generally. *Perdition* means 'destruction,' carrying the connotation of being eternally lost. Lucifer is the name borne by the adversary in the premortal existence. It refers to one of renown, a morning star, literally the 'shining one.' Before his fall, Lucifer was 'a son of the morning' (Isaiah 14:12; D&C 76:26). A devil is a demonic being, the name meaning 'slanderer'" (*Gospel Symbolism*, p. 192).

*12:10.* **Now is come salvation, and strength, and the kingdom of our God, and the power of his Christ:** The voice proclaims that the great day of the Lord is at hand and the kingdom of God will return to the earth. Those things which people have waited for throughout the ages are now set to come to pass.

*12:11.* The adversary (dragon) has been overcome **by the blood of the Lamb** and **by the word of their testimonies** (those of the faithful Saints). The only way we can overcome all that Satan has brought about here on the earth is through the blood of Jesus Christ—through his atonement. If we do not express our faith and belief in him there is no way for us to overcome all things. Remember, the first principle of the gospel is "faith in the

Lord Jesus Christ." Without faith it is impossible to cultivate a relationship with him.

*12:12.* Another **woe** is now set to come. The devil is cast to the earth and he knows that he must carry out his work quickly because **he hath but a short time.** It is important to take a moment to discuss what the earth is doing while all of this is going on. The earth has a role in the eternal existence of man for it will become a celestial kingdom for those who are worthy. However, until that time it must endure wickedness, bloodshed, filthiness, famine, and every other vile thing caused by the wicked desires of man and Satan. We can only imagine the desires of the earth to cleanse itself from all wickedness in order to become a pure and holy place on which the Lord may dwell.

"But a short time" suggests two unique ideas. One, with regards to eternity, the earth's existence is short and Satan's influence here is for a short time. Two, concerning Satan's temptations of us, an even shorter time exists because our life expectancy is only seventy to eighty years.

## Applicability

The battle we are engaged in is real and deadly. There were no neutrals in the War in Heaven, which means that if we are here upon the earth, we chose the Father's plan. Our adversary, and his followers, were cast to the earth. What does that mean for us? Consider the beautiful message and warning of the following verse: "And now, my sons, remember, remember that it is upon the rock of our Redeemer, who is Christ, the Son of God, that ye must build your foundation; that when the devil shall send forth his mighty winds, yea, his shafts in the whirlwind, yea, when all his hail and his mighty storm shall beat upon you, it shall have no power over you to drag you down to the gulf of misery and endless wo, because of the rock upon which ye are built, which is a sure foundation, a foundation whereon if men build they cannot fall" (Hel. 5:12).

We are guaranteed that Satan will cause his storms to beat upon us while here in this mortal life, but we can overcome through our testimonies of and faithfulness to the gospel of Jesus Christ. It is not too difficult to learn who is on the Lord's side and who is working for the adversary, but we must also use wisdom to realize that at times there will be wolves in sheep's clothing who will attempt to turn us from our covenants with Christ. We have the opportunity to choose whom we will follow and whether we will be advocates of the Father and the cause of Christ, or whether we will be accusers like the adversary and seek to shift blame for our actions to others. The choice is truly ours. If we are built upon the rock, who is Christ, we shall not fall.

## REVELATION 12:13–17

13 And when the dragon saw that he was cast unto the earth, he persecuted the woman which brought forth the man child.

14 And to the woman were given two wings of a great eagle, that she might fly into the wilderness, into her place, where she is nourished for a time, and times, and half a time, from the face of the serpent.

15 And the serpent cast out of his mouth water as a flood after the woman, that he might cause her to be carried away of the flood.

16 And the earth helped the woman, and the earth opened her mouth, and swallowed up the flood which the dragon cast out of his mouth.

17 And the dragon was wroth with the woman, and went to make war with the remnant of her seed, which keep the commandments of God, and have the testimony of Jesus Christ.

### Verse Commentary

*12:13–17.* The dragon persecutes the woman and she is given **two wings of a great eagle** to **fly into the wilderness** for a set period of time. As explained previously, the dragon persecutes the woman in an attempt to destroy righteousness from off the earth. She is then given two wings, representing the idea that she is no longer bound to the earth in her flight and can seek refuge in the heavenly places of protection. The set period of time is known by God, who is the only one who knows when the day will come that the kingdom of God in heaven and the kingdom of God on earth will be joined together once again. Finally, the use of the wilderness or "desert illustrates that the church has become inaccessible to humans" (Draper, p. 137).

The serpent then casts water as a flood to try to destroy her. The flood is used by the serpent in mimicking something the Lord has used previously. Satan attempts to flood the earth with water to destroy righteousness, in the same way the Lord cleansed the earth of wickedness at the time of Noah. Consider other comparisons also. The earth is to be flooded with the Book of Mormon, thereby wiping away wickedness. Satan will attempt to flood the earth with lies, temptation, tribulation, evil, and wickedness in order to sweep away righteousness.

President Ezra Taft Benson said, "The Book of Mormon is the instrument that God has designed to 'sweep the earth as with a flood, to gather out His elect unto the New Jerusalem.' This sacred volume of scripture has not been, nor is it yet, central in our preaching, our teaching, and our missionary work" (*Teachings*, p. 60). Similarly, the Lord told Moses, "And righteousness will I send down out of heaven; and truth will I send forth out of the earth, to bear testimony of mine Only Begotten; his resurrection from the dead; yea, and also the resurrection of all men; and righteousness and truth will I cause to sweep the earth as with a flood, to gather mine elect from the four quarters of the earth, unto a place which I shall prepare, an Holy City, that my people may gird up their loins, and be looking forth for the time of my coming; for there shall be my tabernacle, and it shall be called Zion, a New Jerusalem" (Moses 7:62).

The earth then opens up her mouth and helps the woman by swallowing the flood sent forth from the serpent. The earth has now become a part of the battle against wickedness and swallows those who are evil and who are attempting to destroy the woman or her child. At the time prior to the coming of Christ in the Americas we gain a brief glimpse of one way in which this statement is fulfilled and a flood of wickedness is swallowed up by the earth (see 3 Ne. 8:9–10, 14; 9:4–5, 7–8). The earth also helped at the time of the flood—water came from within her to add to that which God had sent from the heavens to cleanse the wicked from the earth (see Gen. 7:11).

After failing to destroy the woman or devour the man child, the dragon has one alternative left—to **make war with the remnant** of the woman's seed. In other words, all those who remain on the earth and are a part of the Church will be persecuted by the dragon as he uses every possible means to overcome the remnant of her seed with his flood of wickedness.

Speaking of wickedness in the last days Paul cautions us saying, "This know also, that in the last days perilous times shall come. For men shall be lovers of their own selves, covetous, boasters, proud, blasphemers, disobedient to parents, unthankful, unholy, Without natural affection, trucebreakers, false accusers, incontinent, fierce, despisers of those that are good, Traitors, heady, highminded, lovers of pleasure more than lovers of God; Having a form of godliness, but denying the power thereof: from such turn away. For of this sort are they which creep into houses, and lead captive silly women laden with sins, led away with divers lusts, Ever learning, and never able to come to the knowledge of the truth" (2 Tim. 3:1–7).

Compare the previous statement of counsel regarding this war, with the following guarantee of what can be done to overcome all things. "And they said unto me: What meaneth the rod of iron which our father saw, that led to the tree? And I said unto them that it was the word of God; and whoso would hearken unto the word of God, and would hold fast unto it, they would never perish; neither could the temptations and the fiery darts of the adversary overpower them unto blindness, to lead them away to destruction" (1 Ne. 15:23–24).

## Applicability

We see two powerful opposing forces at work on the earth at this time. One is attempting to flood the earth with righteousness through the Book of Mormon and conversion to the gospel of Jesus Christ. The other is flooding the earth with lies, deceit, hatred, envy, moral infidelity, and every other conceivable sin known to man. What is the answer to these opposing forces? It is to remain faithful to the covenants which protect us from the power of Satan. Where are those covenants found? In our homes, the Church, and the temple. We are at war with the adversary and his servants. It would be extremely foolish to think that we could go onto his turf or enter his lair and come out unscathed. We must avoid the very appearance of evil.

The serpent cast a flood after the woman and failed. Now he makes war with all of her remnant. There is one certain way to guarantee protection against the powers of Satan and that is to remain faithful to your covenants with Christ. That doesn't mean we won't have trials and storms, but we will be able to weather them.

Dragons look extremely fierce and mean but do not really exist. Satan looks and acts powerful but he has no hold on us; he has no power to drag us down if we are built upon the rock of Christ. Finally, the serpent may have power to bite us and bruise our heel, but we have power to crush his head (see Gen 3:15; Moses 4:21). In other words, the battle is won, the victory is assured, but the adversary has not and will not give up the fight until the end.

## SUMMARY

This chapter provides a deep and informative description of the war which rages between the forces for good and for evil. It is evident that one of the major reasons for the war is that Satan and his hosts were cast out of heaven and lost whatever opportunities previously existed for them. Because of being cast out, Satan (the dragon) will use whatever means are at his control in an attempt to destroy or devour the woman, her child, and her seed.

The battle did not just take place in heaven, and did not end when Satan was cast out. This chapter is significant in all ages of the earth's existence during which the forces of evil are allowed to roam upon the earth seeking to destroy the souls of men. The adversary persecuted the woman, the Church of God, with such vigor that the Church was removed from the earth. In the wilderness, her place of refuge, the woman was strengthened and prepared to come again in the Restoration.

Any time that the Church is here upon the earth, whether in the days of Adam, Noah, Elijah, or Moses, in the days of Christ, John the Baptist, and the Twelve Apostles, or finally in the early days of the restored Church, whenever we see the truth upon the earth, with all of its rights, powers, privileges, and keys, we are assured that the adversary is close at hand and ready to wage war with the Saints. The message here is that the Lord will deliver his people—though they may pass through perilous times. To those who are true and faithful, the Lord gives hope that they will be victorious.

"And if thou shouldst be cast into the pit, or into the hands of murderers, and the sentence of death passed upon thee; if thou be cast into the deep; if the billowing surge conspire against thee; if fierce winds become thine enemy; if the heavens gather blackness, and all the elements combine to hedge up the way; and above all, if the very jaws of hell shall gape open the mouth wide after thee, know thou, my son, that all these things shall give thee experience, and shall be for thy good. The Son of Man hath descended below them all. Art thou greater than he? Therefore, hold on thy way, and the priesthood shall remain with thee; for their bounds are set, they cannot pass. Thy days are known, and thy years shall not be numbered less; therefore, fear not what man can do, for God shall be with you forever and ever" (D&C 122:7 9).

# 13

## THE BEASTS OF REVELATION
## AND SATAN'S REIGN

At times when it seems as though we can't hold on any longer, and the battle seems too fierce, we must remember that John saw the whole series of events described in Revelation. The vision of wickedness continues. Remember all of the various forces of evil which have already been swept off the earth? John has seen the exact opposite of the Savior, in the heavenly realm, as he beheld the dragon and the forces which followed him. He now beholds a new beast come upon the earth, a beast which is in subjection to the dragon and which attempts to draw all nations of the earth unto the dragon.

Explaining this beast, Elder McConkie says, "John is here seeing a beast in heaven, which is 'in the likeness of the kingdoms of the earth' ([JST], verse 1), that is, the beast is being used to symbolize certain unnamed kingdoms on earth and to show their dealings toward the saints and the cause of righteousness" (*DNTC*, 3:520). All beasts in this chapter represent the kingdoms of the world which rise up and give battle to the Saints.

The beast comes up out of the sea and stands upon the sands of the sea. If we relate the Lord's promise to Abraham that "I will multiply thy seed as the stars of the heaven, and as the sand which is upon the sea shore" (Gen. 22:17), to the beast who stands upon the sand of the sea, we may illuminate Satan's purpose. It could be that the beast standing on the sand represents Satan's desire to cause us to break our covenants, hoping that we would deny ourselves the blessings of Abraham, of having posterity as numerous as the sands of the sea. In reality, when we subject ourselves to Satan we become his posterity, his sands of the sea.

# REVELATION 13:1–10

1 ¶ And I stood upon the sand of the sea, and saw a beast rise up out of the sea, having seven heads and ten horns, and upon his horns ten crowns, and upon his heads the name of blasphemy.

2 And the beast which I saw was like unto a leopard, and his feet were as the feet of a bear, and his mouth as the mouth of a lion: and the dragon gave him his power, and his seat, and great authority.

3 And I saw one of his heads as it were wounded to death; and his deadly wound was healed: and all the world wondered after the beast.

4 And they worshipped the dragon which gave power unto the beast: and they worshipped the beast, saying, Who is like unto the beast? who is able to make war with him?

5 And there was given unto him a mouth speaking great things and blasphemies; and power was given unto him to continue forty and two months.

6 And he opened his mouth in blasphemy against God, to blaspheme his name, and his tabernacle, and them that dwell in heaven.

7 And it was given unto him to make war with the saints, and to overcome them: and power was given him over all kindreds, and tongues, and nations.

8 And all that dwell upon the earth shall worship him, whose names are not written in the book of life of the Lamb slain from the foundation of the world.

9 If any man have an ear, let him hear.

10 He that leadeth into captivity shall go into captivity: he that killeth with the sword must be killed with the sword. Here is the patience and the faith of the saints.

## Verse Commentary

**13:1–3. Another sign, in the likeness of the kingdoms of the earth** (JST Rev. 13:1). Once again we find another sign being used to show forth the power of something. This sign is in the "likeness" of the kingdoms of the earth. There is no particular kingdom it is representing but it is in the likeness of all kingdoms which follow after Satan, blaspheme God, and fight against the work of the Lord.

**I saw . . . a beast rise up out of the sea and he stood upon the sand of the sea** (JST Rev. 13:1). This beast is not the dragon, but is one of his agents through which the work of Satan will be carried out. The actual Greek word, *thēriŏn*, describes a dangerous beast (see *Strong's,* Greek Dictionary, p. 36). This beast will represent all of the classes of things here upon the earth that follow after the dragon, in the same way that the four living beasts, denoted by the word *zōŏn* in Greek, represented classes of things (see *Strong's,* Greek Dictionary, p. 35) that followed the Lord (see Rev. 4:6–11).

The beast here has **seven heads and ten horns, and upon his horns ten crowns, and upon his heads the name of blasphemy.** Each of these features indicate the power which the beast possesses. He has seven heads and ten horns, and with the head symbolizing control and the horns symbolizing power, we find that the beast has complete control and complete power, but not whole power over his dominion (see Symbols Guide). Remember, the Lord is the one who has ultimate control of the keys of the bottomless pit. The crowns represent rule, authority, or dominion over a kingdom, and here again we see the number ten symbolizing complete but not whole power over something. Although Satan has power to do many mighty works, he is unequal to God or Christ.

To carry the "name of blasphemy" is to do one of three things. First, it is to say that you are God when you are not. Second, it is to attempt to be worshipped as a God. Third, it is to do things in the name of God without the authority to do so. Even some so-called religious organizations carry the name of blasphemy as their leaders supposedly forgive sins, heal the sick, and divine, all for profit. By doing these things, they commit priestcrafts in the supposed name and authority of Christ (see 2 Ne. 26:29).

The beast has blasphemy written on his heads. The beast is marked in a manner similar to those who follow the Lord. The head is the center of thought and so those who have blasphemy written upon their heads are directly opposed to those who have the name of God written upon theirs. In this verse, the proper translation of name is *names* (see Vincent, p. 526), and so each head may have a different name of blasphemy written upon it, or in other words, the heads illustrate the various ways blasphemy can be manifest.

"And the angel said unto me: Behold the foundation of a church which is most abominable above all other churches, which slayeth the saints of God, yea, and tortureth them and bindeth them down, and yoketh them with a yoke of iron, and bringeth them down into captivity. And it came to pass that I beheld this great and abominable church; and I saw the devil that he was the foundation of it" (1 Ne. 13:5–6). Obviously, one of the best ways for Satan to fight against the Saints of God is to set up his own church here upon the earth. The adversary's church will not carry his name, but will do its acts of wickedness in the name of God. This church may appear to do a righteous work, but it will actually harden the hearts of its members and will persecute the Saints. The church may teach about Jesus Christ, but will not tell a person to seek God in prayer. The professors will say that the heavens are closed, that God does not reveal things to man on earth anymore but only gives us his word through the Bible.

13:2. The beast is described **like unto a leopard, and his feet were as the feet of a bear, and his mouth as the mouth of a lion.** This symbolism is used to express the fierceness and ferociousness of the beast. **And the dragon gave him his power, and his seat and great authority.** The dragon will use the beast to perform his works here upon the earth, as evidenced by people here who use wickedness to accomplish their ends. It is interesting to note that the beast does not have the authority himself, but must receive it from the dragon.

Richard Draper writes, "The Bible uses the term *beast* to translate three Greek words: *zōon*, *ktēnos*, and *thērion*. *Zōon* describes living creatures, often those connected with God like the seraphim of Isaiah 6:2–3 and the four living beings in Revelation 4:6–9. *Ktēnos* refers to domesticated animals, especially beasts of burden and animals used for food as in Revelation 18:13. *Thērion*, on the other hand, characterizes wild beasts, especially beasts of prey. John calls the sea monster *thērion*, and the term aptly fits. The beast's three components—leopard, bear, and lion—are all untameable and flesh-devouring" (Draper, p. 143).

It may seem like the beast has more power than the dragon

because he has ten horns and the dragon has only seven, but one must remember that ten is symbolic of a complete portion of power whereas the dragon has the complete perfect power, denoted by the number seven, which pertains specifically to his kingdom (see Symbols Guide). Satan does not match the ultimate power possessed by the Savior and is in subjection to him since Christ controls the keys of the bottomless pit.

One of the most important messages of this section of scripture is that even though the dragon and various beasts make war with the Saints, their destructive forces are limited and they have no power over the children of God, unless the children of God submit themselves to the enticings of the devil. Essentially, we cannot lose unless we give in to the adversary. We must remember, however, that opposition must be here upon the earth to allow us agency to choose who we will opt to follow.

13:3. One of the heads of the beast is wounded unto death, but the deadly wound is healed, causing the whole world to wonder after the beast. The word for wounded, *sphazō,* means to "kill" or "slaughter" (*Strong's,* Greek Dictionary, p. 70). Marvin Vincent considers the wounding and subsequent healing to be significant. "Professor Milligan rightly observes that the statement is the counterpart of that in ver. 6 [Rev. 5:6], where we read of *the Lamb as though it had been slaughtered.* In both cases there had been actual death, and in both revival. The one is a mocking counterpart of the other" (p. 527).

We must realize that although one of the heads is "wounded to death," it does not kill the beast and the head is healed. Numerous attempts have been made by scholars to relate this head to one individual person, such as Nero, Nebuchadnezzar, Constantine, or even the Roman Catholic Church (see *TPJS,* p. 293; *DNTC,* 3:521), but there is no definitive answer. It seems that when one of Satan's "heads," or leaders of his program, is killed or removed from power, Satan will "heal" that head by placing a new devotee in its place. The cycle is repeated throughout history as shown in the Book of Mormon where Satan enacts his secret combinations and covenants with the Gadianton robbers (see 2 Ne. 9:9; 4 Ne. 1:42, 46; Ether 8:20–23).

**All the world wondered after the beast.** This part of the vision is in direct opposition to the Lamb who was slain and then raised (see Rev. 5:6). We can be guaranteed that wherever we find truth in one form, we will find a counterfeit nearby. As God gives the Lamb the power over death, allows him to receive the throne of God, and grants him all authority, so the dragon gives power to the beast to be healed of his wound and also bestows upon him his seat, and great authority. It is impossible for the beast to heal himself. Christ possesses the key to the bottomless pit, thereby having authority and power over the beast and the dragon.

We will continue to see, through the rest of chapter 13, similar comparisons made between the Savior and the beasts (see vv. 1, 11).

13:4. People begin to worship **the dragon which gave power unto the beast,** and they also worship the beast. This is Satan's true desire, to be worshipped like God the Father. He desires to have all of the Father's honor (see Moses 4:1).

The comparisons of Lamb and beast continue. Previously we heard the question, "Who is worthy to open the book, and to loose the seals thereof?" (Rev. 5:2). No one was found until the Lamb of God, "the Lion of the tribe of Juda" (Rev. 5:5), came along. In direct opposition to that phrase, here we see, **Who is like unto the beast? who is able to make war with him?** Here, the beast that had "his mouth as the mouth of a lion" (v. 2) is the one that makes war. It appears that no one is able to counteract the advances of the beast. This semblance of great power is all that Satan has and he wields it over only those who are willing to follow after him.

13:5–8. The beast is given a mouth to speak **great things and blasphemies.** He has this power for the space of **forty and two months** (see Rev. 11:2–3). The beast will speak those things that make him appear to have the power of God, but in reality he will be blaspheming all holy things; yet, "forty and two months" indicates that his blasphemies will be cut short.

It is important to note the things which will be blasphemed by the beast. He will blaspheme God's **name, . . . his tabernacle,**

**and them that dwell in heaven.** All things which are sacred and holy will be the subject of derision by the beast. Of the particular things the beast blasphemes against, Henry Alford says, "The meaning is to enhance the enormity of the blasphemy by bringing out the lofty nature of God's holy name and dwelling-place" (as quoted in Vincent, pp. 527–28). In other words, the blasphemies which are cried out by the beast will be in direct opposition to all of the things representing God, his people, and his tabernacle.

*13:7–8.* The beast is given power **to make war with the saints, and to overcome them: and power was given him over all kindreds, . . . tongues, and nations.** The beast makes war with the Saints, overcoming them in one or the other of two drastically different ways.

First, if a righteous person's work here has been accomplished, Satan, through his followers, may be allowed to kill him and end the Saint's mortal existence. This was the case with Abinadi (see Mosiah 17:20), the women and children who were cast into the fire before Alma and Amulek (see Alma 14:9–10), the two prophets (see Rev. 11:7), and Joseph Smith (see D&C 135:4), but Satan's power is only temporary. Second, if the righteous give in to his enticements and he overcomes them, he then rules over them for eternity except they repent. These are the ones spoken of which become servants and angels of the devil, to dwell with him forever. "Wherefore, he maketh war with the saints of God, and encompasseth them round about. And we saw a vision of the sufferings of those with whom he made war and overcame, for thus came the voice of the Lord unto us: Thus saith the Lord concerning all those who know my power, and have been made partakers thereof, and suffered themselves through the power of the devil to be overcome, and to deny the truth and defy my power—They are they who are the sons of perdition, of whom I say that it had been better for them never to have been born; For they are vessels of wrath, doomed to suffer the wrath of God, with the devil and his angels in eternity" (D&C 76:29–33).

The Savior would be excluded from the group that is subject to the adversary's temporary power over life, because the

Savior voluntarily gave his life. Satan's servants had not the power to take it from him.

*13:8.* **All that dwell upon earth shall worship him,** with the exception of those whose names are **written in the book of life of the Lamb slain from the foundation of the world.** The beast will have such power that all who dwell here, and do not follow the Savior, will worship him because of the power he possesses. Elder McConkie discusses this phenomenon: "Who worships the devil? An immediate and superficial reaction is: Why, no one, or at least scarcely anyone. But more mature reflection leads to the realization that just as the true worship of God consists in keeping his commandments, and in emulating those characteristics and attributes which he possesses, so to pursue a Godless course of rebellion against the truth, to revel in wickedness, and to live carnal and unclean lives is, in the very nature of things, to worship Satan" (*DNTC*, 3:522).

A vital element of the plan of salvation is that it provides for an eternal sacrifice—a Lamb, unblemished by the world, offered for all those willing to accept it as payment for their sins. Even though this offering was not made until the meridian of time, it was an integral part of the foundation for the entire plan of salvation from the beginning of time and throughout all eternity. President Joseph Fielding Smith explains: "Therefore, he is called the 'Lamb of God,' who was chosen to be slain 'from the foundation of the world.' The only way this atonement could be made was for Jesus who was chosen to pay the debt to justice and mercy, and redeem us from the grasp of Satan, to come into the world with power over death, for no one who was under the bondage of death could pay the debt and restore us to live forever. Jesus was the only person who ever came into this world who had power over death, and having that great power, by the shedding of his blood on the cross he could redeem us and get the power of the resurrection. After he came forth from the tomb he had all power to call every other person forth from the grave" (*AGQ*, 1:32).

*13:9–10.* **If any man have an ear, let him hear.** All have ears, so we must listen to the prophecies. The judgments of verse 10

mete out an eye for an eye (see Deut. 19:21) to the followers of
Satan. Our Father is just and his punishments are the same;
therefore, those who **leadeth into captivity shall go into captivity**, and those who **killeth with the sword must be killed with
the sword.** This is the most equitable form of judgment there is;
the punishment or judgment inflicted by the wicked upon others is the same form of judgment which will be inflicted upon
them.

**The patience and the faith of the saints** is described in the
previous part of this verse in that some of them will be placed
into captivity by those who follow after the beast, and some will
be slain by the sword, in order that their testimonies may stand
against the wicked at the last day. Alma and Amulek encountered this type of adversity when they stood by and watched as
the righteous were cast into the fire and burned by the wicked
(see Alma 14:10–13). The adversary has always used these
means to try the patience of the Saints.

## Applicability

There are times that the power of wickedness and the servants of Satan seem so overwhelming that nothing can stop
them from sweeping the earth. This previous section of verses
gives us a good idea of some of the trials and challenges we may
face, even to the point of being killed, but that does not mean
Satan has won. When a righteous person dies at the hand of the
wicked, it is to provide a witness against him who was wicked,
to ensure the judgments of God are just. When the righteous die,
they return to that God who gave them life and then rest in a
state of happiness (see Alma 40:11–14). Mortal existence is but a
momentary segment of their eternal advancement. The Lord
will never allow the wicked to take the life of a righteous person
who has not completed his earthly mission. (Consider Nephi;
Abinadi; Shadrach, Meschach, and Abidnago; Alma and
Amulek; Joseph Smith; and so forth.)

## REVELATION 13:11–18

11 ¶ And I beheld another beast coming up out of the earth; and he had two horns like a lamb, and he spake as a dragon.

12 And he exerciseth all the power of the first beast before him, and causeth the earth and them which dwell therein to worship the first beast, whose deadly wound was healed.

13 And he doeth great wonders, so that he maketh fire come down from heaven on the earth in the sight of men,

14 And deceiveth them that dwell on the earth by the means of those miracles which he had power to do in the sight of the beast; saying to them that dwell on the earth, that they should make an image to the beast, which had the wound by a sword, and did live.

15 And he had power to give life unto the image of the beast, that the image of the beast should both speak, and cause that as many as would not worship the image of the beast should be killed.

16 And he causeth all, both small and great, rich and poor, free and bond, to receive a mark in their right hand, or in their foreheads:

17 And that no man might buy or sell, save he that had the mark, or the name of the beast, or the number of his name.

18 Here is wisdom. Let him that hath understanding count the number of the beast: for it is the number of a man; and his number is Six hundred threescore and six.

## Verse Commentary

**13:11. And I beheld another beast coming up out of the earth; and he had two horns like a lamb, and he spake as a dragon.** This beast comes up out of the earth, or appears to be made by the earth. It would seem to indicate that Satan's influence is not just over the seas (consider the first beast), but is also covering the earth. This beast has two horns like a lamb (see Symbols Guide). This is a direct counterfeit of the Lamb of God. He is recognized as a counterfeit because of his words: "he spake as a dragon." The beast is like a lamb, not like *the Lamb*, but his appearance would make some believe that this is the Christ. In reality this is anti-Christ and goes about working miracles and teaching false doctrines as though he were doing it by the power of God.

We now have a trinity of evil, in direct opposition to the trinity of the Godhead. All three of these evils, though separate and distinct, have the desire to overthrow the kingdom of God, and they are the complete imitation of the Father, Son, and Holy Ghost. Satan has given his power to the things he has created, and both bear witness of him, and he will kill all who do not worship the image of the beast (see v. 15). "Thou shalt have no other gods before me" (Ex. 20:3) is the righteous statement by our Father because he *is* our creator. The dragon, on the other hand, desires the awe and worship of those who subject themselves to him, but he has no legal claim to such adoration. He is not their creator, he is not their savior, he is just their oppressor. The Lord and our Father do not force subjection, but allow all men their agency to choose whom they will follow.

13:12–17. **He,** the second beast, **exerciseth all the power of the first beast,** and causes all that dwell in his presence to **worship the first beast.** With his power he begins to perform many miracles comparable to those performed by the Lord's prophets throughout the ages. First, **he maketh fire come down from heaven in the sight of men,** very much like the power exhibited by Elijah over the wicked priests of Baal (see 1 Kgs. 18:26–38). **Whose deadly wound was healed** gives the impression that this beast was wounded unto death but was brought back in some way, to portray a type of resurrection, in imitation of Christ's resurrection. Satan and his servants, however, do not have power over the resurrection, this being another of their counterfeits of truth.

Each of the miracles the beast performs are specifically designed to bring attention to himself. These miracles are used to deceive those who dwell on the earth to such a degree that **they should make an image to the beast, which had the wound by a sword, and did live.** The image comes from the Greek word *eikon* and is a figure or likeness (see Vincent, pp. 528–29). This icon is something which Satan has caused to be brought forth and is in the likeness of himself. Once again we find Satan imitating the Creators, Father and Son. God said, "Let us make man in our image, after our likeness" (Gen. 1:26). Satan has imi-

tated the things which he saw performed from the creation of
the worlds, he has no other plan.

Unlike the Savior who bled from every pore and even gave
his life for mankind, the beast was wounded in but one of his
heads. Christ had power and authority over death, laying down
his own life and taking it up again. The beast tries to imitate this
power, but without authority it is just a sham and a fraud.

The image of the beast is given life and then speaks and
sends forth a decree that all who will not worship him shall be
killed. The beast is forcing himself on those of the earth. They
have lost all agency and must worship him or be killed.

13:16. All are caused **to receive a mark in their right hand,
or in their foreheads.** Those who follow after the Son receive the
seal of God in their foreheads (see Rev. 7:3; 9:4; 14:1) and are
found on the right hand of God (see Matt. 25:34), while those
who desire to follow after Satan must also make a covenant with
him and mark it in their right hand, or in their foreheads. Here
the adversary causes a mark to be placed upon those who follow him. Marvin Vincent compares the marks placed upon the
followers of God and those of Satan with identifiers commonly
used in the ancient world. "Commentators find illustrations in
the brand set upon slaves by their masters, or upon soldiers by
their monarchs, and in the branding of slaves attached to certain
temples" (Vincent, p. 529).

Those who follow the Lord receive the mark in their foreheads, the center of their thoughts, that they are found worthy
to enter his presence after having participated in the sealing cer-
emonies as found in the temples of God here on earth. They are
then found on the right hand of God, as a part of their covenant,
if they have kept the commandments and have endured to the
end. In the situation with the beast, those who follow after Satan
have now made a pact or covenant with Satan in which they
have also marked themselves, symbolizing their covenant with
him.

13:17. All agency is lost. **No man might buy or sell, save he
that had the mark, or the name of the beast, or the number of
his name.** The beast now requires all people to carry his mark,

name, or number if they are to deal with others who dwell on
the earth. There is no agency. It has been forfeited on account of
the people desiring to follow after the beast.

*13:18.* **Here is wisdom.** A powerful introduction to the following information of how to identify the beast and the number
of his name. **Count the number of the beast: for it is the number of a man; and his number is Six hundred threescore and
six [666].** There is much symbolism in the number. First, it is
imperfection magnified. The number six is one short of seven,
thereby symbolizing coming short of perfection, and since it is
magnified, it follows to surmise that this beast has intensified its
lack of perfection. In the same way that the Lord had a name
and number attributed to him anciently, we find a name and
number for the adversary.

The following explanations help one to understand the significance of the numbers as associated with their names, and
help to intensify how Satan has become so inferior to the Lord,
even in the representations of their names. "The method of reading generally adopted is that known as the *Ghematria* of the Rab-
bins, or in Greek, *isopsephia numerical equality,* which assigns
each letter of a name its usual numerical value, and gives the
sum of such numbers as the equivalent of the name. Thus, in the
Epistle of Barnabas, we are told that the name *Iesous Jesus* is
expressed by the number 888. $I = 10$; $e = 8$; $s = 200$; $o = 70$; $u = 400$; $s = 200$. The majority of the commentators use the Greek
alphabet in computation; others, however, employ the Hebrew;
while a third class employ the Roman numerals" (Vincent, p.
531).

The Lord's number is a complete and total perfection, even
surpassing that expressed by the number seven, as symbolized
by the number eight, repeated three times. It is a representation
of all of his powers and abilities. The number eight, or Hebrew
*sh$^e$môwnâh,* represents "a surplus above the 'perfect' seven"
(*Strong's,* Hebrew Dictionary, p. 118) thereby implying the greatness of the Lord's name.

As to the number of the beast, it is imperative that we
understand that there is no definitive answer as to who the

name identifies, other than being a representation of evil. Any person, society, people, or government who set as their desires the worship of men fall into the category of having the number.

Note that it is the number of a man. "This famous number has been made to yield almost all the historical names of the past eighteen centuries: Titus, Vespasian, and Simon Gioras; Julian the Apostate and Genseric; Mahomet and Luther; Benedict IX. and Louis XV.; Napoleon I. and the Duke of Reichstadt; and it would not be difficult, on the same principles, to read in it one another's names" (Reuss, as quoted in Vincent, p. 531; see also Draper, pp. 149–50).

In view that the number 666 is in reference to the beasts and the dragon, it is a suitable representation of the imperfection that each of these figures exhibits when compared with their counterparts in the Godhead. Each of them fall far short of the perfection associated with the Father, Son, and Holy Ghost, and therefore their infamous number is correctly expressed.

**Applicability**

Satan is the great imitator, the father of all lies. In the previous verses we have seen that he will go as far as appearing "like a lamb" (v. 11). It is at this point that we find ourselves today. We face a myriad of choices, and through each choice we either do good or evil. If we follow the promptings and guidance of the Holy Ghost, we will be led to choose good (see Mosiah 3:19) and will be given answers to our prayers (see D&C 112:10). On the other hand, if we give in to the enticings and subtleties of Satan, he will lead us "away carefully down to hell" (2 Ne. 28:21). Sooner or later we will become subject to the devil if we continue to make choices which support him.

We have all been born with the Light of Christ, or in other words, our conscience, and with that light we have the ability to discern truth from error. The Lord has revealed the processes Satan uses to show his power and make it appear that he is more powerful than the Lamb. All Lucifer can do is imitate. All of his workings are false imitations of the truth. Our responsibility is to use the wisdom we have been blessed with to weigh the facts placed before us as we make our decisions. We know that any man who tempts us to do that which is evil in the sight of God fits the description of the number 666, and we must shy away from that person. It is imperative to our own eternal salvation that we stop approaching those things which we know are evil, and begin focusing on those things in life which bring lasting joy and happiness. It is complete foolishness to continue reaching down to pick up the serpent when we know that the serpent's only goal and desire is to strike and kill.

## SUMMARY

Chapter 13 has provided an excellent comparison between the workings of the Father and his Son, and the relationships of the dragon (Satan) and his beasts. All that the Savior has done is copied by the adversary and then is brought forth in counterfeit. In the same way that the Son of God was born and "brought forth on the earth," the adversary brings forth his supposed creations, beasts, one from the sea and one from the earth.

The wounds inflicted upon the beast, his supposed power and authority, and appearance like unto a lamb, are all symbolic counterparts to the Savior of the world. The dragon and beast force their servants to worship them, whereas the Lord allows agency and accountability from those who desire to follow after him. Satan cannot get people to routinely follow after him and so he must use deception and subtlety to entice people to become subject unto him. His power is limited, but with the power he possesses he will do everything possible to mislead mankind. In every generation on the earth Satan has found willing associates to carry on the work which he is unable to do for himself.

"Lucifer is the Great Imitator. He patterns his kingdom after that of God the Lord. The Lord proclaims a plan of salvation; Satan sponsors a plan of damnation. Signs follow those who believe and obey the law of the gospel, and false signs, false wonders, false miracles attend the ministry of the Master of Sin.

Knowledge is power, and because he knows more about many things than mortal men, the Great Imitator is able to blind the eyes and deceive the hearts of men and to put his own seal of verity, that of false miracles, on his damning philosophies. Thus those who place themselves wholly at his disposal have power to imitate the deeds of the prophets, as the magicians of Egypt imitated the miracles of Moses and as Simon the sorcerer sought to duplicate the works of Peter" (*DNTC*, 3:523–24).

We have learned many of the ways Satan will mislead the world into thinking that he is the one with the power. There is no question that Satan has power and authority, but we must continually keep in mind that there is a limit to the power and authority which he possesses—the Savior is the one who controls the keys. Our minds and thoughts must always be centered on the fact that the Savior is the Lamb who was chosen from the foundation of the world. Satan's temporary reign is a part of the plan, but as long as we follow the pathway and hold onto the rod we will not succumb to the enticings of the adversary or be swayed by his seemingly miraculous actions.

# 14

## THE LAMB ON MOUNT ZION, THE RESTORATION, AND THE ETERNAL HARVEST

Once again, at a point when we would expect to see a major battle take place between the forces for good and evil, we have an interlude of joy and rejoicing. It is as though the Lord is aware of the pain and sorrow John must feel as he encounters the devil and his legions and thus blesses him with a vision of the glorious things to take place on the earth. This is a time for John to feel joy and happiness as he sees the Lamb standing on Mount Zion, views the restoration of the gospel upon the earth through an angelic ministrant, and observes the preparation of all things to come to pass as the eventual glory of the Lord is unveiled.

The angels are preparing their sickles to reap the harvest. The day of the Lord is at hand and all things will be subdued under his feet. The time has now come that the Lord will harvest the earth and draw up those who are prepared to receive him. It is a time of rejoicing as the faithful Saints of the earth have waited for the Lord to overcome their enemies and the time is at hand. New songs are sung in praise to the Lord, and the fall of Babylon, or in other words, the fall of everything promoting wickedness and the ways of the world is heralded as the angels are loosed to thrust in their sickles and reap the harvest.

### REVELATION 14:1–5

1 ¶ AND I looked, and, lo, a Lamb stood on the mount Sion, and with him an hundred forty and four thousand, having his

Father's name written in their foreheads.

2 And I heard a voice from heaven, as the voice of many waters, and as the voice of a great thunder: and I heard the voice of harpers harping with their harps:

3 And they sung as it were a new song before the throne, and before the four beasts, and the elders: and no man could learn that song but the hundred and forty and four thousand, which were redeemed from the earth.

4 These are they which were not defiled with women; for they are virgins. These are they which follow the Lamb whithersoever he goeth. These were redeemed from among men, being the firstfruits unto God and to the Lamb.

5 And in their mouth was found no guile: for they are without fault before the throne of God.

## Verse Commentary

*14:1.* **A Lamb stood on the mount Sion, and with him an hundred forty and four thousand, having his Father's name written in their foreheads.** There are two different locations for Mount Zion. One is located in Jerusalem and the other in Missouri. The following scriptural account discusses how the Lord will appear in both locations: "Prepare ye the way of the Lord, and make his paths straight, for the hour of his coming is nigh— When the Lamb shall stand upon Mount Zion, and with him a hundred and forty-four thousand, having his Father's name written on their foreheads. Wherefore, prepare ye for the coming of the Bridegroom; go ye, go ye out to meet him. For behold, he shall stand upon the mount of Olivet, and upon the mighty ocean, even the great deep, and upon the islands of the sea, and upon the land of Zion. And he shall utter his voice out of Zion, and he shall speak from Jerusalem, and his voice shall be heard among all people; And it shall be a voice as the voice of many waters, and as the voice of a great thunder, which shall break down the mountains, and the valleys shall not be found. He shall command the great deep, and it shall be driven back into the north countries, and the islands shall become one land; And the land of Jerusalem and the land of Zion shall be turned back into their own place, and the earth shall be like as it was in the days before it was divided. And the Lord, even the Savior, shall stand in the midst of his people, and shall reign over all flesh" (D&C 133:17–25).

We believe that Zion will be built upon the American continent (see A of F 1:10), while it is simultaneously in existence in
Jerusalem. Zion is a people pure in heart. The Lord calls his
people Zion because they are of one heart and one mind (see
Moses 7:18). The Lord will come to his people in the same way
he did after his resurrection. Will it be in the same order? We
know that the last shall be first and the first shall be last and that
he will visit his people and shall stand in the midst of his people,
and Zion (the city) will be united never to be separated.

The 144,000 (see Rev. 7:4–8) will be there with the Savior and
with the redeemed children of the Lord. What a great opening
for John to behold as he begins to see complete fulfillment of all
that has been promised through the prophets since the beginning of the world.

14:2–5. **I heard a voice from heaven, as the voice of many
waters, and as the voice of a great thunder: and I heard the
voice of harpers harping with their harps: . . . [singing] a new
song before the throne, and before the four beasts, and the
elders.** Once again we hear the power of the heavens proclaiming the glory and honor of the Lord. Those who have learned or,
in other words, understand the song break into singing. All who
understand join into singing the glorious song of redemption.
The words of the song are only known by the 144,000 which
were redeemed from the earth. Could it be comparable to the
following song of redemption?

> The Lord hath brought again Zion;
> The Lord had redeemed his people, Israel,
> According to the election of grace,
> Which was brought to pass by the faith
> And covenant of their fathers.
> The Lord hath redeemed his people;
> And Satan is bound and time is no longer.
> The Lord hath gathered all things in one.
> The Lord hath brought down Zion from above.
> The Lord hath brought up Zion from beneath.
> The earth hath travailed and brought forth her strength;

And truth is established in her bowels;
And the heavens have smiled upon her;
And she is clothed with the glory of her God;
For he stands in the midst of his people.
Glory, and honor, and power, and might,
Be ascribed to our God; for he is full of mercy,
Justice, grace and truth, and peace,
Forever and ever, Amen (D&C 84:99–102).

14:4. It is imperative to understand that verse 4 is not saying that the 144,000 will have never had sexual relations with females. The reference of **not** being **defiled with women; for they are virgins** means that they are pure and holy with an eye single to the glory of God, whether they are single or married (see *DNTC*, 3:527). In order for these 144,000 to have received the highest degree of the Father's kingdom and to be in his presence, they would have had to be married. Their total focus is on the Lord and so the application of being virgins and not being defiled is that they are pure in all thoughts and are faithful and true to the Lord, their King and God. They will be directly focused on their leader, and on no other thing, in the terrible battle with the adversary.

They are **the firstfruits unto God and to the Lamb.** The firstfruits are the very best offerings of the flocks and fields and are given at the beginning of the sacrifice. The Hebrew root *bâkar* also means "to give the birthright" (*Strong's*, Hebrew Dictionary, p. 21). Thus we see that these 144,000 are the first of them who shall rise up from the resurrection, having been true and faithful in all things here upon the earth. Many of these may be the faithful who were gathered and waiting, in the postmortal spirit world, at the time of the death of Jesus Christ. "And there were gathered together in one place an innumerable company of the spirits of the just, who had been faithful in the testimony of Jesus while they lived in mortality; All who had offered sacrifice in the similitude of the great sacrifice of the Son of God, and had suffered tribulation in their Redeemer's name. All these had departed the mortal life, firm in the hope of a glorious resurrection, through the grace of God the Father and his Only Begotten Son, Jesus Christ. I beheld that they were filled with joy and gladness, and were rejoicing together because the day of their deliverance was at hand" (D&C 138:12–15).

14:5. **In their mouth was found no guile,** or in other words, they stood before the Lord having confessed his name and lived their lives in accordance with his will. These 144,000 had repented of their errors and sins while in the flesh and had stood pure and spotless before the Lord, having his name sealed in their foreheads. Nothing else occupied their mind or escaped from their lips than to give praise and glory to the Lord whom they chose to follow.

### Applicability

The 144,000 are those who have been true and faithful to all of the covenants they have entered into. They have been pure in their thoughts and have the Father's name written in their foreheads. There is only one place on the earth where a person can get to the point that they make these types of covenants and that is in the temple of God. They are pure in their relationships with others, in that they have no guile, and are honest and forthright in their dealings with their fellowman. Essentially, they are pure and holy before God and man and are not swayed by the enticements of the world.

This is an army of righteous people who have chosen to follow after their God and keep his commandments. Surely among the members of the Church throughout eternity we can find this number, and many more, who have been faithful to their covenants and who serve the Lord with an eye single to his glory. They will be from all walks of life and will lead the throngs in proclaiming the great day of the Lord. We, too, have the option of being numbered with this great multitude of righteous people in singing praises to our Lord and King when he returns in his glory. The 144,000 are truly without fault before the throne of God.

## REVELATION 14:6–7

6 ¶ And I saw another angel fly in the midst of heaven, having the everlasting gospel to preach unto them that dwell on the earth, and to every nation, and kindred, and tongue, and people,

7 Saying with a loud voice, Fear God, and give glory to him; for the hour of his judgment is come: and worship him that made heaven, and earth, and the sea, and the fountains of waters.

## Verse Commentary

*14:6.* **I saw another angel fly in the midst of heaven, having the everlasting gospel to preach unto them that dwell on the earth.** What greater pronouncement can there be than the declaration of the restoration of the fulness of the gospel? From the time that the woman (Church) was carried into the wilderness (see Rev. 12:6) the earth had been without the fulness of the gospel, and now, at this time, the gospel would be restored. The heavens would be opened again and the everlasting gospel, having no beginning of days or end of years, would be restored to the earth.

This restoration will herald some great eternal truths. First, the truth was taken from the earth and had to be restored through angelic ministrants. There is only one church upon the earth who has claimed that angels from heaven have restored the everlasting gospel to the earth and that is The Church of Jesus Christ of Latter-day Saints. Second, the gospel will be preached to **every nation, and kindred, and tongue, and people.** All will have the opportunity to hear the gospel. "And now, verily saith the Lord, that these things might be known among you, O inhabitants of the earth, I have sent forth mine angel flying through the midst of heaven, having the everlasting gospel, who hath appeared unto some and hath committed it unto man, who shall appear unto many that dwell on the earth. And this gospel shall be preached unto every nation, and kindred, and tongue, and people. And the servants of God shall go forth, saying with a loud voice: Fear God and give glory to him, for the hour of his judgment is come; And worship him that made heaven, and earth, and the sea, and the fountains of waters—Calling upon the name of the Lord day and night, saying: O that thou wouldst rend the heavens, that thou wouldst come down, that the mountains might flow down at thy presence" (D&C 133:36–40).

The first angel comes and proclaims the restoration of the gospel. Why must it be a restoration? Because the Church and its authority were taken from the earth when the woman fled into the wilderness and the man child was caught up unto God (see Rev. 12:5–6). The angel is the one who has the everlasting gospel, and who would that angel be? President Joseph Fielding Smith stated, "Joseph Smith declared that Moroni—an ancient prophet on this continent, and now resurrected—in partial fulfillment of this promise, taught him the gospel, giving him instruction in relation to the restoration of things preceding the coming of Christ (Joseph Smith Hist. 2:29–54). And the Lord said: 'For behold, the Lord God hath sent forth the angel crying through the midst of heaven, saying: Prepare ye the way of the Lord, and make his paths straight, for the hour of his coming is nigh.' (D&C 133:17)" (*DS,* 3:4–5).

The statue of Moroni is placed on the tops of some of the temples to represent the angel flying through the midst of heaven. Moroni brought the message of the gospel back to the earth and numerous angels, or messengers, from our Father's presence also returned to the earth to confer upon Joseph Smith the keys of each of their dispensations. The responsibility then falls upon the members to take the restored gospel out to the nations and people of the earth, and to proclaim it to those who will hear. "Was it one angel or many?" Elder McConkie asks, regarding who was responsible for the Restoration. He then answers: "It is traditional (and true!) to reply: 'Moroni, son of Mormon, the now resurrected Nephite prophet, who holds the keys of the "stick of Ephraim" (D&C 27:5), the one through whose ministry the Book of Mormon was again brought to light.' The reasoning is that the Book of Mormon contains 'the fulness of the everlasting gospel' (D&C 135:3); that therein is

God's message of salvation for all of the earth's inhabitants; and that this gospel message is now being taken by the Lord's witnesses to one nation, and kindred, and tongue, and people after another" (*DNTC*, 3:528–29).

14:7. The angel now declares **with a loud voice, Fear God, and give glory to him; for the hour of his judgment is come: and worship him that made heaven, and earth, and the sea, and the fountains of waters.** This is the everlasting gospel, that which has been from eternity to eternity but was taken away because of the wickedness of the world, and it is restored! "Another trump shall sound, which is the fifth trump, which is the fifth angel who committeth the everlasting gospel—flying through the midst of heaven, unto all nations, kindreds, tongues, and people; And this shall be the sound of his trump, saying to all people, both in heaven and in earth, and that are under the earth—for every ear shall hear it, and every knee shall bow, and every tongue shall confess, while they hear the sound of the trump, saying: Fear God, and give glory to him who sitteth upon the throne, forever and ever; for the hour of his judgment is come" (D&C 88:103–4).

### Applicability

The restoration of the gospel of Jesus Christ is the single most important event to occur upon the earth since the time of the Atonement. With the Restoration came the dispensation of the fulness of times in which all of the priesthood keys ever held upon the earth were restored by the proper authority. The keys of the gathering of Israel, the sealing powers, the remembrance of the covenant of Abraham, the Book of Mormon, and many other wonders, have all been restored in our day. We, like no other people who have ever existed upon the earth, have the gospel in its fulness.

With the blessings of the Restoration come great responsibilities. Those who are parents today are raising the children who will herald the Second Coming, and through the righteous posterity we bring forth will come those who have been chosen for the last days. It is our opportunity, blessing, and challenge to live in a day and age when the forces for good and evil are making themselves manifest so openly. The lines are being drawn and the so-called gray area is dissipating. The two directly opposing forces are evident. The coming of Moroni, heralding the dispensation of the fulness of times, is a blessed and hallowed event for all of our Father's children. It is this event that ushers in the coming of the Savior.

## REVELATION 14:8–11

8 And there followed another angel, saying, Babylon is fallen, is fallen, that great city, because she made all nations drink of the wine of the wrath of her fornication.

9 And the third angel followed them, saying with a loud voice, If any man worship the beast and his image, and receive his mark in his forehead, or in his hand,

10 The same shall drink of the wine of the wrath of God, which is poured out without mixture into the cup of his indignation; and he shall be tormented with fire and brimstone in the presence of the holy angels, and in the presence of the Lamb:

11 And the smoke of their torment ascendeth up for ever and ever: and they have no rest day nor night, who worship the beast and his image, and whosoever receiveth the mark of his name.

**Verse Commentary**

*14:8.* Another angel follows after and says: **Babylon is fallen, is fallen, that great city, because she made all nations drink of the wine of the wrath of her fornication.** Babylon is representative of all wickedness. Gospel scholar Hugh Nibley writes, "Babylon is a state of mind, just like Zion. Like Zion, Babylon is a city: 'Babylon is fallen, is fallen, that great city' (Rev. 14:8). It's a world center of commerce and business. . . . She leads the world, and nations have drunk of her wine. Here Jeremiah talks (not John the Revelator yet): 'The nations have drunken of her wine; therefore the nations are mad. Babylon is suddenly fallen and destroyed' (Jer. 51:7–8). All the world is involved. At the noise of the taking of Babylon, the earth is moved, and a cry is heard among the nations. 'So at Babylon shall fall the slain of all the earth' (Jer. 51:49). Her clever, experienced, unscrupulous men will be helpless. She thinks that she can get away with anything, so she says, 'None seeth me. Thy wisdom and thy knowledge, it hath perverted thee' (Isa. 47:10)" (*Approaching Zion*, p. 324).

In other words, Babylon is everything that uses deceit, blasphemy, subtlety, and lying. She will beguile anyone to carefully lead their souls down to hell. She has "made all nations drink of the wine of the wrath of her fornication" (Rev. 14:8). The wine represents the enticements offered to seduce the nations of the earth and draw them away from worshipping the true God. The wrath to be poured out upon her (and all who dwell with her) is a consequence of the covenants she has turned from, the fornication she has committed. Rousas John Rushdoony, an authority on biblical law, writes that "even as infidelity in the O[ld] T[estament] typified the forsaking of the true God in order to worship idols, so fornication is used in Revelation 2:21; 14:8; 17:2, 4; 18:3 and 19:2 to describe rebellion against and insubordination to God and the religion and life of such rebellion" (p. 407). It is the wrath that God will pour out upon the wicked who have turned from their covenants and sought the things of the world.

*14:9–11.* The third angel then follows with a loud voice and serious warning: **If any man worship the beast and his image,** (as spoken in chapter 13) **and receive his mark in his forehead, or in his hand** (those who have made their covenant with Satan), **The same shall drink of the wine of the wrath of God** (the judgment which is to be meted out as justice), **which is poured out without mixture into the cup of his indignation** (there is nothing to lessen or distill the severity of the judgments)**; and he shall be tormented with fire and brimstone in the presence of the holy angels, and in the presence of the Lamb** (vengeance is the Lord's, and the punishment is a torture of the soul with everlasting burnings and fires, this fire and brimstone are the sufferings of those who must suffer for their own sins)**: And the smoke of their torment** (similar to the incense of the Saints and their prayers) **ascendeth up for ever and ever: and they have no rest day nor night, who worship the beast and his image, and whosoever receiveth the mark of his name.** They will receive the cursing placed upon the devil, whom they choose to obey. Those who choose to worship the beast will do so everlastingly because that is what he requires of them; they have forfeited their agency.

### Applicability

With the coming of the gospel and the advent of the Savior comes a heralding of different sorts: "Babylon is fallen" (v. 8). It is impossible for Babylon and the heavenly city to exist in the same sphere—one must fall. Because this is our Father's plan, Babylon must be the one to be utterly wasted. The personal application to each of us is that we must rid ourselves of all that represents Babylon, and focus on the things of eternity. If we are still in subjection or bondage to things sold in Babylon, whatever their enticements may be, we will be comparable to Lot's wife who turned her heart towards the things found in Sodom and Gommorah and received the reward of that which she truly desired (see Gen. 19:26). The Lord looks on the heart (1 Sam. 16:7) for the desires of the heart reveal our aspirations.

### REVELATION 14:12–13

12 Here is the patience of the saints: here are they that keep the commandments of God, and the faith of Jesus.

13 ¶ And I heard a voice from heaven saying unto me, Write, Blessed are the dead which die in the Lord from henceforth: Yea, saith the Spirit, that they may rest from their labours; and their works do follow them.

### Verse Commentary

*14:12.* **Here is the patience** (endurance and constancy) **of the saints.** Those who not only say that they believe in Jesus Christ but who **keep the commandments of God, and the faith of Jesus.** It is not by merely proclaiming a belief in Christ that makes one a disciple. A disciple believes fully in the same gospel truths which the Savior taught and manifests that belief in word and deed. As the Savior said, "If ye love me, keep my commandments" (John 14:15). Can it be expressed any more succinctly than that?

*14:13.* Another voice commands John to write: **Blessed are the dead which die in the Lord from henceforth: Yea, saith the Spirit, that they may rest from their labours; and their works do follow them.** According to the Doctrine and Covenants, "those that die in me shall not taste of death, for it will be sweet unto them" (42:46). And Alma says, "Then shall it come to pass, that the spirits of those who are righteous are received into a state of happiness, which is called paradise, a state of rest, a state of peace, where they shall rest from all their troubles and from all care, and sorrow" (Alma 40:12).

The comfort and assurance of these verses should help us to remember that nothing we do is in vain, if it is done to glorify the Lord, or to draw ourselves closer to him. Our works follow after us, because they truly typify who we are. A person may say he believes in Jesus Christ and may proclaim his name, but the true showing of faith in the Lord is to keep his commandments and walk in his paths. A demonstration of the faith one has is how he performs in the face of adversity; obviously, from what is taking place in this chapter, the adversity which comes out from Babylon is almost overwhelming.

## Applicability

This promise of chapter 14 gives us the assurance that those who keep the commandments, even unto death, will be granted a place in the "rest of the Father" where they shall rest from their labors. Our obedience and faithfulness while here in this existence will weigh heavily in determining the kingdom of glory we receive at the time of judgment. Of course we are saved by grace, but our works indicate the real commitment we have to the gospel.

## REVELATION 14:14–20

14 And I looked, and behold a white cloud, and upon the cloud one sat like unto the Son of man, having on his head a golden crown, and in his hand a sharp sickle.

15 And another angel came out of the temple, crying with a loud voice to him that sat on the cloud, Thrust in thy sickle, and reap: for the time is come for thee to reap; for the harvest of the earth is ripe.

16 And he that sat on the cloud thrust in his sickle on the earth; and the earth was reaped.

17 And another angel came out of the temple which is in heaven, he also having a sharp sickle.

18 And another angel came out from the altar, which had power over fire; and cried with a loud cry to him that had the sharp sickle, saying, Thrust in thy sharp sickle, and gather the clusters of the vine of the earth; for her grapes are fully ripe.

19 And the angel thrust in his sickle into the earth, and gathered the vine of the earth, and cast it into the great winepress of the wrath of God.

20 And the winepress was trodden without the city, and blood came out of the winepress, even unto the horse bridles, by the space of a thousand and six hundred furlongs.

**Verse Commentary**

*14:14.* John now looks and beholds **a white cloud, and upon the cloud one sat like unto the Son of man.** The white cloud represents the purity and presence of God, thus the one that sat upon the cloud would be the resurrected Lord returning to earth, displaying the fulness of his power. He has **on his head a golden crown, and in his hand a sharp sickle.** The golden crown is the symbol of victory and incorruptible rule, and the sharp sickle is that tool representing judgment and the harvest. The day is now past for the peoples of the earth to change their ways. The harvest of the earth is now at hand, and the angels are calling for judgment to be spread over the face of the land. "In the last days, even now while the Lord is beginning to bring forth the word, and the blade is springing up and is yet tender— Behold, verily I say unto you, the angels are crying unto the Lord day and night, who are ready and waiting to be sent forth to reap down the fields; But the Lord saith unto them, pluck not up the tares while the blade is yet tender (for verily your faith is weak), lest you destroy the wheat also. Therefore, let the wheat and the tares grow together until the harvest is fully ripe; then ye shall first gather out the wheat from among the tares, and after the gathering of the wheat, behold and lo, the tares are bound in bundles, and the field remaineth to be burned" (D&C 86:4–7).

*14:15–16.* **Another angel came out of the temple crying** to the Lord on the cloud, **Thrust in thy sickle, and reap: for the time is come for thee to reap; for the harvest of the earth is ripe.** This angel from the temple is now asking for the work of harvest to begin. There is no longer time for repentance. The Lord then **thrust[s] in his sickle on the earth; and the earth [is] reaped.** The Lord has harvested his righteous Saints and they are gathered up as the wheat is gathered from the field before the tares are burned. "Behold, the field is white already to harvest; therefore, whoso desireth to reap, let him thrust in his sickle with his might, and reap while the day lasts, that he may treasure up for his soul everlasting salvation in the kingdom of God" (D&C 6:3).

Theologian Ethelbert Stauffer observes, "We read that the final subjection of God's enemies will only take place at the end of the days, though it is presupposed, in saying this, that the fundamental beginning has already been made (Mark 14:62; Rev. 3:21; 14:14). We read again that the subjection has already taken place, though here the celebration of the triumph is held back until the time of the end (Eph. 1:20 ff.; Heb. 1:13; 10:12 f.; 12:2). But wherever the emphasis falls, this much is clear: The Lord has from now on all authority in heaven and on earth, and he is 'with' his Church always, even unto the end of the world (Matt. 28:18 ff.)" (as quoted in Rushdoony, p. 729).

All enemies will be put under his feet and he will come forth to meet those Saints who are prepared for his coming. The responsibility for meeting him and being worthy to endure his presence, as well as enjoying the harvest of the righteous, rests squarely on our shoulders.

*14:17–20.* **And another angel came out of the temple which**

**is in heaven, . . . also having a sharp sickle.** The Lord is sending forth his servants from his temple on high, to bring judgment upon the face of the earth. We have been told that the
angels will assist in the judgments poured out upon the wicked
on the earth. From here through the end of the revelation the
angels take an active role in the judgments enacted upon the
inhabitants of the earth.

**Another angel came out from the altar, which had power
over fire.** This angel will bring forth the fire prepared to burn
the field once it is harvested. This angel comes forth from the
altar, where all of the sacrifices of the Saints have been offered.
All things are before the Lord. He will not just bring forth
destructions out of anger towards the wicked, but these things
will come forth on account of the acts which the wicked have
performed and which were recorded in heaven.

The angel with the sickle is commanded to **thrust in thy
sharp sickle, and gather the clusters of the vine of the earth;
for her grapes are fully ripe.** The earth is prepared, the vineyard
has been allowed to grow for enough time, and now the time of
the harvest has come. To be fully ripe means that the earth is at
the highest point of preparation for the coming of the Son of
Man, both in righteousness and wickedness. *Sharp sickle* is the
English rendering of the Greek *"drepanon,* an all purpose blade
used for pruning, cutting clusters of grapes, and harvesting
grains. Its roughly foot-long curved blade made it easy to
handle with clean cutting power" (Draper, p. 163).

Once the fruit is gathered it is **cast into the great winepress
of the wrath of God.** A winepress is for the purpose of treading
grapes. Here, in the winepress of the wrath of God, judgment
will come down upon the wicked with full force. There will be
no escaping his judgments. Joel says, "Put ye in the sickle, for
the harvest is ripe: come, get you down; for the press is full, the
fats overflow; for their wickedness is great. Multitudes, multitudes in the valley of decision: for the day of the Lord is near in
the valley of decision" (3:13–14).

The **winepress [is] trodden without the city, and blood
came out of the winepress, . . . by the space of a thousand and**

**six hundred furlongs.** The winepress is outside the city. Those who remain in the city, within the bounds set by God, will be protected. Blood comes out of the winepress. The destructions will be such that the slaughter is something never before seen upon the earth. Blood will flow for 1,600 furlongs, or about 184 miles. Here again, John is using symbolism to describe the bloodshed and destruction to take place.

The number 1,600 is four times four times one hundred (1600 = 4 x 4 x 100), or, in other words, geographic fulness multiplied by itself, suggesting a complete geographic inclusion, and then multiplied by one hundred to portray an increasing magnitude of worldwide destruction. All those who remain wicked upon the earth after so many opportunities to repent will now incur the fulness of the wrath of God in complete devastation.

## Applicability

Everything we have read to this point directs us towards the great day of the Lord when all things are put under his feet. When the angels are loosed upon the earth they will go forth to harvest the vineyard. The great day of judgment that the righteous have been praying for since the fall of man is now at hand. Wickedness shall no longer prevail. Those who love to lie and corrupt shall be cut off from the face of the earth. The righteous need not fear this judgment for the Lord has promised that he will protect his Saints, even if he must do so by fire (see 2 Ne. 30:10). We will be protected. Only those who do not have the seal of the living God in their foreheads will be cut down and cast into the great winepress of the Lord. Throughout Revelation we have seen that the choice of happiness or misery is ours to make.

## SUMMARY

Chapter 14 has been used to portray the manner in which the righteous are protected and the wicked are judged during the great harvest. The angels have been kept in check until this time, and now they are released to assist in the harvest. All of these declarations shout forth the destruction of Babylon and all of her worldly ways. Nothing will hinder or prevent this offensive of righteousness brought about by the Bridegroom of the Church. The wicked will suffer in ways that only those who participate may understand.

We must remember that the Lord will ultimately fight the battles and that the Saints will be victorious, but there must be a period of opposition first. All those who desire to accept the word of the Lord have the opportunity to receive the gospel and to accept the ordinances therein. Those who are converted will be saved when the Lord sends forth his servants to harvest the earth. The Savior will gather the righteous out from among the wicked and will spread his arms to protect them, "even as a hen gathereth her chickens under her wings" (Matt. 23:37).

The angels are loosed with their destructive forces. Those who are wicked are cast into the "great winepress of the wrath of God" (Rev. 14:19). The wrath of God is brought about as a direct result of the disobedience of those upon the earth who will not hearken to the voice of the Lord, nor the voice of his servants (see D&C 1:38). Our simple message in all of this is that the righteous need not fear because the Lord will protect those who have kept the commandments and followed him.

# 15

# EXALTATION OF THE RIGHTEOUS

Everything has now been prepared and the Lord is beginning the final cleansing of the earth. John is now seeing a new portion of the vision in heaven, with the angels preparing to bring their plagues and destructions upon the earth. Seven angels, having the seven last plagues, are now ready to carry out their work against the wicked. The righteous have been spared and the wicked have had their opportunities to repent. From here on, the plagues are directed specifically towards the wicked as they incur the full wrath of a just God. The whole plan of the Lord has reached its climax and is now prepared to be fulfilled.

The chapter begins with the praises of the righteous Saints as they glorify that God who will now fight their final battle for them. Their patience has been tried and their faith has been tested, but they are victorious as the enemy is put under their feet by he who holds the keys over the bottomless pit, even the Savior of the world. What a joyous event this will be to see the fruition of our faithfulness and trust in the Lord! His promises are sure.

## REVELATION 15:1–4

1 ¶ And I saw another sign in heaven, great and marvellous, seven angels having the seven last plagues; for in them is filled up the wrath of God.

2 And I saw as it were a sea of glass mingled with fire: and them that had gotten the victory over the beast, and over his image, and over his mark, and over the number of his name, stand on the sea of glass, having the harps of God.

3 And they sing the song of Moses the servant of God, and the

song of the Lamb, saying, Great
and marvellous are thy works,
Lord God Almighty; just and true
are thy ways, thou King of saints.
   4 Who shall not fear thee, O Lord,

and glorify thy name? for thou
only art holy: for all nations shall
come and worship before thee; for
thy judgments are made manifest.

## Verse Commentary

*15:1.* **Another sign in heaven, great and marvelous,** is now
seen: **seven angels having the seven last plagues.** Once again
we have a sign shown forth from heaven as a token to those who
dwell on earth that the Lord will fulfill his promises. The angels
that hold the seven plagues are now allowed to begin their
work. In these angels **is filled up the wrath of God.** Vincent
says this phrase is "more correctly, brought to an end (telos)" (p.
537). The angels bear the completion or culmination of the
wrath of God. The seven last plagues will be expounded upon
in chapters 16–18, but here we see a brief glimpse into the marvelous works of the Lord as he prepares to unleash his terrible
fury.

*15:2–4.* The glorious, victorious Saints stand on, as it were, **a
sea of glass mingled with fire.** We know that the sea of glass
represents the celestialized earth (see Rev. 4:6; D&C 77:1) and
the fire is the purifying power of the Lord. These are the righteous Saints who have gained **the victory over the beast, and
over his image, and over his mark, and over the number of his
name**; in other words, Satan, his servants, and all evil things
have been overcome by those who have followed after the Lord.
The celebration of the Saints is glorious; they have the **harps of
God** and sing their song of praise to the Being who helped them
gain their victory over the adversary.

First, **they sing the song of Moses,** the song of he who was
a type of the Savior and led the children of Israel from bondage.
Then the Saints sing a song that is even greater, it is **the song of
the Lamb** because he has led all of Israel, all of his people, from
the bondage of the adversary. The Doctrine and Covenants
states that "the graves of the saints shall be opened; and they
shall come forth and stand on the right hand of the Lamb, when

he shall stand upon Mount Zion, and upon the holy city, the New Jerusalem; and they shall sing the song of the Lamb, day and night forever and ever" (133:56). The song is expressive of the hopes of all the faithful Saints as their prayers are now brought to pass in the final triumph of the Lamb, and both Old and New Testament churches are now combined.

**Great and marvellous are thy works, Lord God Almighty; just and true are thy ways, thou King of saints. Who shall not fear thee, O Lord, and glorify thy name? for thou only art holy: for all nations shall come and worship before thee; for thy judgments are made manifest.** The works of the Lord are recognized and praised. He is the King of Saints, the King of Kings, and the Lord of Lords. He is the King over the whole world and all that dwell therein, and his ways are righteous and true. In contrast, the fear that came upon some because of the beast was out of concern for his destructive ways; whereas, all shall fear, meaning respect, the Lord and glorify his name out of honor and praise for his accomplishments. Being holy is a reference of his purity and righteousness. Because of their sinfulness, the Lord is truly justified in bringing these judgments to pass upon the wicked. The judgments are not arbitrary decisions made by the Lord, but are righteous consequences which must come to pass to meet the requirements of justice. The judicial assessment passed down from the Judge must be executed or he would cease to be God. All of his judgments are just and true and any consequences brought upon the children of the earth are on account of their obedience or disobedience to the word of the Lord. Mormon taught, "For behold, the Spirit of Christ is given to every man, that he may know good from evil; wherefore, I show unto you the way to judge; for every thing which inviteth to do good, and to persuade to believe in Christ, is sent forth by the power and gift of Christ; wherefore ye may know with a perfect knowledge it is of God. But whatsoever thing persuadeth men to do evil, and believe not in Christ, and deny him, and serve not God, then ye may know with a perfect knowledge it is of the devil; for after this manner doth the devil work, for he persuadeth no man to do good, no, not one; neither do his

angels; neither do they who subject themselves unto him"
(Moro. 7:16–17).

## Applicability

The victory over the adversary is quickly being brought to
pass. The seven angels with the seven last plagues are awaiting
the command to go and cleanse the earth from the wickedness
it has endured for so long. If we truly believe that Moses and all
other biblical prophets were men of God, and if we have a testimony that latter-day prophets are also men of God, we will sing
the song of Moses and the song of the Lamb. Those who are
valiant in their testimony of the Lord know their own personal
faithfulness. They look forward to this proclaimed day and its
deliverance. Their testimony of the Savior is indelibly written
upon their hearts.

### REVELATION 15:5–8

5 ¶ And after that I looked, and, behold, the temple of the tabernacle of the testimony in heaven was opened:

6 And the seven angels came out of the temple, having the seven plagues, clothed in pure and white linen, and having their breasts girded with golden girdles.

7 And one of the four beasts gave unto the seven angels seven golden vials full of the wrath of God, who liveth for ever and ever.

8 And the temple was filled with smoke from the glory of God, and from his power; and no man was able to enter into the temple, till the seven plagues of the seven angels were fulfilled.

## Verse Commentary

*15:5.* **I looked, and, behold, the temple of the tabernacle of
the testimony in heaven was opened:** The tabernacle of the testimony, or the ark of the covenant, is where the covenant and
law of God is kept. It was kept anciently within the temple and
was where Moses placed the Ten Commandments. The temple
of the tabernacle is the most holy place within the temple. From

this imagery we see that these judgments, the plagues borne by the seven angels, come forth from the most holy place in heaven, the actual place where God resides. The final judgments of the Lord upon this earth will flow from his temple over the nations of the earth. All those who refuse to hear his voice will reap the judgments flowing therefrom.

15:6-7. **The seven angels came out of the temple.** They have now received the Lord's approval to carry on their work and thus depart from the temple of God. They have **the seven plagues,** the complete divine judgments which God will loose, through his angels, upon the earth to cleanse it from sin. Following the cleansing, all of the earth will see the coming of the Firstborn. In similitude of Christ, Moses released ten (see Symbols Guide) plagues upon Egypt as a consequence of their rejection of the Lord (see Ex. 7:19–25 [water to blood]; 8:5–7 [frogs upon land]; 8:16–18 [lice]; 8:20–24 [flies]; 9:1–7 [death of cattle]; 9:8–12 [boils on men]; 9:22–25 [hail]; 10:12–15 [locusts]; 10:21–23 [darkness]; with the final plague being the death of the firstborn of all those who were not protected by the blood of the Lamb [Ex 12:29–30]). In Revelation, however, we find seven (see Symbols Guide) plagues sent forth upon the whole wicked world.

To be **clothed in pure and white linen** is to wear the clothing of the temple and to have **their breasts girded with golden girdles** seems to represent that the righteous are wearing golden girdles very similar to that which the Savior wears when he is spoken of earlier, wherein he is "girt about the paps with a golden girdle" (Rev. 1:13) indicative of the temple and priesthood blessings. The girdle is one eternal round and represents the eternal nature of the temple covenant.

**One of the four beasts** (*zōōn*, living beasts) now gives **the seven angels seven golden vials full of the wrath of God.** The angels now hold the vials, a vial being, according to *The New Strong's Exhaustive Concordance of the Bible,* "a broad shallow cup" (Greek Dictionary, p. 75). These vials are full of the wrath of God that has been prophesied by all of God's holy prophets. His wrath is about to be loosed upon the earth as a direct fulfillment of all that has been spoken of concerning the dreadful day of the Lord. For those who have chosen to be wicked it will truly be a "dreadful day." Another word for wrath is vengeance: "Vengeance is mine; I will repay, saith the Lord" (Rom. 12:19).

*15:8.* **The temple was filled with smoke from the glory of God.** The smoke is similar to the cloud of Exodus which covered the tent of the congregation and no one could enter into the tent (see 40:34–35). Here **no man was able to enter into the temple.** In ancient Israel, the high priest could enter the temple and "make atonement" for the children of Israel and then return and provide mercy for Israel through the use of the scapegoat (see Lev. 16). There will be no mercy here until the Lord has executed all of his judgments against the unjust. None are allowed to enter the temple because the Day of Atonement is passed and his justice shall now be fulfilled.

There will be no mercy shown and none will enter the presence of the Lord until **the seven plagues of the seven angels [are] fulfilled.** In place of atonement we have judgment and this is a complete judgment and destruction to be poured out upon the wicked because they have chosen to reject any saving power offered to them. They have rejected the Lord, and in so doing, have rejected any of the saving blessings he promised for their protection. They must now incur the wrath of a just God upon them.

Alma taught, "Therefore, whosoever repenteth, and hardeneth not his heart, he shall have claim on mercy through mine Only Begotten Son, unto a remission of his sins; and these shall enter into my rest. And whosoever will harden his heart and will do iniquity, behold, I swear in my wrath that he shall not enter into my rest" (Alma 12:34–35).

### Applicability

These angels come out of the temple dressed in the temple clothing as they are prepared to fulfill their obligations before the Lord. The angels are servants of God who have the injunction to pour out their vials upon the wicked. We have similar responsibilities based upon covenants we have entered into at baptism: "To stand as witnesses of God at all times and in all things, and in all places that [we] may be in, even until death" (Mosiah 18:9). Once clothed in the robes of the temple, having received the purifying ordinances associated therewith, we have the obligation to stand for truth and defend the righteous in whatever battle they may be in. As we are faithful to the Lord his protective influences will shelter us and our families, and he will preserve us throughout eternity through the priesthood powers and ordinances.

## SUMMARY

The righteous are now preserved and are able to witness the ultimate victory which the Lamb provides. They are on the sea of glass, the celestialized earth, and are singing praises to their Lord and their King. It is almost impossible to express the gratitude and joy we will feel for the Savior who has delivered us from death and the chains of the adversary. The Firstborn Lamb has provided the ultimate sacrifice for all who would accept it, but he must now rain judgment down upon those who reject him.

We must remember that the judgments and justice which come forth from our Father's temple are not based upon revenge. Our God is a God of mercy (see Isa. 30:18). These judgments are part of the law and are the consequences of disobedience (see Jacob 6:8–9). Consistently, in all of scripture, we are told that the righteous shall be blessed, shall prosper, and shall be delivered and the disobedient or unrighteous shall be cut off from his presence (see 1 Kgs. 8:32; Ps. 1:6; Isa. 26:2; 1 Ne. 1:20; Alma 34:35–36; D&C 20:14–15). He must fulfill his law in perfectness, or he ceases to be God. The wage of sin is death (see Alma 5:42), and the sure way to avoid this death is through repentance and enjoying the mercy of the Atonement.

The Lord's vengeance spoken of in the scriptures (see Rom. 12:19; Heb. 10:30) is from the Greek *ĕkdikēsis* and means "vindication" or "retribution" (*Strong's*, Greek Dictionary, p. 26), thus symbolizing that the Lord does not get revenge for wrongs committed against him or his people, but seeks retribution, or fair payment to meet the demands of justice for those wrongs. When the Lord begins to execute these judgments from his holy temple, none will be able to enter his presence until all things have been fulfilled and the earth is cleansed.

We should take comfort knowing that the righteous will be under the protective arm of the Lord when these destructions come forth upon the earth. God is not only a God of mercy, but he is also a God of justice. We should strive to be "them that had gotten the victory over the beast" (Rev. 15:2) and leave the judgments to the Lord. It is our choice to be among those singing "the song of the Lamb" (Rev. 15:3).

# 16

## THE SEVEN VIALS AND
## PLAGUES UPON THE WICKED

As the Lord begins the cleansing of the earth, he will do so from his temple, and will cleanse from the inside out. There are some who call themselves members of the Lord's Church, act as though they are righteous, and even enter into his temples, but inwardly they are ravenous wolves, and these shall be cut off from his presence. The Doctrine and Covenants warns, "Vengeance cometh speedily upon the inhabitants of the earth, a day of wrath, a day of burning, a day of desolation, of weeping, of mourning, and of lamentations; and as a whirlwind it shall come upon all the face of the earth, saith the Lord. And upon my house shall it begin, and from my house shall it go forth, saith the Lord; First among those among you, saith the Lord, who have professed to know my name and have not known me, and have blasphemed against me in the midst of my house, saith the Lord" (112:24–26).

The wrath of God is now come forth to be poured out upon the earth. John has seen that the righteous are protected and the destructions coming upon the earth will only affect the wicked. The previous chapters have been forewarning us of the impending judgments to come upon the rebellious. Throughout history God has used prophetic messengers to continually forewarn his children of the impending destruction. He has proclaimed repentance to help them avoid the judgments which are to be poured out prior to the Savior's coming.

The seven angels now pour out their vials. They are directed by the voice from the temple to "go your ways, and pour out the vials of the wrath of God upon the earth" (Rev. 16:1). Can any of us even imagine the wrath of God? Why does he take so much time to warn his children of the plagues to fill the earth? Obviously, he tries to get them to change their ways, to repent and return to him. To procrastinators Samuel the Lamanite says, "But behold, your days of probation are past; ye have procrastinated the day of your salvation until it is everlastingly too late, and your destruction is made sure; yea, for ye have sought all the days of your lives for that which ye could not obtain; and ye have sought for happiness in doing iniquity, which thing is contrary to the nature of that righteousness which is in our great and Eternal Head. O ye people of the land, that ye would hear my words! And I pray that the anger of the Lord be turned away from you, and that ye would repent and be saved" (Hel. 13:38–39).

The warning voice has been raised time after time, and now the time for repentance is past. All those who remain and are not protected by the Lord must incur the wrath of God upon them. His merciful arm has been extended time and again, but they would not, therefore they must now endure the justice of God brought forth upon them.

## REVELATION 16:1–16

1 ¶ And I heard a great voice out of the temple saying to the seven angels, Go your ways, and pour out the vials of the wrath of God upon the earth.

2 And the first went, and poured out his vial upon the earth; and there fell a noisome and grievous sore upon the men which had the mark of the beast, and upon them which worshipped his image.

3 And the second angel poured out his vial upon the sea; and it became as the blood of a dead man: and every living soul died in the sea.

4 And the third angel poured out his vial upon the rivers and fountains of waters; and they became blood.

5 And I heard the angel of the waters say, Thou art righteous, O Lord, which art, and wast, and shalt be, because thou hast judged thus.

6 For they have shed the blood of saints and prophets, and thou hast given them blood to drink; for they are worthy.

7 And I heard another out of the altar say, Even so, Lord God Almighty, true and righteous are thy judgments.

8 ¶ And the fourth angel poured

out his vial upon the sun; and power was given unto him to scorch men with fire.

9 And men were scorched with great heat, and blasphemed the name of God, which hath power over these plagues: and they repented not to give him glory.

10 And the fifth angel poured out his vial upon the seat of the beast; and his kingdom was full of darkness; and they gnawed their tongues for pain,

11 And blasphemed the God of heaven because of their pains and their sores, and repented not of their deeds.

12 ¶ And the sixth angel poured out his vial upon the great river Euphrates; and the water thereof was dried up, that the way of the kings of the east might be prepared.

13 And I saw three unclean spirits like frogs come out of the mouth of the dragon, and out of the mouth of the beast, and out of the mouth of the false prophet.

14 For they are the spirits of devils, working miracles, which go forth unto the kings of the earth and of the whole world, to gather them to the battle of that great day of God Almighty.

15 Behold, I come as a thief. Blessed is he that watcheth, and keepeth his garments, lest he walk naked, and they see his shame.

16 And he gathered them together into a place called in the Hebrew tongue Armageddon.

## Verse Commentary

*16:1.* **A great voice out of the temple** says to the seven angels, **Go your ways, and pour out the vials of the wrath of God upon the earth.** This command, similar to the command given the angels who loosed their destructive forces in chapters 8 and 9 and those who proclaim various messages in chapter 14, is for them to carry out the work that God has assigned them. This third time that the angels go forth represents that the powers of God are now covering the heavens and the earth including all of God's earthly creations. "The term translated 'vial' (Greek *phialē*) means 'bowl,' especially one used in making sacred offerings" (Draper, p. 173). The Greek word used for cup, *pŏtēriŏn*, may figuratively mean a "lot or fate" (*Strong's*, Greek Dictionary, p. 59). The Jews felt that by drawing lots God's will was allowed to be manifest. In contrast to the bitter cup of our sins that Christ symbolically drank of in the Garden of Gethsemane, fulfilling his role as the chosen offering, the wicked must drink from the bitter vial of the wrath of God that is filled with their own offenses. The sacrificial offering of Christ's blood in atonement for our sins is in contrast to the blood that will be shed by the wicked as a result of their disobedience to and disregard for God's commands.

*16:2.* **The first went, and poured out his vial upon the earth; and there fell a noisome and grievous sore upon the men which had the mark of the beast, and upon them which worshipped his image.** The two Greek words for noisome (*kakon*) and grievous (*poneron*) suggest malice and wickedness occurring together (see Vincent, p. 539). These sores represent the embodiment of all spiritual and physical suffering that can be passed upon mankind. They are the pains that the wicked must endure themselves because they have refused the atonement of the Savior. The Lord has commanded us to "repent, lest I smite you by the rod of my mouth, and by my wrath, and by my anger, and your sufferings be sore—how sore you know not, how exquisite you know not, yea, how hard to bear you know not. For behold, I, God, have suffered these things for all, that they might not suffer if they would repent; But if they would not repent they must suffer even as I; Which suffering caused myself, even God, the greatest of all, to tremble because of pain, and to bleed at every pore, and to suffer both body and spirit— and would that I might not drink the bitter cup, and shrink—" (D&C 19:15–18).

The sore only affects those which have the mark of the beast and worship his image. It is a direct result of their allegiance to the beast and their disobedience to God.

*16:3.* **The second angel poured out his vial upon the sea, and it became as the blood of a dead man: and every living soul died in the sea.** The Lord cursed the sea for the last days: "Behold, I, the Lord, in the beginning blessed the waters; but in the last days, by the mouth of my servant John, I cursed the waters. Wherefore, the days will come that no flesh shall be safe upon the waters" (D&C 61:14–15).

Nothing will be safe in or upon the waters. Although the embodiment of life is in blood, in this case the flow of blood is such that it brings about death rather than life. With the sea becoming as "the blood of a dead man," there is no life in it. The blood of a dead man decays and stinks and is wasted; it is useless.

*16:4.* **The third angel poured out his vial upon the rivers and fountains of waters; and they became blood.** All sources of water are now bringing forth blood and are polluted. There is no life-saving water on the earth. The Savior has the water from which, if we drink, we will never thirst (see John 4:14), but at this time there is none of that water to be found because the earthly inhabitants have rejected the Source.

*16:5–6.* The angel of the waters then proclaims, **Thou art righteous, O Lord, which art, and wast, and shalt be, because thou hast judged thus. For they have shed the blood of saints and prophets, and thou hast given them blood to drink; for they are worthy.** The wicked have desired in their hearts to drink the blood of the Saints and prophets; as a direct result of their desires, God grants what they wish. The cup that the Savior drinks from is the offering he made for the sins of the world. The wicked, however, desire to drink the blood of the Saints to fulfill their oaths of revenge. Consider Amalickiah's oath: "Yea, he was exceedingly wroth, and he did curse God, and also Moroni, swearing with an oath that he would drink his blood; and this because Moroni had kept the commandments of God in preparing for the safety of his people" (Alma 49:27).

In contrast to the Savior being the only one "worthy" (see Rev. 5:5) to open the book, those who are allowed to drink the blood are "worthy" of their sufferings, because that is what they have desired.

*16:7.* Another angel then proclaims from the altar, **Even so, Lord God Almighty, true and righteous are thy judgments.** All those beings which have been engaged in wickedness will receive their just reward. All of the judgments of God are in harmony with the laws that he has established through all eternity, and the punishments which follow are merely a fulfillment of what was already written. The punishments represent justice for all those who were martyred for the Lord at the hands of evil and designing men.

The first three vials have brought about God's will in

execution of justice—the third angel proclaims this truth. After the fourth and fifth angels pour out their vials those upon the earth, in vain desperation, blaspheme God's name.

*16:8–9.* **The fourth angel poured out his vial upon the sun; and power was given unto him to scorch men with fire.** All of creation is now getting involved in the destruction of the wicked. The sun scorched men **with great heat.** This heat results from the fire that cleanses and purifies the earth by burning off the dross. Those who are tithed and have made their offerings will be protected from the burning (see D&C 64:23–24).

A sad commentary on the lives of the wicked is expressed as men **blasphemed the name of God** instead of turning to him in repentant humility. Rousas Rushdoony says that "blasphemy is more than taking the name of God profanely. It is defamatory, wicked, and rebellious language directed against God (Ps. 74:10–18; Isa. 52:5; Rev. 16:9, 11, 21). It was punishable by death (Lev. 24:16)" (p. 108).

The men who are incurring these judgments do not repent; instead, they turn further from their God to the point of profaning his name. As Nephi stated to his brothers, "Ye were past feeling, that ye could not feel his words" (1 Ne. 17:45). These men have lost all desire to repent and will pridefully reap as the rewards of their earthly labors, the judgments of God. **They repented not to give him glory** means that they would not glorify the Lord nor acknowledge his divinity by repenting.

*16:10–11.* **The fifth angel poured out his vial upon the seat of the beast[s].** The resultant affliction is a grave darkness. Those who must endure this darkness **gnawed their tongues for pain.** The seat of the beast is the place where Satan dwells and the plague is the darkness that comes up from the bottomless pit to afflict and torment man (see Rev. 9:2). With this darkness comes a loss of light. The two cannot exist together for wherever there is light, darkness must flee; but whenever spiritual darkness is allowed to enter, the spiritual light one possesses is diminished. One can never associate with the things of the adversary without being affected to some degree.

These men then **blasphemed the God of heaven because of**

**their pains and their sores, and repented not of their deeds.**
Once again blasphemy is shouted forth toward heaven. Men
who will not accept responsibility for their actions and must
blame someone else for their suffering blaspheme God. Even
this darkness does not cause them to repent of their deeds;
rather, pride prevents them from doing so.

In Revelation 13:6 it was the beast that was uttering blasphemies out of his mouth, now evil men have joined in. All of
wickedness are profaning the name of God, as a direct opposite
to all of the righteous who are continually praising God and glo-
rifying his name. These wicked men are past feeling and will be
swept off from the earth in consequence of their continued rejection of the very being who can forgive them.

*16:12.* **The sixth angel poured out his vial upon the great
river Euphrates; and the water thereof was dried up.** As the
vials are poured out, a sore that cannot be cleansed by any form
of water, a heat that cannot be quenched by water, and a main
river that is devoid of water are all symbolic of the living water
being taken from the earth. In the first few verses we saw that
the sore came about, then the sea became as the blood of a dead
man, the rivers and fountains then became blood, followed by
the fourth and fifth angels and their vials that brought burning
and darkness. No pure water can be found, and life must soon
end if there is no water. In a consummate end to all of this
destruction and death the Euphrates is dried up. The resultant
wickedness is unlike anything ever before seen on the face of the
earth. All of hell has broken loose for a final battle. Vincent
observes, "The Euphrates was known as *the great River, the River,
the Flood. . . .* It was the boundary-line of Israel on the northeast
(Gen. 15:18; Deut. 1:7; Josh. 1:4. Compare 2 Sam. 8:3–8; 1 Kings
4:21). It thus formed the natural defence of the chosen people
against the armies of Assyria. . . . To the prophets the Euphrates
was the symbol of all that was disastrous in the divine judgments" (p. 511).

With the Euphrates being dried up there is nothing to keep
the armies from coming upon the Holy City and surrounding
areas. They will come in a way never imagined, but will come in

a manner that **the way of the kings of the east might be prepared.** The "kings of the east" are those who come as the rising of the morning, the dawning of a new day, and with them bring a newness of life. Kings saw the Savior's star in the East (see Matt. 2:2) and came to worship him. It is imagined that the kings seen by John will come to do the same (worship the Savior). All wickedness must be swept off and the earth must be cleansed before these kings will come.

*16:13–14.* John sees **three unclean spirits like frogs come out of the mouth of the dragon . . . of the beast . . . and . . . of the false prophet.** This is the only place in the New Testament where any reference is made to frogs, and it appears very similar to when Moses commanded frogs to come upon the earth and afflict Pharaoh (see Ex. 8:1–14). This was the last plague that Moses brought upon the land that the magicians of the Pharaoh could duplicate. It must be remembered that these things are "unclean spirits" like frogs and they come out of the mouths of the dragon, the beast, and the false prophet. In the Mosaic law frogs were not to be eaten nor touched or one would become unclean, but no other information has been provided as to what frogs may have represented.

There is only one purpose for these unclean evil spirits—to do the work of the devil in gathering every wicked person together for battle. They gather the kings of the earth and go about **working miracles** in order to sway those who follow after them to believe that they will win the battle. Though many destructions have occurred on the earth, these spirits now convince the kings of the earth, through supposed miraculous power, that there is still hope for them to overcome God and his servants. The battle lines are drawn and the sides have been determined, but this is God's conflict. He will judge the wicked nations of the earth as they assemble against him to do battle. This is the final battle. There will be no other and God will be victorious.

*16:15.* Once again we see a brief warning to those who read this record. The second coming of Christ will be **as a thief.** It will come at a time least expected. **Blessed is he that watcheth** (keeps an eye on the signs of the times), **and keepeth his garments** (remembers his covenants and honors them), **lest he walk naked** (without the protection of covenants one is essentially naked), **and they see his shame.** The sins of the wicked will be uncovered and the real truth of their iniquities will be revealed. "And the rebellious shall be pierced with much sorrow; for their iniquities shall be spoken upon the housetops, and their secret acts shall be revealed" (D&C 1:3).

*16:16.* Hosts of armies are gathered together into the place **called in the Hebrew tongue Armageddon.** The Greek form of the word is *Harmagdon* and many scholars have interpreted this word to be *Har-megiddon,* meaning "the mountain of Megiddo," but there is no definitive answer as to one specific location of this battle. For all of these forces to be gathered together it must be a place large enough to accommodate all of them at once. In *The Life and Teachings of Jesus and His Apostles* we find the following description of the location. "Lying about sixty miles north of Jerusalem is the site of Megiddo, a great mound or hill commanding the northern entrance to the broad plain called the valley of Esdraelon. The mountain or hill of Megiddo (*Har Megiddo* in Hebrew, of which *Armageddon* is the Greek transliteration) guarded the strategic pass that cuts through the mountain range separating the coastal plains from the inland plains and hill country of Galilee. Because of this fortress or Mount of Megiddo, the valley and surrounding areas have also come to be known as Armageddon.

"One of the most important highways of the ancient world— the main link between Egypt and Asia—ran through this valley and near the fortress of Megiddo. Because of that strategic location, Megiddo and the valley of Esdraelon have seen some of history's bloodiest battles. Egyptian pharaohs, Roman legions, British troops, and Israeli tanks all have struggled in the valley of Megiddo. Prior to the second coming of Christ, all nations of the earth shall be gathered together to battle against Jerusalem. This tremendous war, one of the final great events prior to the Savior's second coming, has been foreseen and described in detail by many of the Lord's ancient prophets. (See, for example, Ezekiel 38,

39; Joel 2, 3; Isaiah 34; Jeremiah 25; Daniel 11, 12; Zechariah 12–14.)
Jerusalem will be under siege and great suffering will be the lot of
her inhabitants. Evidently, Armageddon, which is north of
Jerusalem, will be the site of the great decisive battle of this war.
'During this siege, when the nations are gathered and the Lord
comes, there will be great destruction. The armies will become so
confused they will fight among themselves. There will be great
slaughter. Then the Lord comes to the Jews. He shows Himself.
He calls upon them to come and examine His hands and His feet,
and they say, "What are these wounds?" And He answers them,
"These are the wounds with which I was wounded in the house
of my friends. I am Jesus Christ."

" 'Then they will accept Him as their Redeemer, which they
have never been willing to do.' (Smith, *Signs of the Times*, p.
171)" (*Life and Teachings*, p. 463).

The battle will progressively move towards Jerusalem and
the "mountain of the Lord's house," or in other words, not to the
Mount of Megiddo, but to the temple of the Lord, and his judgments will come forth from there. The battle must come to the
house of the Lord, for if the dragon, the beast, and the false
prophet are to have dominion over the earth, they must destroy
the seat, or resting place, of their foe, the Lord. It is from this
place that the final vial will be poured out upon the earth or
"into the air" (Rev. 16:17), unleashing the ultimate destruction.
Elder McConkie expounds: "It is incident to this battle of
Armageddon that the Supper of the Great God shall take place
(Rev. 19:11–18), and it is the same battle described by Ezekiel as
the war with Gog and Magog. (Ezek. 38; 39; *Doctrines of Salvation*, vol. 3, p. 45)" (*MD*, p. 74).

## Applicability

Prior to the seventh angel pouring out his vial the other six
plagues will have been poured out upon the earth and the
wicked will suffer in ways never before endured by man. Some
would wonder why, in the face of all of these destructions, the
people won't repent and turn to that God who gave them life?

The answer is found in their lives. They have worshipped the things of the earth and the things brought forth by the beast. They are past feeling, they cannot *feel* the word of the Lord (see 1 Ne. 17:45). They have been so overcome by the things of Babylon that they will only blaspheme God when they see his judgments come upon the earth. In these verses (1–16) we are again reminded that "blessed is he that watcheth, and keepeth his garments" (v. 15) and we see that the Lord will always remember and protect those who are faithful to their covenants. Hopefully by this time we would understand the saving power that is possessed by those who have entered into the temple and received the ordinances available to them.

## REVELATION 16:17–21

17 ¶ And the seventh angel poured out his vial into the air; and there came a great voice out of the temple of heaven, from the throne, saying, It is done.

18 And there were voices, and thunders, and lightnings; and there was a great earthquake, such as was not since men were upon the earth, so mighty an earthquake, and so great.

19 And the great city was divided into three parts, and the cities of the nations fell: and great Babylon came in remembrance before God, to give unto her the cup of the wine of the fierceness of his wrath.

20 And every island fled away, and the mountains were not found.

21 And there fell upon men a great hail out of heaven, every stone about the weight of a talent: and men blasphemed God because of the plague of the hail; for the plague thereof was exceeding great.

### Verse Commentary

*16:17.* **The seventh angel poured out his vial into the air; and there came a great voice out of the temple of heaven, from the throne, saying, It is done.** The seventh angel represents completeness. All things are fulfilled with the pouring out of this vial. The voice proclaims directly from the throne in the temple, or in other words, straight from the mouth of God: It is done! No greater pronouncement could be made. In the same way that the Savior proclaimed, "It is finished" (John 19:30) when his work upon the earth was completed, the Father proclaims from his throne in heaven that his work here upon the earth is finished. What a great message for the righteous inhabitants of the earth! The will of God is fulfilled.

*16:18.* **There** are **voices, and thunders, and lightnings; and there was a great earthquake.** All of the natural forces of the earth are involved in the Second Coming. Powerful manifestations of nature, including an earthquake the likes of which men have never before seen, proclaim the great day of the Lord.

*16:19.* **The great city was divided into three parts.** The term parts "comes from an obsol[ete] but more prim[itive] form of [the Greek] *mĕirŏmai*" which means "to get as a section or allotment" (*Strong's*, Greek Dictionary, p. 47). It seems that the reference to the city must be to Babylon and not to Jerusalem because Jerusalem is to be united and become as one whereas Babylon will be broken up and destroyed. In Revelation 14:8 we are told, "Babylon is fallen!" From chapter 14 we also receive a full description of all that Babylon is.

**The cities of the nations fell.** All worldly things that seem to have so much power are as nothing compared to the destruction caused by the natural powers of earth. Each of the cities of the nations shall fall. Through the Prophet Joseph Smith, the Lord tells us that "with the sword and by bloodshed the inhabitants of the earth shall mourn; and with famine, and plague, and earthquake, and the thunder of heaven, and the fierce and vivid lightning also, shall the inhabitants of the earth be made to feel the wrath, and indignation, and chastening hand of an Almighty God, until the consumption decreed hath made a full end of all nations" (D&C 87:6).

**Babylon came in remembrance before God, to give unto her the cup of the wine of the fierceness of his wrath.** The Lord forgives our sins saying, "Though your sins be as scarlet, they shall be as white as snow" (Isa. 1:18) and "I, the Lord, remember them no more" (D&C 58:42). Because the wicked refuse to repent, the remembrance of all that Babylon has done will come back presently before the Lord, and with that remembrance will come the fierceness of his wrath. Babylon is to receive all that she is due. The division of Babylon into three parts is the beginning of the process for her destruction. She will receive the full proportion of the fierceness of his wrath.

*16:20.* **And every island fled away, and the mountains were not found.** This passage is speaking specifically of the drastic changes that will take place upon the surface of the earth. From the Doctrine and Covenants we learn more detail about these changes. "Wherefore, prepare ye for the coming of the Bridegroom; go ye, go ye out to meet him. For behold, he shall stand upon the mount of Olivet, and upon the mighty ocean, even the great deep, and upon the islands of the sea, and upon the land of Zion. And he shall utter his voice out of Zion, and he shall speak from Jerusalem, and his voice shall be heard among all people; And it shall be a voice as the voice of many waters, and as the voice of a great thunder, which shall break down the mountains, and the valleys shall not be found. He shall command the great deep, and it shall be driven back into the north countries, and the islands shall become one land; And the land of Jerusalem and the land of Zion shall be turned back into their own place, and the earth shall be like as it was in the days before it was divided" (133:19–24).

Obviously, the changes to take place upon the earth will be such that it will be impossible for men to seek safety in any building. The only safety will be found in turning to the Lord. For someone who does not believe in God or who blasphemes his name, there is nowhere to hide during these overwhelming earthly movements.

*16:21.* **There fell upon men a great hail out of heaven, every stone about the weight of a talent.** Since Moses' day the use of hail has been one way in which God brings the wrath of his judgments upon men (see Ex. 9:18–26; Josh. 10:11; Rev. 8:7). According to Richard Draper, a talent is generally thought to be "between 60 to 80 pounds" (p. 182).

Once again, though, **men blasphemed God because of the plague of the hail.** As each of these elements of the wrath of God are unleashed upon the earth, there is still no sign of repentance from the mouths or hearts of men. It is unbelievable that the people could have fallen so low. The Spirit, or Light of Christ that was in them, has flickered and gone out. Unrepentant, they must now await the awful sentence of the consequences of their sins.

## Applicability

At the Savior's coming, when the proclamation sounds, "It is done," the power of God will be manifest in the upheaval of the forces of nature incomparable to anything ever before experienced. The battle of Armageddon is over possession of the earth. The forces of the righteous will overcome and wickedness will be swept from the earth. How many warnings have men been given to repent and turn back to their God? Is it any wonder that the Lord is grieved after he has attempted for so long, through his prophets and servants, to get his children to turn from their wicked ways and return to him? His promises are sure and as a result the wicked must incur the displeasure of a just God upon them. He is bound by his own law to bring his judgments upon the wicked. Of all those who, even in the face of such ominous destructions, refuse to repent, all we can ask is Why?

## SUMMARY

Time and again the Lord has warned that his destructive forces will be loosed upon the earth if the children of men do not repent. How long will his judgments remain in check? The time has now come. The execution of all that has been promised is now coming to pass. Chapter 16 has shown the wrath of God being "poured" out upon the earth by his angels. The plagues are the work of the Lord—this is his battle. He sounds the decrees and declares what is to be done.

The Saints were warned to watch and to keep their garments so as to be ready. We have the guarantee that as long as we watch and are ready, the wrath of God will not affect us in this world, nor in the world to come. The whole purpose of watchtowers in ancient times was to provide the city with an opportunity to see the adversary from afar in time to prepare for the battle. We, too, must watch and be ready as these scriptures indicate. "Therefore be ye also ready, for in such an hour as ye think not, the Son of Man cometh" (JS—M 1:48). And again, "Watch ye therefore: for ye know not when the master of the house cometh, at even, or at midnight, or at the cockcrowing, or in the morning: Lest coming suddenly he find you sleeping. And what I say unto you I say unto all, Watch" (Mark 13:35–37).

The judgments which come upon Babylon have been promised throughout the ages. In their fulfillment we see Babylon broken up and the fall of the cities of the nations of the earth. Nothing can withstand the power of God. The forces of nature must obey his will and do so to the destruction of Babylon and all that she represents. Once again, however, all those who associate with Babylon do not repent of their sins—even in the face of such a destructive onslaught. They still blaspheme God. There is little wonder at this point if God is justified in all of his judgments. The wicked are out of time and there is no hope for a release from their sufferings. Relief will surely not be provided by the dragon.

# 17

## Babylon, the Beast, and the Great and Abominable Church

Very little time has actually elapsed since we first became acquainted with the dragon, the beasts, and all of the forces of evil, and their representations. For the last five chapters more has been explained of the devil and his followers than in other parts of the scriptures. It is important to realize that the Lord has shown us these things to teach us who the adversary is, what he represents, and how he goes about his work in his futile attempt to thwart the work of God.

For every good thing in the world—the things that lead us to believe in God—we can be guaranteed that the adversary has brought about something that is a close counterfeit to the truth. In earlier chapters we have seen a beast with crowns (see Rev. 13:1), a beast like a lamb (see Rev. 13:11), and so forth; and now we see the complete antithesis, or opposite, of the woman (see Rev. 12) brought forth in the form of "a great whore that sitteth upon many waters" (Rev. 17:1).

Chapter 12 presented the bride (the woman) awaiting the Bridegroom (Christ), and as chapter 17 unfolds to our view we see a blasphemous woman committing fornication with the kings of the earth. In the same way that we saw the righteous come forth from the woman, we now see what is brought forth from this great whore. As terrible as the word *whore* may sound, it is perfectly expressive of all that this harlot brings forth and of the manner in which she does so.

We will also see how the kings and nations of the earth, offspring of the mother of abominations, shall then turn against her and prove to be her destruction. The very entity that created the kings and nations in all of their wickedness shall be destroyed by her own, fulfilling the word of the Lord.

<h2 style="text-align:center">REVELATION 17:1–6</h2>

1 ¶ And there came one of the seven angels which had the seven vials, and talked with me, saying unto me, Come hither; I will shew unto thee the judgment of the great whore that sitteth upon many waters:

2 With whom the kings of the earth have committed fornication, and the inhabitants of the earth have been made drunk with the wine of her fornication.

3 So he carried me away in the spirit into the wilderness: and I saw a woman sit upon a scarlet coloured beast, full of names of blasphemy, having seven heads and ten horns.

4 And the woman was arrayed in purple and scarlet colour, and decked with gold and precious stones and pearls, having a golden cup in her hand full of abominations and filthiness of her fornication:

5 And upon her forehead was a name written, MYSTERY, BABYLON THE GREAT, THE MOTHER OF HARLOTS AND ABOMINATIONS OF THE EARTH.

6 And I saw the woman drunken with the blood of the saints, and with the blood of the martyrs of Jesus: and when I saw her, I wondered with great admiration.

## Verse Commentary

*17:1–2.* **One of the seven angels which had the seven vials** comes and talks with John and says, **Come hither; I will shew unto thee the judgment of the great whore that sitteth upon many waters: With whom the kings of the earth have committed fornication, and the inhabitants of the earth have been made drunk with the wine of her fornication.** The judgment of God is about to come to pass. *The Life and Teachings of Jesus and His Apostles* says that "the kingdom of Satan, in all its opulent and wicked splendor, is depicted as a harlot, lavishly dressed and riding on a beast. The obvious representation is that of impurity, evil, wickedness. But the symbolism goes much deeper than that. The figure of a harlot as a metaphor for Satan's dominions is appropriate, for Satan prostitutes all that is noble and good" (p. 464).

She **sitteth upon many waters**—her influence and wicked-ness has stirred the hearts of kings and nations throughout the world. Though some have supposed that the symbolism is only to Babylon, pagan Rome, Papal Rome, or Jerusalem, it is neces-sary to realize that the whore has many names. Anyone she sways to follow after her enticements becomes known by her name.

**The kings of the earth have committed fornication** with her and her enticements have drawn the inhabitants of the earth away from their covenants with God. Rousas Rushdoony explains: "Even as infidelity in the O[ld] T[estament] typified the forsaking of the true God in order to worship idols, so for-nication is used in Revelation 2:21; 14:8; 17:2, 4; 18:3 and 19:2 to describe rebellion against and insubordination to God and the religion and life of such rebellion" (p. 407).

The inhabitants of the earth having been **made drunk with the wine of her fornication** means that the peoples of the earth have succumbed to her enticements. It is not wine that is draw-ing them away and causing them to stagger and fall, but a turn-ing from the truth they possessed. Isaiah says, "They are drunken, but not with wine; they stagger, but not with strong drink. For the LORD hath poured out upon you the spirit of a deep sleep, and hath closed your eyes: the prophets and your rulers, the seers hath he covered" (29:9–10).

They no longer see the things of God and of the prophets because they have turned their eyes from the gospel. The Lord has covered the truths they have received. Their walk in life is therefore unsteady and they reel, stagger, and fall.

*17:3–6.* **So he carried me away . . . into the wilderness.** John is carried away by the angel into the wilderness and sees **a woman sit upon a scarlet coloured beast, full of names of blas-phemy, having seven heads and ten horns.** The woman is on the back of the beast, therefore she controls it. The beast is simi-lar to the one seen in Revelation 13:1 with its heads and horns, and carrying its names of blasphemy. Satan himself is neither the beast nor the whore, but these two figures represent the adversary's wickedness and kingdom. Scarlet is the color of blood, and the blood of the Saints and Christian martyrs rests upon the shoulders of the beast.

**The woman was arrayed in purple and scarlet colour, and decked with gold and precious stones and pearls.** All of the symbols of the pride of the world and imagery of supposed greatness are put on by the harlot. All that she uses to entice the hearts of men is evident as she is "decked with," or wearing, these treasures of the world. The wealth of the world is flaunted as she uses all that is possible to seduce and beguile the nations of the earth to forsake their covenants and follow after her. In a vision similar to John's, Nephi reported that he saw "gold, and silver, and silks, and scarlets, and fine-twined linen, and all manner of precious clothing; and I saw many harlots. And the angel spake unto me, saying: Behold the gold, and the silver, and the silks, and the scarlets, and the fine-twined linen, and the precious clothing, and the harlots, are the desires of this great and abominable church" (1 Ne. 13:7–8). Later, an angel showed Nephi the church of the devil: "Look, and behold that great and abominable church, which is the mother of abominations, whose foundation is the devil" (1 Ne. 14:9; see Rev. 17:5).

In her hand, mimicking the seven angels, she holds a **golden cup . . . full of abominations and filthiness of her fornication.** The seven angels poured out their vials upon the earth, and these vials held the judgments reserved for the wickedness of man. The harlot holds in her cup the very things for which man is to be judged. The cup represents offerings. Its golden color symbolizes riches and the nature of the sins and filthiness of the corruption she offers to those who follow her. "Babylon hath been a golden cup in the LORD's hand, that made all the earth drunken: the nations have drunken of her wine; therefore the nations are mad" (Jer. 51:7).

17:5. The harlot is the epitome of evil. She represents the lusts of the flesh and the treasures of the world. Her appeal is based entirely on appearance; the satisfaction she offers is fleeting.

On her forehead we see an explicit name written: **MYS-TERY, BABYLON THE GREAT, THE MOTHER OF HAR-LOTS AND ABOMINATIONS OF THE EARTH.** This "woman" carries on her forehead her name, which is perfectly descriptive of all that she is and does. Conversely, we wish to have the name of God written or sealed upon our foreheads (see Rev. 9:4; 14:1). Such a seal perfectly describes all that we represent and believe.

Her name is **Mystery.** How appropriate. The Greek word *mustēriŏn* speaks of the mysteries being a sort of silence imposed by initiation into religious rites (see *Expository Dictionary*, sv. "mystery"). Each time the word is used in the New Testament, it is speaking of these rites. Even as the Lord has his sacred covenants and vows within his holy temples, Satan also uses secret oaths and covenants to bind the hearts of men to him. In Book of Mormon times we find continual infestation of the secret oaths administered through the Gadianton society. "And it came to pass that they did have their signs, yea, their secret signs, and their secret words; and this that they might distinguish a brother who had entered into the covenant, that whatsoever wickedness his brother should do he should not be injured by his brother, nor by those who did belong to his band, who had taken this covenant" (Hel. 6:22).

Whenever the Lord has developed a process to allow those who righteously desire to learn more of his "mysteries," the great imitator will then develop similar initiation rites. Rather than being sacred, however, Satan's rites are secret.

The ordinances performed in latter-day temples are not secret, but are extremely sacred. They are covenants with God. All who desire to be obedient to the word of God and to accept the ordinances set forth in The Church of Jesus Christ of Latter-day Saints are allowed to enter the temple and participate in those ordinances. They are sacred and are made in a building dedicated as the house of God.

The woman also bears the name **Babylon the Great, the Mother of Harlots and Abominations of the Earth.** She represents all wickedness. As a mother she brings forth those things which seduce the hearts of men and cause them to follow after the abominations of the earth. An abomination is "a loathsome act or thing" (Webster, sv. "abomination"). In other words, she represents all disgusting, revolting things that man can participate in here on the earth.

Kingdoms, organizations, societies, or churches that set their hearts to lead away captive the souls of men are all offspring of this woman and are subject to Satan's power. "And behold, others he flattereth away, and telleth them there is no hell; and he saith unto them: I am no devil, for there is none—and thus he whispereth in their ears, until he grasps them with his awful chains, from whence there is no deliverance. Yea, they are grasped with death, and hell; and death, and hell, and the devil, and all that have been seized therewith must stand before the throne of God, and be judged according to their works, from whence they must go into the place prepared for them, even a lake of fire and brimstone, which is endless torment" (2 Ne. 29:22–23).

Evil is not one specific entity, it is any form of wickedness. Evil deeds bring forth more wickedness. In this manner wickedness becomes a "mother" of more evil designs. It is an extremely sad commentary on Satan's purposes that he mocks the sacred role of mothers in bringing forth the wicked things of the world.

*17:6.* The woman is **drunken with the blood of the saints, and with the blood of the martyrs of Jesus.** The wicked of Babylon rejoice in injuring the righteous. The woman has become intoxicated, not with alcohol, but with the enjoyment she receives from killing those who profess a belief in Jesus Christ. The martyrs are those who were killed because of the testimonies they bore of Jesus Christ. They were witnesses of the truth, and the woman, and her followers, took great joy in putting the righteous Saints to death.

When John saw the woman he **wondered with great admiration.** The actual term is an indication of marvel, and not specifically admiration. "The Greek word *thaumazō*, translated 'admiration' in the KJV, means to be amazed, to wonder, to be astonished. The common element seems to be incredulous surprise" (Draper, p. 191).

## Applicability

We now know what the great whore of all the earth repre-sents. All of those things of the world which people place their hopes and dreams on are merely temporary forms of a false sense of security. When we die, as is seen by those who worship the things of the earth, we will only take that which is inside us, our spirit, when we go before the Lord to be judged. For every pure and holy thing which our Father creates we can be guar-anteed that Satan will attempt to imitate him. The Church is to be the bride of the Lamb, so Satan comes along and brings forth the whore of all the earth. Each pure creation has its opposite in one of Satan's imitations.

In the previous verses we find that the whore of all the earth is drunken with the blood of Saints and martyrs. Even today we find those who are mocked and treated with derision because of their attempts to choose the right. At times we find those who strive to be faithful and keep the commandments are treated with contempt or are considered "holier than thou," even by members of the Church. The people who cause the most dam-age to the Church are not those from without but those from within—those who say they are sheep, but are actually ravenous wolves. This is not meant to be derisive of the membership of the Church but its occurrence even once is far more often than should be the case.

## REVELATION 17:7–18

7 ¶ And the angel said unto me, Wherefore didst thou marvel? I will tell thee the mystery of the woman, and of the beast that carri-eth her, which hath the seven heads and ten horns.

8 The beast that thou sawest was, and is not; and shall ascend out of the bottomless pit, and go into perdition: and they that dwell on the earth shall wonder, whose names were not written in the book of life from the foundation of the world, when they behold the beast that was, and is not, and yet is.

9 And here is the mind which hath wisdom. The seven heads are seven mountains, on which the woman sitteth.

10 And there are seven kings: five are fallen, and one is, and the other is not yet come; and when he cometh, he must continue a short space.

11 And the beast that was, and is not, even he is the eighth, and is of the seven, and goeth into perdition.

12 And the ten horns which thou sawest are ten kings, which have received no kingdom as yet; but receive power as kings one hour with the beast.

13 These have one mind, and shall give their power and strength unto the beast.

14 ¶ These shall make war with the Lamb, and the Lamb shall overcome them: for he is Lord of lords, and King of kings: and they that are with him are called, and chosen, and faithful.

15 And he saith unto me, The waters which thou sawest, where the whore sitteth, are peoples, and multitudes, and nations, and tongues.

16 And the ten horns which thou sawest upon the beast, these shall hate the whore, and shall make her desolate and naked, and shall eat her flesh, and burn her with fire.

17 For God hath put in their hearts to fulfil his will, and to agree, and give their kingdom unto the beast, until the words of God shall be fulfilled.

18 And the woman which thou sawest is that great city, which reigneth over the kings of the earth.

## Verse Commentary

*17:7.* John marvels at what he sees before him, but in no way admires the woman or the beast. The angel asks, **Wherefore didst thou marvel?** His astonishment towards the woman and the beast will be placated as the angel now tells the **mystery of the woman, and of the beast that carrieth her.**

*17:8.* The beast is similar to the beast John saw in chapter 13 and in opposition to the Lamb. This beast **was, and is not; and shall ascend out of the bottomless pit, and go into perdition.** The Savior will descend from heaven in his glorious second coming, and then inherit celestial glories on high; conversely, the beast will ascend from the bottomless pit, and then go into perdition. "Perdition, in the Greek is *apōléia*, and is presumed to be from the Greek *apóllumi*, 'meaning to destroy fully'" (*Strong's*, Greek Dictionary, p. 14). The word *apōléia* means "ruin or loss," (physical, spiritual, or eternal) and also is related to "damnation, destruction, die, perdition, perish, pernicious ways, waste" (*Strong's*, Greek Dictionary, p. 15).

To go into perdition then, would seem to represent being cast off forever to a complete physical, spiritual, and eternal destruction. This would represent a complete loss of hope for all of those who would follow after Satan and be called "sons of perdition" (see D&C 76:31–38). Perdition also seems to logically indicate that if one is not progressing toward eternal life, then he must be digressing from the blessings offered therein.

We learn from this verse that the beast is only temporary: it was, and is not. The beast is unlike "the Lord, which is, and which was, and which is to come" (Rev. 1:8). The Lord is eternal, and he shall return again to the earth. Our Savior is counterfeited in the form of the beast. Even the comparison of the two symbols for these powers helps us understand what they represent. The Lord is known as both the Lion (see Rev. 5:5) and the Lamb (see Rev. 5:6), while the terms for Satan and his servants are the dragon (see Rev. 12:3), the beast (see Rev. 13:1), and the serpent (see Rev. 20:2).

**They that dwell on the earth shall wonder, whose names were not written in the book of life . . . when they behold the beast that was, and is not, and yet is.** Satan will be upon the earth for a period of time and many will worship the beast, or in other words, "he was" (see Rev. 13:8). At the Second Coming the adversary shall be bound, otherwise stated, "he is not." And finally he is loosed for a short season at the end of the Millennium, "and yet is," meaning that he shall return. The resiliency of the adversary to keep coming back and trying to fight is what will cause those on earth to wonder after this beast with so much power. Satan is eternal but his power and presence are temporary. The higher power of the Lord will cause Satan to be cast out, or go into perdition.

Those "whose names were not written in the book of life" (Rev. 17:8) will wonder after the beast as they see his supposed power upon the earth. They will be amazed by what he can do, yet the reason they will be in such awe is that they do not comprehend the power of the Lord. They have rejected the Lord their God and do not repent of their sins, therefore their names are not written in the book of life.

*17:9.* **Here is the mind which hath wisdom.** Deciphering all that the beast represents requires wisdom from God. We must not identify only one specific entity as the beast. The moment that we specify one particular person or thing as the beast, we close our eyes to all others of similar design. For example, many scholars have said that the woman of Revelation represents Rome because of the seven mountains surrounding Rome. They assert that John was alluding to this being the center of "Babylon" because of Rome's idolatry, false worship, and the wickedness of her emperors.

Rome, however, has not been the only great and idolatrous city. Although it is true that many parts of Revelation were perfectly applicable to John's period and to the Saints of his day, it is a revelation disclosing details of the battle between the forces for good and evil from the beginning till the end of time. The times revealed through John have not all passed, and we should be cautious in saying that some of these calamities are behind us. Consider the battle around us. The woman and the beast surround us at this moment, and therefore, Revelation was not just for the Saints in the meridian of time.

Here is wisdom then: **The seven heads are seven mountains, on which the woman sitteth.** A head represents power or control over the body and seven represents completeness. Reason, therefore, suggests that the "seven heads" represents a complete control over a certain kingdom's domain. Next we find the woman sitting, comparable to a queen on her throne, on the "seven mountains." Mountains are often used to portray the temple, or the place where God reveals his will to man. If Satan and his servants are the great imitators, we would then see that the great harlot will sit on the mountains—her thrones, or temples—to reveal her mind and will to the nations and kingdoms of the earth. Some of the largest temples built in ancient times were those dedicated to Greek, Roman, and other pagan gods. Today's temples may be represented by the large structures dedicated to war, prestige, money, or in other words, those things made by our own hands that we worship or idolize.

*17:10–11.* **There are seven kings.** Again we see completeness as associated with kings, or the power to rule. It is even possible that the kings are those leaders responsible for carrying out the work of the adversary during each of the thousand-year periods of the earth. **Five** of the kings **are fallen, and one is, and the other is not yet come.** A possible reading of this is that "five are fallen" because the first five dispensations are past; "one is" because we are currently in the sixth thousand years; and "one is not yet come" because Satan's final manifestation is not yet upon us. We don't know who this is speaking of, but although there is much speculation on actual identities, we can find numerous kings, rulers, emperors, and presidents throughout history who resemble the kings mentioned. Whenever a king or kingdom is overthrown it is almost always the result of a terrible battle in which many lives are lost. Five of these kings are fallen, and with them their servants. The other is not yet come and he will continue but a short space prior to the ending of the reigns of the kings.

What would be the cause of an end to the reign of kings which had occurred for six millennia? Nothing but the coming of the King of Kings, and Lord of Lords, even Jesus Christ returning in his glory. The **beast that was, and is not, even he is the eighth [king], and is of the seven.** The beast is one of the seven, but he is "the eighth," or in other words, he is the consummate fulfillment, the embodiment, of all that the wicked kings of the earth represent. In the end, wickedness is cast into perdition. There is only one true king over the earth. It is Jesus Christ. He will come in his glory and will put all other things under his feet. The other kings must be cast off and go into a place prepared for them where they become subjects to Satan, the supposed king they chose to follow.

*17:12–13.* The **ten horns . . . are ten kings.** Here we see the number ten expressing a part of the whole. These ten kings, a group of wicked men who desire to rule in wickedness but have not yet received their kingdoms, will share power over the things of the earth **as kings one hour with the beast.** They will rule over the earth with the beast, but for a very limited time. They have **one mind, and shall give their power and strength**

**unto the beast.** Even though they are desirous to be kings, they still are in subjection to the beast and will give all that they have to serve him. As they do so, they will be allowed to rule as kings and to bring more glory, and power, and might to themselves. They are all self-serving and have one desire: to rule and reign.

*17:14.* These ten kings, or in other words, the kingdoms of the world excluding the Saints of the Church, **shall make war with the Lamb.** In vision, Nephi sees the armies gather: "And it came to pass that I beheld the church of the Lamb of God, and its numbers were few, because of the wickedness and abominations of the whore who sat upon many waters; nevertheless, I beheld that the church of the Lamb, who were the saints of God, were also upon all the face of the earth; and their dominions upon the face of the earth were small, because of the wickedness of the great whore whom I saw. And it came to pass that I beheld that the great mother of abominations did gather together multitudes upon the face of all the earth, among all the nations of the Gentiles, to fight against the Lamb of God" (1 Ne. 14:12–13). The realization has come to them that if they are to be kings as they desire, and rule over the earth completely, they must defeat the Lamb. It is an impossible battle for them. **The Lamb shall overcome.** What an awesome message in the middle of all of this wickedness! As John sees complete decay upon the earth, even among kingdoms, thrones, and principalities, he sees that the Lamb shall win the battle and will overcome. **He is Lord of lords, and King of kings.** Jesus Christ is the King and Lord over us all. He shall rule and reign forever.

**They that are with him are called, and chosen, and faithful.** Those who follow after the Lord are called by him. The term *called* comes from the Greek *klētŏs* meaning invited or appointed, specifically as a saint (see *Strong's*, Greek Dictionary, p. 42). They know his voice and he has shepherded them as his Saints. They are chosen, or in other words, selected from the best. They are the elect of the earth, they are the faithful Saints who have been willing to give all things, even their lives if necessary, in defense of the truth.

*17:15.* The angel then gives to John the interpretation of the things he has seen in this part of the vision: **The waters which thou sawest, where the whore sitteth, are peoples, and multitudes, and nations, and tongues.** In this explanation we find that the whore is ruling over the flood of people inhabiting the earth in what appears to be her hour of glory. In the last days evil will abound on the earth. President Joseph Fielding Smith said, "There is more sin and evil in the world now than there has been at any time since the day of Noah, when the Lord felt disposed to destroy the world by a flood so that He could send His spirit children to earth in a better and more righteous environment" (Ricks College Baccalaureate Services, 7 May 1971, as quoted in *Life and Teachings*, p. 464). President Smith was more explicit in *Doctrines of Salvation*. "*Satan has control now.* No matter where you look, he is in control, even in our own land. *He is guiding the government as far as the Lord will permit him.* That is why there is so much strife, turmoil, and confusion all over the earth. One master mind is governing the nations. It is not the President of the United States; it is not Hitler; it is not Mussolini; it is not the king or government of England or any other land; it is Satan himself" (3:315).

*17:16.* **The ten horns which thou sawest upon the beast . . . shall hate the whore, and shall make her desolate and naked, and shall eat her flesh, and burn her with fire.** The very powers of the wicked that she has controlled and placed in subjection shall turn on her and bare all of her sins to her utter destruction. This is a part of the Lord's plan. He allows the wicked to fight against the wicked to bring about their own destruction and to preserve his righteous armies from the battlefield. Nephi was allowed to see in vision the wars and destruction of the wicked. "And as there began to be wars and rumors of wars among all the nations which belonged to the mother of abominations, the angel spake unto me, saying: Behold, the wrath of God is upon the mother of harlots; and behold, thou seest all these things—And when the day cometh that the wrath of God is poured out upon the mother of harlots, which is the great and abominable church of all the earth, whose founder is the devil, then, at that day, the work of the Father shall commence, in preparing the way for the fulfilling of his covenants, which he hath made to his people who are of the house of Israel" (1 Ne. 14:16–17).

The great whore will be destroyed by her own people. Nations will rise up against her and she will be made desolate— nothing will be left of those who make up the church of the devil. She will have no gold, or silver, or precious jewels, or things of the earth which lead away the hearts of men. She will be stripped and her abominations will be exposed for all to see. She will be punished for her fornications. In Leviticus we find the following judgment exacted for the crime of fornication by the daughter of the priest: "And the daughter of any priest, if she profane herself by playing the whore, she profaneth her father: she shall be burnt with fire" (21:9).

The great whore who sitteth upon the waters has received the same judgment. Her nakedness is exposed and she has profaned the Father. She will reap the consequences of her sins. Her own seed, whom she has raised to fight against the Lamb and his Saints, now turn on her and destroy her as they destroy each other. By contrast, the seed of God, his covenant children, will honor him, praise him, and ultimately strive to be like him.

**17:17. God hath put in their hearts to fulfil his will, and to agree, and give their kingdom unto the beast, until the words of God shall be fulfilled.** The Interpreter's Bible explains: "The imperial tyranny indeed contains seeds of destruction which God uses for his own purposes of judgment. It is a sobering and yet an inspiring thought that God bends evil men to his own purposes as a part of his great reign" (12:497).

The Lord grants unto men according to the desires of their hearts, and when their hearts are set upon the things of the world, the Lord will use their desires to further his work. Nephi taught that "the blood of that great and abominable church, which is the whore of all the earth, shall turn upon their own heads; for they shall war among themselves, and the sword of their own hands shall fall upon their own heads, and they shall be drunken with their own blood. And every nation which shall war against thee, O house of Israel, shall be turned one against another, and they shall fall into the pit which they digged to ensnare the people of the Lord. And all that fight against Zion shall be destroyed, and that great whore, who hath perverted the right ways of the Lord, yea, that great and abominable church, shall tumble to the dust and great shall be the fall of it" (1 Ne. 22:13–14). An integral part of the plan of salvation is the agency that each of us must have. Agency, however, could not exist without some type of opposition. The opposition was provided when Satan chose to rebel against the Father and drew the third part of heaven with him. "The works, and the designs, and the purposes of God cannot be frustrated, neither can they come to naught" (D&C 3:1).

The kings of the earth will continue in wickedness. Their lusts and greed will not provide them with what they expect. They will war amongst themselves, destroying each other and fulfilling the Lord's will. This is part of their downfall and judgment.

*17:18.* **The woman which thou sawest is that great city.** She is Babylon, the epitome of all wickedness, the place where all the wicked dwell. Spiritually there are only two cities in the last days: 1) Babylon, the city of wickedness **which reigneth over the kings of the earth,** and 2) Zion, the city of righteousness and the pure in heart (see Moses 7:18). We must decide where our citizenship will be. "For where your treasure is, there will your heart be also" (Luke 12:34). The kings of the earth have given their hearts to Babylon and she rules over them, in purpose, in word, and in deed.

## Applicability

Throughout the Book of Mormon the people were warned against choosing kings to lead them. Mosiah taught that when a wicked king received power, great iniquities would accompany his reign (see Mosiah 29:35–36). The elixir of power can often change the heart of a righteous man, causing him to lose sight of the true purposes for which he desires to lead a group of people. The Doctrine and Covenants teaches that "many are called, but few are chosen" because their hearts are so set upon the things of the world and the honors of men (121:34–36, 40). The kings discussed in these verses make war with Jesus Christ, the King of Kings in a vain attempt to preserve their power. Often, people say how wonderful it would be to have Jesus Christ reign as king. Some claim they would find it easier to follow him because he is perfect and so all of his judgments and decisions would be perfect. Yet, in Book of Mormon times, as well as today, men trample the God of heaven under their feet as they set at naught, or fail to heed, his counsels as given through the scriptures and latter-day prophets. The scriptures contain Christ's perfect counsel for us. Too many members of the Church, however, claim to follow Jesus Christ but fail to keep the Sabbath day holy, continue to watch inappropriate videos or movies, or do not live up to the temple covenants they have made. We must avoid worshipping the "beast." Babylon is anything that draws our attention away from the Lord and the principles of salvation—anything that keeps us from acknowledging our allegiance to the King of Kings. We look forward to our Savior's coming with repentant hearts and contrite spirits.

## SUMMARY

"Babylon the Great" is wickedness in all of its ugly glory. Evil servants are born of her and come forth to do her bidding. She uses her seductive practices to lead away the hearts of men, and causes them to marvel at her worldly grandeur. John must have ached as he saw the worldly influence of this harlot who sat upon the waters and the powerful effect she had on the souls of the children of men.

Verse 14 confirmed to John that the Lord would triumph over evil. This, too, must be our encouragement. If we are true and faithful the time will come that we will be called up, chosen, and pronounced faithful. Then we will receive all that the Father hath. We will not have to fight the final battle for it will be the Lord's and he will be victorious. Remember, "Wherefore, he will preserve the righteous by his power, even if it so be that

the fulness of his wrath must come, and the righteous be preserved, even unto the destruction of their enemies by fire.
Wherefore, the righteous need not fear; for thus saith the
prophet, they shall be saved, even if it so be as by fire. Behold,
my brethren, I say unto you, that these things must shortly
come; yea, even blood, and fire, and vapor of smoke must come;
and it must needs be upon the face of this earth; and it cometh
unto men according to the flesh if it so be that they will harden
their hearts against the Holy One of Israel. For behold, the righteous shall not perish; for the time surely must come that all
they who fight against Zion shall be cut off" (1 Ne. 22:17–19).

Even in the face of so much corruption, as has been
expressed in chapter 17, the righteous must remain faithful and
realize that Babylon, in all of her wickedness, shall be destroyed,
and she will be destroyed by her own, in fulfillment of the will
of the Lord.

# 18

# The Fall of
# Babylon the Great

Babylon has been described in every detail. We will now see the fall of that great church, the whore of all the earth, and "the destruction of the wicked, which is the end of the world" (JS—M 1:4). "And the great and abominable church, which is the whore of all the earth, shall be cast down by devouring fire, according as it is spoken by the mouth of Ezekiel the prophet, who spoke of these things, which have not come to pass but surely must, as I live, for abominations shall not reign" (D&C 29:21).

All that the Saints have waited for is now to come to pass. The fall of all things wicked, represented by Babylon, will take place as the Lord remembers the inquities of those who have chosen to follow Satan. This grand judgment upon Babylon will cause joy and rejoicing among the righteous, as vindication comes from the Lord for the suffering they have endured at her hands. The persecutions of the Saints will be no more. Babylon will be destroyed and righteousness will rule in its stead. Figuratively speaking, a millstone is hanging around the necks of the wicked and it will drag them down as it is cast into the sea. The Savior said, "But whoso shall offend one of these little ones which believe in me, it were better for him that a millstone were hanged about his neck, and that he were drowned in the depth of the sea" (Matt. 18:6). Could we not imagine such a fate for all unrepentant sinners?

## REVELATION 18:1–8

1 ¶ And after these things I saw another angel come down from heaven, having great power; and the earth was lightened with his glory.

2 And he cried mightily with a strong voice, saying, Babylon the great is fallen, is fallen, and is become the habitation of devils, and the hold of every foul spirit, and a cage of every unclean and hateful bird.

3 For all nations have drunk of the wine of the wrath of her fornication, and the kings of the earth have committed fornication with her, and the merchants of the earth are waxed rich through the abundance of her delicacies.

4 And I heard another voice from heaven, saying, Come out of her, my people, that ye be not partakers of her sins, and that ye receive not of her plagues.

5 For her sins have reached unto heaven, and God hath remembered her iniquities.

6 Reward her even as she rewarded you, and double unto her double according to her works: in the cup which she hath filled fill to her double.

7 How much she hath glorified herself, and lived deliciously, so much torment and sorrow give her: for she saith in her heart, I sit a queen, and am no widow, and shall see no sorrow.

8 Therefore shall her plagues come in one day, death, and mourning, and famine; and she shall be utterly burned with fire: for strong is the Lord God who judgeth her.

### Verse Commentary

*18:1.* John now sees **another angel come down from heaven, having great power; and the earth was lightened with his glory.** Once again the light of the gospel and the message of the Lord is seen as the brightness of an angel's glory lightens the earth. This will represent the eventual overcoming of righteousness as the fall of Babylon is imminent. Ezekiel records a similar description of the glory of the Lord: "The earth shined with his glory" (43:2).

*18:2.* The angel cries, **Babylon the great is fallen, is fallen, and is become the habitation of devils, and the hold of every foul spirit, and a cage of every unclean and hateful bird.** The moment of victory and truth has arrived. Babylon is fallen! She has become the habitation, the dwelling place, of all evil things.

Devils, or those who follow after the devil, and every foul spirit is now placed in a hold. The Greek word, *phulakē,* means a guarding place or prison (see *Strong's,* Greek Dictionary, p. 76). Thus, every devil or unclean spirit is placed in a prison. The "unclean and hateful bird[s]" are those that pick away at the souls of men. Richard Draper explains that "the Old Testament associates fowl with the judgment of God upon a rebellious people. Out of this grew the association of something feeding upon the souls of men (see e.g., Deut. 28:26; 1 Sam. 17:44; 1 Kgs. 14:11; Ps. 79:2; Isa. 18:6; Jer. 16:4; Ezek. 29:5). The birds thus probably symbolize in general those incorporeal forces that destroy the souls of men" (p. 199).

*18:3.* The angel continues its proclamation in verse 3 with, **For all nations have drunk of the wine of the wrath of her fornication, and the kings of the earth have committed fornication with her, and the merchants of the earth are waxed rich through the abundance of her delicacies.** These are the reasons for the judgments that are to come upon Babylon. The major sins men have committed are highlighted here as lustful desires for the things of the world. The enticements of the flesh and promises of wealth cause men to commit fornication with her as they turn from those sacred covenants made with God and seek after those things that are of little worth in the eternities. Marvin R. Vincent declares that "the abundance of her delicacies" is literally "the power of her luxury." He also says that the interpretation "over-strength, luxury, wantonness" can be applied, but "only here in the New Testament." In addition, Vincent notes that a similar verb, *streniao,* meaning "to live deliciously," occurs in Revelation 18 verses 7 and 9 (p. 549).

The merchants of the earth have lusted after wealth. It must be recognized that money is not bad, but the lust or all-encompassing desire for money is. Remember Paul's words to Timothy: "The *love of money* is the root of all evil" (1 Tim. 6:10, emphasis added). The merchants of the earth have become rich through the powers of Babylon's luxurious enticements.

*18:4–5.* John now hears another voice from heaven, saying, **Come out of her, my people, that ye be not partakers of her**

**sins, and that ye receive not the plagues. For her sins have reached unto heaven, and God hath remembered her iniquities.** The command is given to all that follow after the Lord, who desire to free themselves from the downfall of Babylon, to "come out of her." The call to go out of Babylon is not just speaking of the Rome of John's time, but is referencing every wicked city that men dwell in, whether it be Sodom and Gomorrah, Rome, or any other city. The call to flee Babylon has come in every dispensation. Hugh Nibley writes, "In every dispensation of the Gospel, the Lord has insisted on segregating his covenant people from the rest of the world: if they were not ready to 'come out of her, [O] my people' (Revelation 18:4) willingly, he saw to it that the world was more than willing to persecute and expel them" (*Approaching Zion*, p. 341).

Jeremiah recorded one of the Old Testament calls to flee: "Flee out of the midst of Babylon, and deliver every man his soul: be not cut off in her iniquity; for this is the time of the LORD's vengeance; he will render unto her a recompence. Babylon hath been a golden cup in the LORD's hand, that made all the earth drunken: the nations have drunken of her wine; therefore the nations are mad. Babylon is suddenly fallen and destroyed: howl for her; take balm for her pain, if so be she may be healed. We would have healed Babylon, but she is not healed: forsake her, and let us go every one into his own country: for her judgment reacheth unto heaven, and is lifted up even to the skies" (51:6–9). The Prophet Joseph Smith recorded a similar commandment to the Saints of the latter days: "The voice of the Lord is unto you: Go ye out of Babylon; gather ye out from among the nations, . . . even from Babylon, from the midst of wickedness, which is spiritual Babylon" (D&C 133:7, 14).

The only way to avoid the plagues that flow upon Babylon is to flee from her. You cannot "sit on the fence," participating both in the things of Babylon and in the things of God.

The choice must be made of whom you will follow. President Joseph Fielding Smith said, "If you think the world is getting better, just observe and witness the vulgarity and the near-approach to indecency that we find published in some pictorial magazines and so frequently on the screen. Think of the corruption and the debasing conditions due to the indulgence in liquor and tobacco and other narcotics and drugs. Think of the immorality which is so prevalent throughout the country" (*DS,* 3:30–31).

The battle lines are being drawn. If we are not for the Lord and the truth we are fighting for the adversary. The decree of the Lord has been made. We must go out from Babylon to escape the wrath of God and the judgment Babylon will incur. Isaiah foretold of the Lord's vengeance to be brought upon Babylon. "And Babylon, the glory of kingdoms, the beauty of the Chaldees' excellency, shall be as when God overthrew Sodom and Gomorrah. It shall never be inhabited, neither shall it be dwelt in from generation to generation: neither shall the Arabian pitch tent there; neither shall the shepherds make their fold there. But wild beasts of the desert shall lie there; and their houses shall be full of doleful creatures; and owls shall dwell there, and satyrs shall dance there. And the wild beasts of the islands shall cry in their desolate houses, and dragons in their pleasant palaces: and her time is near to come, and her days shall not be prolonged" (Isa. 13:19–22).

No people will dwell in Babylon. The remains of what once stood as the pride of the world shall be inhabited only by the unclean animals of the earth. Doleful creatures, owls, and satyrs (he-goats) are all used to represent uncleanness in the law of Moses.

*18:6.* **Reward her even as she rewarded you, and double unto her double according to her works: in the cup which she hath filled fill to her double.** Babylon is to be rewarded in double measure for the sins she has committed. Some might think that this does not seem just, to be rewarded double, but she is accountable for sins of commission and omission. She is not only accountable before the Lord for those things which she purposely did (sins of commission), but also for all of those things which came about as a result of her inaction (sins of omission). The Levitical law required that double recompense be given for certain trespasses against another (see Ex. 22:4, 7, 9).

*18:7.* Babylon's judgments shall be just. **She hath glorified herself, and lived deliciously.** Babylon has desired a fulfillment of her pleasures and luxuries, and she glories in that which she portrays. A noted Bible commentary suggests that "men's carnal mind relishes a religion like that of the apostate Church, which gives an opiate to conscience, whilst leaving the sinner license to indulge his lusts" (Jamieson, Fausset, and Brown, p. 594).

**Torment and sorrow give her.** This is the judgment she will receive, to reward her with the very things she has brought upon the souls of men who have been drawn in by her beguiling traps. Think of alcoholism, pornography, various types of abuse, idolatry in its many forms, and all the other Babylonian seductions. Consider all of the torment and sorrow which has come upon mankind because of these things. Babylon shall receive just recompense for the things she has brought upon mankind.

**She saith in her heart, I sit a queen, and am no widow, and shall see no sorrow.** She is puffed up in the pride of her heart as she imagines herself sitting in a queen's regality. She is "married" to those she has drawn after her. To her followers she says that they have not died, that she is not a widow, and that they shall see no sorrow. They are dead to their belief in Christ, however, and to the ordinances which will save them and give them eternal life.

We see Babylon being the complete opposite, or inverse, of Zion and the Church. The following chart may help clarify how Satan counterfeits some of the symbolism of the Lord as pertaining to Zion:

| Item | Zion | Babylon |
|---|---|---|
| King | Christ | Satan |
| Bride | Church of God | Church of devil |
| Representation of woman | Bride | Widow/Harlot |
| Enticements | Things of the Spirit | Things of the earth |
| Last days | Church is raised up | Babylon is fallen |
| Relationship to mankind | Make covenants | Commit fornication |

Thus, for all of the glories and blessings awaiting those who dwell in Zion, only condemnations and curses await those who dwell in Babylon. When she falls they shall fall with her.

*18:8.* **Her plagues come in one day, death, and mourning, and famine.** Her fall shall come in one day! It will not be delayed over time, but shall be executed quickly **and she shall be utterly burned with fire.** The cleansing process will burn all the dross and wickedness out of Babylon. She shall be utterly destroyed! In place of riches and all the "imagined" luxuries of the world, she shall now represent death, mourning, and famine. There will not be anything joyful in her possessions as the judgments of a **strong** God rain down upon her. Isaiah prophesied of the destructions to come upon the residents of Babylon. "Therefore hear now this, thou that art given to pleasures, that dwellest carelessly, that sayest in thine heart, I am, and none else beside me; I shall not sit as a widow, neither shall I know the loss of children: But these two things shall come to thee in a moment in one day, the loss of children, and widowhood: they shall come upon thee in their perfection for the multitude of thy sorceries, and for the great abundance of thine enchantments. For thou hast trusted in thy wickedness: thou hast said, None seeth me. Thy wisdom and thy knowledge, it hath perverted thee; and thou hast said in thine heart, I am, and none else beside me" (Isa. 47:8–10).

The Lord has continuously proclaimed that the earth will be cleansed by fire, preparatory to the second coming of the Savior. "All the proud and they that do wickedly shall be as stubble; and I will burn them up, for I am the Lord of Hosts; and I will not spare any that remain in Babylon" (D&C 64.24). This is the reason that the Lord commands his children, specifically those who follow after him, to come out of Babylon and to flee from her presence.

## Applicability

The destruction of Babylon will be swift and all-inclusive. She has provided the things of the earth to all those who lusted after them. She extends the riches and luxuries of the earth and pretends that they will provide all the satisfaction that men will ever need. All too often her pretenses succeed and men are led to believe that even without the Savior in their life they have all that they could ever want and don't need more. She calls herself a queen, says that she has a husband and is not a widow, and boasts that she will not see sorrow. These are lies! Sadly, there are still some who choose to follow her enticements. Her destruction will come in one day, and if we are involved in her wicked ways we will not have time to flee.

## REVELATION 18:9–19

9 ¶ And the kings of the earth, who have committed fornication and lived deliciously with her, shall bewail her, and lament for her, when they shall see the smoke of her burning,

10 Standing afar off for the fear of her torment, saying, Alas, alas, that great city Babylon, that mighty city! for in one hour is thy judgment come.

11 And the merchants of the earth shall weep and mourn over her; for no man buyeth their merchandise any more:

12 The merchandise of gold, and silver, and precious stones, and of pearls, and fine linen, and purple, and silk, and scarlet, and all thyine wood, and all manner vessels of ivory, and all manner vessels of most precious wood, and of brass, and iron, and marble,

13 And cinnamon, and odours, and ointments, and frankincense, and wine, and oil, and fine flour, and wheat, and beasts, and sheep, and horses, and chariots, and slaves, and souls of men.

14 And the fruits that thy soul lusted after are departed from thee, and all things which were dainty and goodly are departed from thee, and thou shalt find them no more at all.

15 The merchants of these things, which were made rich by her, shall stand afar off for the fear of her torment, weeping and wailing,

16 And saying, Alas, alas, that great city, that was clothed in fine linen, and purple, and scarlet, and decked with gold, and precious stones, and pearls!

17 For in one hour so great riches is come to nought. And every shipmaster, and all the company in ships, and sailors, and as many as trade by sea, stood afar off,

18 And cried when they saw the smoke of her burning, saying, What city is like unto this great city!

19 And they cast dust on their heads, and cried, weeping and wailing, saying, Alas, alas, that great city, wherein were made rich all that had ships in the sea by reason of her costliness! for in one hour is she made desolate.

**Verse Commentary**

*18:9–10.* **The kings of the earth, who have committed fornication and lived deliciously with her, shall bewail her, and lament for her.** What a sad commentary on the state of the souls of men who have associated with Babylon! The kings (vv. 9–10), merchants (vv. 11–16), and all of those involved in trafficking the lucrative products of Babylon (vv. 17–19), shall cry out and lament the destruction of their true love. The sight of **smoke** signals the **burning** and destruction of their city.

The kings must stand **afar off for the fear of her torment.** These men, rulers of the earth, cry out because they have lost their opportunity to continue to live with their harlot, yet they stand afar off. They try to avoid the judgments being placed upon her, but they do not regret their wickedness. There will be no more personal satisfaction as the source of their wickedness is destroyed and they lament her destruction.

**Alas, alas, that great city Babylon, that mighty city! for in one hour is thy judgment come.** The judgment brought down upon Babylon is swift and final, there will be no escaping that which shall come upon her.

If it had been possible, the kings of the earth would have healed their mistress in order to continue their life of luxury with her. Once they see her demise they, like Satan when he draws down a person after him, forsake her and go into their own country.

*18:11–13.* **The merchants of the earth shall weep and mourn over her; for no man buyeth their merchandise any more.** All of these people are self-serving. The kings want to satisfy their lustful desires, the merchants sorrow because no one will buy their wares, and the men of the sea (see vv. 17–19) lose the source of their wealth.

Anything could be bought in Babylon—for a price. Lustful desires were satisfied with sexual immorality; riches of the world could be found in **the merchandise of gold, and silver, and precious stones, and of pearls;** those who desired to exalt themselves by the wearing of costly apparel could purchase **fine**

**linen, and purple, and silk, and scarlet;** craftsmen would supply **thyine wood . . . vessels of ivory, and . . . vessels of most
precious wood, and of brass, and iron, and marble.** Sellers of
**cinnamon, and odours (perfumes), and ointments, and frank-
incense** could all peddle their spices and scents; **wine, and oil,
and fine flour, and wheat** could all be purchased; **beasts, and
sheep, and horses, and chariots** were readily available; and
finally, the most vital of all, **slaves, and souls of men** could be
had. This was a consumers' paradise—all of the things of the
world could be had for money.

Lives were spent simply pursuing those things which are
temporary and do not last past this mortal life. Men had spent
their lifetimes creating and satisfying pretended needs. The
economy of the wicked is based upon gluttony and greed, and
when it collapses as Babylon is destroyed the unrighteous
mourn **for no man buyeth their merchandise any more.**
Richard Draper comments on Babylon's pretended needs. "The
whole of their marketing enterprise is built upon a pretense sustained by the creation of artificial needs. They do this by simple
tricks of marketing through which warmth becomes mink; shelter becomes marble and brass; food becomes escargot and
caviar. And when the bottom falls out of the market, the kings
are left without taxes, armies, or treasuries, and the merchants
with rotting cargos and glutted stockpiles that no one will buy"
(pp. 202–3).

*18:14.* **The fruits that thy soul lusted after are departed
from thee, . . . and thou shalt find them no more at all.** All of
the things that their souls craved are no longer available. The
lusts of the flesh will continue with the wicked beyond the veil.
They will not, however, have the wherewithal to satisfy those
desires. The **dainty and goodly** are those things which represent
the fat of the earth, such as oils, perfumes, and clothing (see Vincent, p. 553). They are the things of excess, worldly extrava-
gances which are not needful but are used as measurements of
the wealth and stature one has. Consider how the Lord has used
the term *fruits* before. In the Sermon on the Mount, Jesus said,
"Ye shall know them by their fruits. . . . A good tree cannot bring

forth evil fruit, neither can a corrupt tree bring forth good fruit. Every tree that bringeth not forth good fruit is hewn down, and cast into the fire. Wherefore by their fruits ye shall know them" (Matt. 7:16–20).

*18:15–17.* **The merchants . . . shall stand afar off for the fear of her torment,** and shall be **weeping and wailing.** Their cries are for what they have lost: **Alas, alas, that great city, that was clothed in fine linen, and purple, and scarlet, and decked with gold, and precious stones, and pearls! For in one hour so great riches is come to nought.** They are not sorrowing for the destruction of the city, but for their financial losses. Their thoughts are only concerned with their great riches.

*18:17–19.* **The shipmaster, and all the company in ships, and sailors, and as many as trade by sea, stood afar off.** These souls are just like the kings and the merchants; their concern is not that the city is destroyed, but that the source of their trading has become a thing of nought. Their investments in the riches of the world are gone. They mourn, weep, and wail over the fall of Babylon. She is destroyed, she has fallen and taken her treasures with her. Their hope is also gone. They have procrastinated the day of their repentance, and now it is too late (see Alma 34:32–35). The destruction is incomprehensible for them as they state, **What city is like unto this great city!**

**They cast dust on their heads,** as an outward display of mourning and sorrow for their city. These men are not concerned with the sins they committed in Babylon, but think only of what more they might have made monetarily. They too, like the kings and merchants, cry out—weeping and wailing—saying, **Alas, alas, that great city, wherein were made rich all that had ships in the sea by reason of her costliness! for in one hour is she made desolate.**

All they focus on is what she gave to them as to the riches of the earth. Once again we see the use of multiple witnesses who bear testimony to the purposes for which the judgments of the Lord were brought upon Babylon. In the mouths of these three witnesses—kings, merchants, and seafarers—we see why God's judgments are just.

## Applicability

As Babylon represents worldliness, there is little wonder that mankind will react so vehemently to her destruction. All of the temporary satisfaction is gone, but instead of turning from their wicked ways and directing their attention to the Lord, their only response is to blaspheme his name. Today, we are continually bombarded with the things of Babylon as we view commercials, billboards, and every other enticement to "enjoy" the finer things in life. When the lives of those of the world are not based on spiritual things, and then earthly wealth and pleasure are taken away, there is nothing to fall back on.

"In one hour so great riches is come to nought" (Rev. 18:17). This phrase is indicative of how quickly the things of the world disappear. Consider the effects of numerous recent natural disasters. Homes are swallowed up in the earth, floods sweep away everything in their path, fires destroy most of what they touch, tornadoes annihilate everything that they contact. The physical riches of the world should seem trivial compared to life and personal safety, yet so much is sacrificed in the accumulation of those temporary riches which cannot withstand the destructive forces of nature! Truly, where our heart is, there will be our treasure also.

## REVELATION 18:20–24

20 Rejoice over her, thou heaven, and ye holy apostles and prophets; for God hath avenged you on her.

21 And a mighty angel took up a stone like a great millstone, and cast it into the sea, saying, Thus with violence shall that great city Babylon be thrown down, and shall be found no more at all.

22 And the voice of harpers, and musicians, and of pipers, and trumpeters, shall be heard no more at all in thee; and no craftsman, of whatsoever craft he be, shall be found any more in thee; and the sound of a millstone shall be heard no more at all in thee;

23 And the light of a candle shall shine no more at all in thee; and the voice of the bridegroom and of the bride shall be heard no more at all in thee: for thy merchants were the great men of the earth; for by thy sorceries were all nations deceived.

24 And in her was found the blood of prophets, and of saints, and of all that were slain upon the earth.

**Verse Commentary**

*18:20*. Her destruction is imminent! The call goes up. **Rejoice over her, thou heaven, and ye holy apostles and prophets; for God hath avenged you on her.** Justice has been served and the cries sent forth by those who have suffered at the hands of the wicked from the beginning of time are now answered upon the head of the queen of the wicked.

*18:21*. **A mighty angel took up a stone like a great millstone, and cast it into the sea.** In Jeremiah we find a mighty angel takes a millstone and casts it into the river Euphrates also as a symbol of the judgment which would come upon Babylon (see Jer. 51:62–64). In the same manner that the stone would never rise up again from the depths of the river, or from the sea, **that great city Babylon [shall] be thrown down, and shall be found no more at all.** Her destruction shall be complete and she will not rise up again to bring her destructive vices upon the souls of the children of men.

*18:22–23*. **The voice of harpers, and musicians, and of pipers, and trumpeters, shall be heard no more at all in thee.** All of the music that was part of the fanfare of this city will cease. Worldly music, which today, as anciently, can fuel lustful desires, will cease. **No craftsman . . . shall be found . . . and the sound of a millstone shall be heard no more.** There will be no private enterprise taking place in Babylon. All work that was occurring, in preparation for peddlers to sell their wares, will cease; and the noise of this preparation will also cease.

**The light of a candle shall shine no more at all in thee.** This is not just speaking of the physical light which brightens our day, but the light of the Spirit and the Light of Christ is found no more at all in Babylon. She has lost all that was given her as she seduced herself. **The voice of the bridegroom and of the bride shall be heard no more at all in thee.** This is explained by the following verse from Jeremiah: "Moreover I will take from them the voice of mirth, and the voice of gladness, the voice of the bridegroom, and the voice of the bride, the sound of the millstones, and the light of the candle" (25:10).

Babylon will be desolate. The noises of celebration and industry will be silenced. There will be no joy or music in Babylon. The barren city will host no marriages, no festivities, and no commerce. It will be completely deserted.

**Thy merchants were the great men of the earth; for by thy sorceries were all nations deceived.** Babylon used sorceries to deceive the nations of the earth. Sorceries are the use of power obtained from evil spirits. Because of their relationshp with Satan, the merchants of Babylon became "great men of the earth"—men who were endowed with power from the evil one. Sorceries also can refer to divining, or trying to determine the unknown through ungodly mediums. We must never seek revelations except by the power of the Holy Ghost.

*18:24.* **In her was found the blood of prophets, and of saints, and of all that were slain upon the earth.** One of the reasons for the judgments that have been heaped upon Babylon is the multitude of murders she has committed. Accounts of the torture, persecutions, and slayings of numerous prophets and Saints are recorded throughout the scriptures. Abel (see Gen. 4:8), Abinadi (see Mosiah 17:20), the people of Alma and Amulek (see Alma 14:10–11), the two prophets (see Rev. 11:7), and thousands more have all been slain and their blood bears witness as a testimony against the wicked of Babylon.

### Applicability

The destruction of Babylon and her worldly riches will cause great rejoicing among the righteous upon the earth. They will not rejoice because the wicked are made to suffer, but because the sorrow and suffering Babylon has brought upon the Saints will be done away. The blood of the Saints has cried up from the ground long enough and now vindication is brought to pass. The righteous must understand that the Lord's times are set; neither we nor the wicked can change those times.

At times our trials seem hard to bear. Even Joseph Smith, while in Liberty Jail, asked the Lord how long He would suffer the Saints to be persecuted (see D&C 121–23). But the time will come that the wicked will be put under foot. Then our rejoicings will be in our deliverance and in the destruction of wickedness. We must remember, though, that those we call our enemies are still our brothers and sisters; their demise will bring some feelings of sorrow and sadness to our hearts.

## SUMMARY

What a great and yet sorrowful message has been found in this chapter! The long-sought-after time when Babylon should be destroyed has finally arrived. In the description of all that will happen to Babylon, we see what has taken place among the souls of men. They have spent their lives searching after and working for that which only satisfies temporarily. When one has spent his or her whole life in the search of material wealth, and then in less than "one hour" all is taken away, there is nothing left to hope for. As the Book of Mormon prophet Jacob said, "Before ye seek for riches, seek ye for the kingdom of God. And after ye have obtained a hope in Christ ye shall obtain riches, if ye seek them; and ye will seek them for the intent to do good—to clothe the naked, and to feed the hungry, and to liberate the captive, and administer relief to the sick and the afflicted" (Jacob 2:18 19).

The kings, merchants, and shipmasters had spent their lives trafficking and consuming products that satisfied the desires of the flesh. When Babylon was destroyed, their mourning was that of the damned soul who has chosen the lustful enticements of the world.

There is joyous hope for the righteous Saints. The Lord has delivered his people and has brought his vengeance upon the wicked. Those who have suffered, or who will suffer, the loss of their life for the cause of truth and for their testimonies shall see the justice of the Lord brought down upon those who persecuted them. Saints of the latter days are not exempt. Missionaries have lost their lives to assailants' bullets and have been arrested for preaching the gospel. Righteous believers have been denied the opportunity to worship God. Some have been tortured for their beliefs and many more righteous Saints will be persecuted for the sake of the truth. This is the Lord's work. We are only instruments in his hands. Our sufferings will be rewarded by him.

Once Babylon is cast down, like the millstone cast into the sea never to rise up again or bring wickedness to the earth, righteousness will prevail upon the earth and the Savior will dwell in the midst of his Saints. The earth is prepared for the great wedding feast and marriage of the bride and the groom. All who have been invited shall enter in, the doors will be shut, and the marriage will begin. What a glorious day is at hand! All things will be subdued under the feet of the Savior. Consider the words spoken by the prophet Zechariah: "Sing and rejoice, O daughter of Zion: for, lo, I come, and I will dwell in the midst of thee, saith the LORD. And many nations shall be joined to the LORD in that day, and shall be my people: and I will dwell in the midst of thee, and thou shalt know that the LORD of hosts hath sent me unto thee. And the LORD shall inherit Judah his portion in the holy land, and shall choose Jerusalem again" (Zech. 2:10–12).

We have finally reached the long-awaited day. Babylon is no longer. From this point on John will see the Lord and his servants dwell in righteousness, until the last battle at which the beast will be cast off into a lake of fire and brimstone, but for now it is truly a day of joy and rejoicing, for the coming of the Savior and his angels is at hand.

# 19

## KING OF KINGS AND
## LORD OF LORDS

The great feast of the Lord is now made ready and all of the hosts of heaven who have remained righteous are now proclaiming the glory and honor of the Lamb. It seems as though it was quite a long time ago when the four and twenty elders and the multitudes were surrounding the throne giving praises to him that was worthy to break, or open, the seal (see Rev. 5).

The crescendo of praise that started in chapter 18 now begins to reach over all the earth. The righteous who have waited patiently on the Lord have now seen themselves delivered. Justice and judgment have been brought upon Babylon. The marriage of the Lamb to his bride is finally made ready. The righteous will be allowed to participate in this beautiful covenant of marriage between the Church of faithful Saints and the Lord. Elder Bruce R. McConkie observes that "in this dispensation the Bridegroom, who is the Lamb of God, shall come to claim his bride, which is the Church composed of the faithful saints who have watched for his return. As he taught in the parable of the marriage of the king's son, the great marriage supper of the Lamb shall then be celebrated" (*MD*, p. 469).

This is a glorious moment for the faithful Saints. Each has the testimony of Jesus, and therefore also the spirit of prophecy. The heavens are opened and John sees the Savior, he who is called "Faithful and True" (Rev. 19:11), riding upon a white horse. Now, reminiscent of those riders in chapter 6, we see the Lord sitting upon his own horse, preparing to fight the last battle against the adversary. Soon the adversary will be cast off, as the millstone was cast into the sea, never to return. So shall be the lot of those who have chosen Satan as their king over the Lord, those who are not invited to the great feast. All is in preparation for the millennial reign of Christ.

Ponder the beautiful and comforting words spoken by President Lorenzo Snow at the October general conference of 1900 as he considered the glorious future: "My hopes in reference to the future life are supremely grand and glorious, and I try to keep these prospects bright continually; and that is the privilege and the duty of every Latter-day Saint. I suppose I am talking now to some Latter-day Saints that have been sorely tried and they have thought sometimes, perhaps like the Savior felt, that he had no friends, that his friends had all gone; and everything was going wrong, and everything was disagreeable, and his circumstances were continuing to get worse and worse, and those that he depended upon for assistance failed perhaps to render the assistance expected, and all that sort of thing. Likewise everything sometimes becomes dark to us and we almost forget the relationship that we stand in to the Lord and begin to feel as though it was not what we expected. . . . Think now of how much worse you and I might be, and then think of what superior blessings we actually possess. We know that in the future after we have passed through this life, we will then have our wives and our children with us. We will have our bodies glorified, made free from every sickness and distress, and rendered most beautiful. There is nothing more beautiful to look upon than a resurrected man or woman. There is nothing grander that I can imagine that a man can possess than a resurrected body. There is no Latter-day Saint within the sound of my voice but that certainly has this prospect of coming forth in the morning of the first resurrection and being glorified, exalted in the presence of God, having the privilege of talking with our Father as we talk with our earthly father" (CR, Oct. 1900, p. 4).

The great day of the Lord is at hand and the faithful Saints will participate in the marriage feast of the Lamb.

## REVELATION 19:1–10

1 ¶ And after these things I heard a great voice of much people in heaven, saying, Alleluia; Salvation, and glory, and honour, and power, unto the Lord our God:

2 For true and righteous are his judgments: for he hath judged the great whore, which did corrupt the earth with her fornication, and hath avenged the blood of his servants at her hand.

3 And again they said, Alleluia. And her smoke rose up for ever and ever.

4 And the four and twenty elders and the four beasts fell down and worshipped God that sat on the throne, saying, Amen; Alleluia.

5 ¶ And a voice came out of the throne, saying, Praise our God, all ye his servants, and ye that fear him, both small and great.

6 And I heard as it were the voice of a great multitude, and as the voice of many waters, and as the voice of mighty thunderings, saying, Alleluia: for the Lord God omnipotent reigneth.

7 Let us be glad and rejoice, and give honour to him: for the marriage of the Lamb is come, and his wife hath made herself ready.

8 And to her was granted that she should be arrayed in fine linen, clean and white: for the fine linen is the righteousness of saints.

9 And he saith unto me, Write, Blessed are they which are called unto the marriage supper of the Lamb. And he saith unto me, These are the true sayings of God.

10 And I fell at his feet to worship him. And he said unto me, See thou do it not: I am thy fellowservant, and of thy brethren that have the testimony of Jesus: worship God: for the testimony of Jesus is the spirit of prophecy

## Verse Commentary

*19:1–2.* John now hears **a great voice of much people in heaven, saying, Alleluia; Salvation, and glory, and honour, and power, unto the Lord our God: For true and righteous are his judgments: for he hath judged the great whore, which did corrupt the earth with her fornication, and hath avenged the blood of his servants at her hand.**

The word *Alleluia* means "praise ye the Lord" (see *Strong's*, Greek Dictionary, p. 10). All of the righteous and faithful Saints in heaven now proclaim that which comes from the Lord. Each of the words used by the people in heaven bespeaks of all that he is and does. (He is salvation, and glory, honor, and power are his just blessings because of all that he has overcome.) It is he that sends forth true and righteous judgments, and with these he has judged the whore of all the earth and has brought upon her condemnation for killing his servants.

Drawing from ideas in James H. Moulton and George Milligan's *The Vocabulary of the Greek Testament*, Richard Draper says, "The heavenly host repeat the theme of the nature of God's judgments; they are both 'true and righteous' (v. 2, KJV). The idea behind the term *true* (Greek *althēs*) is 'exact' or 'correct' but goes beyond that. The word conveys the idea of legitimacy" (p. 206).

The judgments which come out against the wicked are legitimate, or justifiable, because the Lord has previously declared them. These judgments are based upon God's eternal law and punishments are meted out for disobedience to the law.

*19:3.* Again, the people cry out, **Alleluia,** for the destruction of Babylon has occurred. The fire described in Revelation 18 witnessed by the kings, merchants, and shipmasters, is still evident as **her smoke rose up for ever and ever.** Those who participate in the fornications and idolatries of Babylon shall go away into everlasting burnings. A similar scene was viewed and recorded by Abraham in Genesis: "And Abraham gat up early in the morning to the place where he stood before the Lord: And he looked toward Sodom and Gomorrah, and toward all the land of the plain, and beheld, and, lo, the smoke of the country went up as the smoke of a furnace" (19:27–28).

*19:4.* Once again we see the **four and twenty elders and the four beasts** (see Rev. 4:4, 6, 7; 5:8) as they **fell down and worshipped God that sat on the throne.** They fall before the Lord in an expression of their humility and gratitude for all that has been accomplished at his hands. They, like all of the people aforementioned, also cry out, **Amen,** signifying both agreement and closure, and then follow with **Alleluia,** praise ye the Lord.

*19:5.* **A voice came out of the throne, saying, Praise our God, all ye his servants, and ye that fear him, both small and great.** What can be said about the joy of this time? Imagine the joy of accomplishing all that you desired to do from before the foundation of the world! Mere words lack the ability to express what will be felt by those who are true and faithful in all things. "Small and great" include all people (see Rev. 20:12) who have been faithful to the Lord.

*19:6.* All gather together as **the voice of a great multitude, and as the voice of many waters, and as the voice of mighty thunderings.** All now proclaim, with a voice that shakes the earth: **Alleluia: for the Lord God omnipotent reigneth.** Continual praises are pouring forth unto the Lord for all that has been and will yet be accomplished. It is truly difficult to express the deep sense of gratitude which will be felt towards our elder brother and his Father for their condescensions to the children of men.

*19:7.* The expressions of praise continue: **Let us be glad and rejoice, and give honour to him: for the marriage of the Lamb is come, and his wife hath made herself ready.** The marriage feast is at hand and the bride is ready for the ceremony to begin. The Church shall now be united with her King and their marriage will last forever. The preparations for the marriage feast began when the true Church of Jesus Christ was restored to the earth in the dispensation of the fulness of times. The invitations are now going out to all who desire in faith to come into the marriage feast and submit themselves to their Savior.

President Joseph Fielding Smith observes that "the vision of John and the revelation to Joseph Smith both have reference to the same event, the second coming of our Lord in his power and glory, to receive his Church or kingdom, the New Jerusalem being the capital city of the Church, and there is no difference in the meaning whether reference is to the Church or the New Jerusalem, for the righteous will have inheritance in the New Jerusalem. Therefore the bride of the Lamb is the organization of the righteous who have inheritance in the holy city" (*AGQ*, 1:25–26).

The union of Church and Christ is a covenant marriage. It is completely different from the adulterous relationship of harlot and beast.

*19:8.* The bride is **arrayed in fine linen, clean and white: for the fine linen is the righteousness of saints.** Everything about her denotes purity and cleanliness. The Church is composed of those who are clean and pure, those whose garments have been made white in the blood of the Lamb (see Rev. 7:14). Alma the Younger says, "There can no man be saved except his garments are washed white; yea, his garments must be purified until they are cleansed from all stain, through the blood of him who it has been spoken by our fathers, who should come to redeem his people from their sins" (Alma 5:21). The righteousness is more specifically the "righteous acts" of the Saints (Vincent, p. 557).

*19:9.* John is told to write the following: **Blessed are they which are called unto the marriage supper of the Lamb.** Those who are like the five wise virgins (see Matt. 25:1–10), those who have overcome all things and are true and faithful to the many covenants they have made, whose lamps are trimmed with oil when the cry goes up that the bridegroom cometh are invited into the feast. We must be called, we cannot just enter in. It is obvious that an invitation must have been sent out, an invitation to come out from Babylon and to keep ourselves unspotted from the world (see D&C 58:6–11). Are we given a personal invitation to attend the marriage feast? Alma declares that we are. "Behold, he sendeth an invitation unto all men, for the arms of mercy are extended towards them, and he saith: Repent, and I will receive you. Yea, he saith: Come unto me and ye shall partake of the fruit of the tree of life; yea, ye shall eat and drink of the bread and waters of life freely; Yea, come unto me and bring forth works of righteousness, and ye shall not be hewn down and cast into the fire—" (Alma 5:33–35).

The voice then says to John, **These are the true sayings of God.** Of this Elder McConkie says, "The angel, in the Lord's name, bears testimony of the truth and divinity of his teachings and ministerial acts—setting a perfect example of testimony bearing for all the Lord's agents in all ages" (*DNTC*, 3:565).

*19:10.* **And I fell at his feet to worship him.** The brightness, glory, and message of this angel is so overwhelming in its grandeur that John falls to worship the angel. The angel forbids him, saying, **See thou do it not: I am thy fellowservant, and of thy brethren that have the testimony of Jesus: worship God: for the testimony of Jesus is the spirit of prophecy.**

What glorious things are spoken from on high! John is being taught by one of his fellowservants and is instructed to worship God. John has the testimony of Jesus and has been prophesying of the things to take place on this earth. It is no different for Saints of the latter days. When we have *the* testimony of Jesus we do not question the divinity of the Savior. This is not merely *a* testimony of the Savior, but a perfect knowledge that Jesus is the Christ, the Eternal Son of God, and the Lamb which was slain from the foundation of the world. In his first epistle John said, "Beloved, now are we the sons [and daughters] of God, and it doth not yet appear what we shall be: but we know that, when he shall appear, we shall be like him; for we shall see him as he is. And every man that hath this hope in him purifieth himself, even as he is pure" (1 Jn. 3:2–3).

## Applicability

Because of the destruction of Babylon the Saints have reason to rejoice. One of the greatest things about entering the temple is that the desire for riches of the world is forgotten. Everyone dresses in white and participates in the same ordinances in the same way. There are no benefits based upon who is known or the wealth one possesses. It is truly a heavenly and restful place. When all wickedness has been swept off the earth and the righteous have been preserved we will praise the Lord with anthems of gratitude and love. Dressed in the garments washed white in the blood of the Lamb, we will witness the everlasting marriage of Christ and his Church.

## REVELATION 19:11–16

11 ¶ And I saw heaven opened, and behold a white horse; and he that sat upon him was called Faithful and True, and in righteousness he doth judge and make war.

12 His eyes were as a flame of fire, and on his head were many crowns; and he had a name written, that no man knew, but he himself.

13 And he was clothed with a vesture dipped in blood: and his name is called The Word of God.

14 And the armies which were in heaven followed him upon white horses, clothed in fine linen, white and clean.

15 And out of his mouth goeth a sharp sword, that with it he should smite the nations: and he shall rule them with a rod of iron: and he treadeth the winepress of the fierceness and wrath of Almighty God.

16 And he hath on his vesture and on his thigh a name written, KING OF KINGS, AND LORD OF LORDS.

## Verse Commentary

*19:11.* John sees **heaven opened** and sees another **white horse** (see Rev. 6:2). The rider is **called Faithful and True, and in righteousness he doth judge and make war.** Once again the horse is symbolic of victory and purity and the name of the rider identifies what he has done. His eternal testimony has been sealed with his blood and his word will come to pass. When the Savior made his triumphal entry into Jerusalem, he rode on the back of a donkey, symbolic of meekness and peace (see Matt. 21:5–7). When he comes the second time, he comes on a horse, symbolic of victory and battle.

All of his judgments are righteous and just. The war which shall be waged against the wicked is because of their disobedience. The Lord is bound to be just in all of his judgments; mercy cannot rob justice. In this situation there shall be no mercy, the day of judgment is at hand. Everyone shall reap the fruits they have sown. The war he is about to undertake will bind the adversary and will free the earth from the wickedness it has endured for so long.

*19:12–13.* The power of the Spirit bears testimony that John saw the glorified, resurrected Christ. The following is John's description of our Savior: **His eyes were as a flame of fire, and on his head were many crowns; and he had a name written, that no man knew, but he himself. And he was clothed with a vesture dipped in blood: and his name is called The Word of God.** Consider the similarity of the description of the Lord recorded by the Prophet Joseph Smith. "His eyes were as a flame of fire; the hair of his head was white like the pure snow; his countenance shone above the brightness of the sun; and his voice was as the sound of the rushing of great waters" (D&C 110:3).

His eyes pierce and burn through every soul he looks upon. He doesn't just wear one crown, but wears many, each representative of the principalities, powers, mights, and dominions he possesses. He has also been given a name which no man knows but himself. Elder McConkie teaches us that "as with all glorified beings, our Lord has a new name in celestial exaltation, a name known to and comprehended by those only who know God in the sense that they have become as he is and have eternal life. See Rev. 2:12–17. Thus, Christ's 'new name' shall be written upon all those who are joint-heirs with him (Rev. 3:12), and shall signify that they have become even as he is and he is even as the Father (3 Ne. 28:10)" (*DNTC*, 3:567).

The Savior is clothed with a vesture, or robe, dipped in blood. It has been stained by the blood the Savior spilt when he took upon himself our sins and suffered the price for those who would repent. The Savior will not forget us. The robe he wears continually reminds him of the price he paid to save his people. Jesus Christ bears other reminders also, as he told Isaiah: "Can a woman forget her sucking child, that she should not have compassion on the son of her womb? yea, they may forget, yet will I not forget thee. Behold, I have graven thee upon the palms of my hands; thy walls are continually before me" (Isa. 49:15–16; 1 Ne. 21:15–16).

His name is called "The Word of God." It is out of his mouth that all things are fulfilled. This name is a complete description of all that Jesus Christ does. He is the Word, a title John used to begin his Gospel (see John 1:1–3, 14). A word, when spoken, tells everyone who hears what is expected of him. Whenever the Savior speaks he is telling those who hear, the mind and will of the Father. He is not here to do his own will but that of the Father.

The Savior will speak judgment, his word being as a two-edged sword loosed upon the face of the earth. The Doctrine and Covenants records: "And it shall be said: Who is this that cometh down from God in heaven with dyed garments; yea, from the regions which are not known, clothed in his glorious apparel, traveling in the greatness of his strength? And he shall say: I am he who spake in righteousness, mighty to save. And the Lord shall be red in his apparel, and his garments like him that treadeth the wine-vat. And so great shall be the glory of his presence that the sun shall hide his face in shame, and the moon shall withhold its light, and the stars shall be hurled from their places. And his voice shall be heard: I have trodden the wine-press alone, and have brought judgment upon all people, and none were with me; And I have trampled them in my fury, and I did tread upon them in mine anger, and their blood have I sprinkled upon my garments, and stained all my raiment; for this was the day of vengeance which was in my heart" (133:46–51). The raiment the Savior will wear at the Second Coming will be crimson, stained with blood, as a reminder to all who see him of the suffering he had to bear in the awful agony of the Atonement.

*19:14.* **The armies which were in heaven followed him upon white horses, clothed in fine linen, white and clean.** Those who follow after the Savior are clothed in white apparel and ride on white horses as their Master does. They are clean from the blood and sins of this generation and are now going forth in their righteousness to do battle against the adversary. The advance will not cease until justice is served.

*19:15.* Judgment comes forth from his mouth in the form of a **sharp sword** and with it he will **smite the nations.** The "sword of the Spirit, which is the word of God" is the only offensive weapon provided with the armor of God (Eph. 6:11–18). Here again we see his word in judgment as it "smite[s] the nations." The sharp sword is one that cuts with exactness, meaning that it will only execute judgment on those who have transgressed the law. A person will never be judged more harshly, or incur more punishment, than they deserve because of the choices they have made.

**He shall rule them with a rod of iron.** The term *rule* is to lead as a shepherd with a rod straight and true and unbending. The rod of iron represents the word of God and is the course that leads us to the tree of life and the paradise of God. Nephi taught this representation to his brothers. "And they said unto me: What meaneth the rod of iron which our father saw, that led to the tree? And I said unto them that it was the word of God; and whoso would hearken unto the word of God, and would hold fast unto it, they would never perish; neither could the temptations and the fiery darts of the adversary overpower them unto blindness, to lead them away to destruction" (1 Ne. 15:23–24).

**And he treadeth the winepress of the fierceness and wrath of Almighty God.** To tread the winepress is to stamp out or subdue the enemy. Consider the words of the Savior as spoken from the mouth of Isaiah: "I have trodden the winepress alone; and of the people there was none with me: for I will tread them in mine anger, and trample them in my fury; and their blood shall be sprinkled upon my garments, and I will stain all my raiment. For the day of vengeance is in mine heart, and the year of my redeemed is come" (Isa. 63:3–4).

Joseph Fielding McConkie describes the symbolism of the winepress: "The device used to press the juice from grapes is figuratively used to represent the vengeance the Lord will take upon the wicked (Isa. 63:3–4; Rev. 19:15; D&C 133:50–51)" (*Gospel Symbolism*, p. 275).

The Lord is treading the winepress on account of the continued wickedness of men and their lack of repentance. How many chances has he given his people to turn from their sins and repent and come unto him? Is it any wonder then that they will have to endure the fierceness and wrath of Almighty God?

*19:16.* **He hath on his vesture and on his thigh a name written.** His name is written on the robe he is wearing and across his thigh where the sword was kept. Perhaps his name was actually written on a sword, especially in light of the idea that his word shall be like a two-edged sword. The sword is a representation of the judgment to come forth upon the children of men. The relationship of sword, word, and name alludes to all things being done in the name of Jesus Christ, especially in matters of judgment.

His name is **KING OF KINGS, AND LORD OF LORDS.** He is King over all kings, both on the earth and in the heavens, and Lord over the whole earth. He has overcome all things and is ready to lead his armies into the final battle. It is imperative to understand that the Lord does not force himself upon the children of men. It is to each to choose for himself, but all men must come before their king to be judged of their works (see Rev. 20:12–13). The judgment of cleansing the earth of wickedness is nigh at hand, and those who are wicked shall now incur his wrath and vengeance.

## Applicability

We have seen a description of the Lord and all of the host who follow him. We should have no greater desire than to live our lives in such a way that when the Savior returns to the earth we will be allowed to be in his presence, to see him as he is. The sword proceeds forth from his mouth and is used to judge and smite the nations. He is the righteous judge. All judgments that are imposed upon us are in direct consequence of obedience or disobedience to his law.

## REVELATION 19:17–21

17 And I saw an angel standing in the sun; and he cried with a loud voice, saying to all the fowls that fly in the midst of heaven, Come and gather yourselves together unto the supper of the great God;

18 That ye may eat the flesh of kings, and the flesh of captains, and the flesh of mighty men, and the flesh of horses, and of them that sit on them, and the flesh of all men, both free and bond, both small and great.

19 And I saw the beast, and the kings of the earth, and their armies, gathered together to make war against him that sat on the horse, and against his army.

20 And the beast was taken, and with him the false prophet that wrought miracles before him, with which he deceived them that had received the mark of the beast, and them that worshipped his image. These both were cast alive into a lake of fire burning with brimstone.

21 And the remnant were slain with the sword of him that sat upon the horse, which sword proceeded out of his mouth: and all the fowls were filled with their flesh.

**Verse Commentary**

*19:17–18.* John now sees **an angel standing in the sun,** or in
such a brightness that one could not stand to look upon him.
The angel **crie[s] with a loud voice, saying to all the fowls that
fly in the midst of heaven, Come and gather yourselves
together unto the supper of the great God; That ye may eat the
flesh . . . of all men.** This gruesome scene is in fulfillment of the
prophecies of the Lord that the fowls of the air would eat the
flesh of the wicked.

Remember that much of the destruction and death upon the
earth results from fighting among the wicked. Elder McConkie
expounds, "So great shall be the slaughter and mass murder, the
carnage and gore, the butchery and violent death of warring
men, that their decaying bodies 'shall stop the noses of the pas-
sengers,' and it shall be a task of mammoth proportions merely
to dispose of them. Then shall Ezekiel's prophecy be fulfilled
that every feathered fowl and every beast of the field shall
assemble to 'eat the flesh of the mighty, and drink the blood of
the princes of the earth.' (Ezek. 39.) . . . That all this is an actual,
literal supper, an horrible but real event yet to be, has been
specifically confirmed in latter-day revelation. (D&C 29:18–21)"
(*MD*, p. 772).

The fowls' menu is disturbingly specific: **ye may eat the
flesh of kings, and the flesh of captains, and the flesh of
mighty men, and the flesh of horses, and of them that sit on
them, and the flesh of all men [who fight against the Lamb
(JST)] both free and bond, both small and great.** These are they
who defy God and refuse to turn from wickedness. They must
be destroyed to appease justice. Those "who fight against the
Lamb" shall receive the proper consequence of their choices.

*19:19.* All is now prepared. John **saw the beast, and the
kings of the earth, and their armies** and they are ready to give
battle to the King and his army. To have any power or glory in
this life, they must destroy the one who holds ultimate authority, the KING OF KINGS AND LORD OF LORDS! They are
**gathered together to make war against him that sat on the**

**horse, and against his army.** There is no hope for these armies of the earth. The decree has already gone forth from heaven for the birds to prepare to feed themselves on the flesh of the men of the earth. How many opportunities has the Lord given them to repent, yet they would not!

*19:20.* **The beast was taken, and with him the false prophet that wrought miracles before him, with which he deceived them that had received the mark of the beast, and them that worshipped his image.** (See Rev. 13:11–18; 16:3–16.) The battle begins and two of the first to fall are the beast and the false prophet. Babylon has fallen, and now the beast and the false prophet are toppled. All who directly fight against the Lamb are taken and cast out. The beast, he who supposedly had so much power and brought such fear upon the hearts of the children of men, and the false prophet, with all of his deceptive, beguiling practices, are **cast alive into a lake of fire burning with brimstone.** The lake of fire is a continual burning, and they are cast alive into it, thereby signifying that they will suffer the burning torment of a seared conscience. The brimstone, with its foul, incense-like smokes, will represent their lamentations, mourning, and weepings as they ascend up to God on high. There is no deliverance for them. In Matthew, the Savior taught of the destination of the wicked. "But the children of the kingdom shall be cast out into outer darkness: there shall be weeping and gnashing of teeth" (8:12). Jesus also said that the unrighteous should be cast "into a furnace of fire: there shall be wailing and gnashing of teeth" (Matt. 13:42).

*19:21.* **The remnant were slain with the sword of him that sat upon the horse, which sword proceeded out of his mouth.** By the word of God all things are brought to pass. From the mouth of the Savior comes a swift and sure judgment. The condemnation and destruction of the adversaries of the Lamb has been foretold throughout history by the prophets. The sharp sword is the word of God that proceeds forth from the mouth of the Lord and his servants. "What I the Lord have spoken, I have spoken, and I excuse not myself; and though the heavens and the earth pass away, my word shall not pass away, but shall all be fulfilled, whether by mine own voice or by the voice of my servants, it is the same" (D&C 1:38).

**All the fowls were filled with their flesh.** The fowls of the air get their fill, feeding off the carcasses of those who followed the beast and the false prophet. (What a sorrowful tale to tell of those who continued to fight against Christ, even when they saw him coming in his glory, but they would not repent, and it is too late.) Prophecy is fulfilled as the birds of the air feast upon the flesh of the kings, captains, and men of the earth who would not repent or turn from their sins.

## Applicability

Once again we are told of the judgments which will come upon those who refuse to repent in the face of such destructions. As the righteous enjoy the marriage feast at the supper of the Lamb the wicked become a feast for the fowls of the earth. The beast and the false prophet are cast in the lake burning with fire and brimstone. Such is the punishment awaiting anyone who refuses to repent of their sins and continues on in their pursuit of wickedness. We have been warned of the consequences of wickedness, yet often we ignore such warnings and continue in our sinful ways. The consequence of choosing sin over righteousness is death. The choice is ours.

## SUMMARY

Praises have rung out to the Lord for his deliverance, his mercy, and his leadership as King of Kings and Lord of Lords. The information contained in this chapter has told of two feasts. The marriage supper of the Lamb is a wonderful and sumptuous feast of the righteous. The Saints who have overcome are invited to come and partake with the Savior. John's description of the Savior is beautiful. To see the Savior we must remain pure and faithful. Those who worship the Lord are invited to participate in the marriage feast, and to enjoy the benefits of faithful living (see D&C 58:11).

The second feast we hear of is the feast of the birds upon the wicked. Here, those who worship the beast are not invited to the feast, but become the feast themselves because they would not repent. The wicked are judged by the word of God, and part of this word is fulfillment of the prophecy that the fowls of the air would feed upon the flesh of the kings and captains of the earth. Long before John had received this vision, Ezekiel had proclaimed: "And, thou son of man, thus saith the Lord God; Speak unto every feathered fowl, and to every beast of the field, Assemble yourselves, and come; gather yourselves on every side to my sacrifice that I do sacrifice for you, even a great sacrifice upon the mountains of Israel, that ye may eat flesh, and drink blood. Ye shall eat the flesh of the mighty, and drink the blood of the princes of the earth, of rams, of lambs, and of goats, of bullocks, all of them fatlings of Bashan. And ye shall eat fat till ye be full, and drink blood till ye be drunken, of my sacrifice which I have sacrificed for you. Thus ye shall be filled at my table with horses and chariots, with mighty men, and with all men of war, saith the Lord God. And I will set my glory among the heathen, and all the heathen shall see my judgment that I have executed, and my hand that I have laid upon them" (Ezek. 39:17–21).

Those who reap bounteous blessings do so because of personal faithfulness. The righteous receive rewards for their righteousness and are invited to the feast. The wicked also receive rewards for their works—misery and destruction.

The work of deliverance has now occurred for the righteous and the wicked. Deliverance was accomplished by the sword, or the word of God. The righteous are delivered to the marriage feast and the wicked are delivered to the feast of the fowls. Those who fight against the Lamb will be delivered up to a terrible suffering. Their leaders, the beast and false prophet, have been cast off to a lake burning with fire and brimstone leaving the wicked to suffer their terrible fate alone.

Think of the marriage feast. All that the prophets have spoken about the second coming of the Savior has now been fulfilled. You shall be invited to sup with the Savior, to participate with him in his eternal union with the Church, and to dwell with him forever. You have overcome all things! The Millennium is here! You see the Lord, you worship him and praise his name. The Lord has fulfilled his covenants.

There are times when, fearful of what man can do, we fail to remember that the promises of the Lord are sure. Throughout this book we have witnessed some of the things which John saw. The Lord is well aware that the view of some of these things may be extremely discouraging, but we must hold on. Like the frightened child who takes hold of his parent's hand when danger approaches, knowing that there is safety in the grasp of the father or mother, we must seek the hand of the Savior. "Be thou humble; and the Lord thy God shall lead thee by the hand, and give thee answer to thy prayers" (D&C 112:10).

We can and will be conquerors. Since we were not placed upon this earth to fail, we must trust in the Lord that he will overcome the adversary. We should have a testimony that the Lord will not fail—there are many things that bear witness to that fact. The end is in sight. A feeling of joy and rejoicing should be in our heart as the hour of deliverance is come.

# 20

## THE MILLENNIAL REIGN

The adversary, Satan himself, must be taken and bound so that the righteous Saints may enjoy a period of tranquillity and peace. Such a peace has not been experienced on the earth since the days of Enoch, and before that, the time Adam and Eve spent in the Garden. The beast and the false prophet have already fallen, but their leader must also fall. As long as Satan is free to roam the earth and influence the hearts of the children of men, there will be no peace. But now the devil is bound, his influence is removed. Those who have chosen to follow the adversary have been destroyed, or cast off, and the earth is prepared to receive the righteous. The Saints will make her their resting place, they will dwell on her for a thousand years in peace and prosperity without sin or corruption.

The great day of deliverance is truly at hand. The spirit of peace and brotherhood must cover the earth. Righteousness must fill the hearts of the Lord's people. There cannot be feelings of hatred, anger, envy, or malice. Any and all things pertaining to Satan must be completely eradicated or peace cannot remain. The words of the prophets in America, shortly after the coming of Christ, suggest what this experience will be like. "And it came to pass that there was no contention among all the people, in all the land; but there were mighty miracles wrought among the disciples of Jesus. . . . And it came to pass that there was no contention in the land, because of the love of God which did dwell in the hearts of the people. And there were no envyings, nor strifes, nor tumults, nor whoredoms, nor lyings, nor murders, nor any manner of lasciviousness; and surely there could not be a happier people among all the people who had been created by the hand of God. There were no robbers, nor murderers, neither were there Lamanites, nor any manner of -ites; but they were in one, the children of Christ, and heirs to the kingdom of God" (4 Ne. 1:13, 15–17).

Can we even begin to fathom what great blessings are in store for us if we are true and faithful in all things before the Lord? Imagine what it would be like to dwell upon this beautiful earth without all of the sin and corruption we currently encounter. Wipe out all that is wicked and this earth is indeed a wonderful place to dwell—even more wonderful as the earth hosts the Savior during his millennial reign.

## REVELATION 20:1–3

1 ¶ And I saw an angel come down from heaven, having the key of the bottomless pit and a great chain in his hand.

2 And he laid hold on the dragon, that old serpent, which is the Devil, and Satan, and bound him a thousand years,

3 And cast him into the bottomless pit, and shut him up, and set a seal upon him, that he should deceive the nations no more, till the thousand years should be fulfilled: and after that he must be loosed a little season.

### Verse Commentary

*20:1–2.* **An angel come[s] down from heaven, having the key of the bottomless pit and a great chain in his hand.** We do not know who the angel is, but it may be Michael, as he is the seventh angel who proclaims the victory of the Lord over the devil (see D&C 88:112). The Doctrine and Covenants documents what news the seventh angel will bring: "And again, another angel shall sound his trump, which is the seventh angel, saying: It is finished; it is finished! The Lamb of God hath overcome and trodden the wine-press alone, even the wine-press of the fierceness of the wrath of Almighty God. And then shall the angels be crowned with the glory of his might, and the saints shall be filled with his glory, and receive their inheritance and be made equal with him" (88:106–7).

This angel has the power, or rather the authority, to cast

Satan into the bottomless pit and to bind him with a chain which will last for one thousand years (see Rev. 20:1–3). The pit is bottomless, or in other words, there is no end to the suffering of those who receive this as their final reward. "The end thereof, neither the place thereof, nor their torment, no man knows; Neither was it revealed, neither is, neither will be revealed unto man, except to them who are made partakers thereof; Nevertheless, I, the Lord, show it by vision unto many, but straightway shut it up again; Wherefore, the end, the width, the height, the depth, and the misery thereof, they understand not, neither any man except those who are ordained unto this condemnation. And we heard the voice, saying: Write the vision, for lo, this is the end of the vision of the sufferings of the ungodly" (D&C 76:45–49).

**And he [the angel] laid hold on the dragon, that old serpent, which is the Devil, and Satan, and bound him a thousand years.** In the same manner that Satan attempted to bind the souls of men with "his awful chains, from whence there is no deliverance" (2 Ne. 28:22), he is now bound by chains from which he cannot escape. This verse also gives us the many names of the adversary. He is the dragon—that creature which attempted to destroy the woman and the man child (see Rev. 12:3–6); that old serpent—the animal that beguiled Adam and Eve to partake of the forbidden fruit (see Gen. 3:13–14; Moses 4:4–7, 19–20); the devil—a name that describes him as the evil author of all sin (see Hel. 6:30); and Satan—the name given to him for his rebellion against the Father (see Moses 4:3–4). In addition to these, the adversary is also called Perdition (see D&C 76:25–26).

After Satan is bound, those who are righteous will dwell upon the earth in a state of peace, joy, and rest. The earth will enjoy paradisiacal glory as Christ personally reigns upon it (see A of F 1:10).

*20:3.* The angel **cast him into the bottomless pit, and shut him up, and set a seal upon him.** It is obvious that Satan will not be able to escape this torment under his own power. The seal will be placed on the door to the bottomless pit and will not be removed until all things are fulfilled. He will be secured there for a thousand years and shall not be able to **deceive the nations** until he is loosed again for a short season. While he is bound, Satan "shall not have power to tempt any man" (D&C 101:28). Elder McConkie states, "However, Satan shall be bound (D&C 43:31; 45:55; 84:100; 88:110–111; Rev. 20:1–3, 7), and for a thousand years he 'shall not have power to tempt any man.' (D&C 101:28.) Accordingly, 'children shall grow up without sin unto salvation' (D&C 45:58), and righteousness and peace be everywhere present. It was this concept that caused Nephi to write, speaking of the period *after the commencement* of the millennium, that: 'Because of the righteousness of his people, Satan has no power; wherefore, he cannot be loosed for the space of many years; for he hath no power over the hearts of the people, for they dwell in righteousness, and the Holy One of Israel reigneth.' (1 Ne. 22:26)" (*MD*, p. 496).

During this millennial period there shall be no deception nor any type of wickedness upon the earth. Not all will be members of the Church, but those who were righteous, who did not worship the beast, or false prophet, shall remain and receive the blessings of the gospel of Jesus Christ. This will be the case until Satan is loosed again for a short season, more of which will be spoken about in Revelation chapter 20.

## Applicability

The Millennium will be a glorious experience for the righteous. The key to the bottomless pit is had by the Lord who solely controls the binding and releasing of Satan. As Satan is bound for the thousand-year period he will have no power over us to bring us down to the gulf of misery and endless woe. Even now, if we are built upon the rock of our Redeemer who is Christ the Lord (see Hel. 5:12), we can effectively bind Satan and cast him out of our lives. Conversely, if we are not built upon that rock, we remain vulnerable to Satan's deceits.

## REVELATION 20:4–6

4 And I saw thrones, and they sat upon them, and judgment was given unto them: and I saw the souls of them that were beheaded for the witness of Jesus, and for the word of God, and which had not worshipped the beast, neither his image, neither had received his mark upon their foreheads, or in their hands; and they lived and reigned with Christ a thousand years.

5 But the rest of the dead lived not again until the thousand years were finished. This is the first resurrection.

6 Blessed and holy is he that hath part in the first resurrection: on such the second death hath no power, but they shall be priests of God and of Christ, and shall reign with him a thousand years.

## Verse Commentary

*20:4.* **And I saw thrones, and they sat upon them, and judgment was given unto them.** The righteous who have been obedient in all things shall be given their just reward as promised in the letters to the seven churches, and shall sit with the Savior in his throne, even as he sits with the Father. They are "joint-heirs with Christ" (Rom. 8:17), and in being joint-heirs they are also given the right and responsibility to judge in some matters. Elder Bruce R. McConkie explains: "Our Lord promised his 12 apostolic ministers in Jerusalem that when he came in glory, they also should 'sit upon twelve thrones, judging the twelve tribes of Israel.' (Matt. 19:28; Luke 22:30.) 'It hath gone forth in a firm decree, by the will of the Father, that mine apostles, the Twelve which were with me in my ministry at Jerusalem, shall stand at my right hand at the day of my coming in a pillar of fire, being clothed with robes of righteousness, with crowns upon their heads, in glory even as I am, *to judge the whole house of Israel, even as many as have loved me and kept my commandments, and none else.*' (D&C 29:12.)" Elder McConkie continues, "Some 600 years before the first coming of our Lord, an angel told Nephi, 'The twelve apostles of the Lamb . . . are they who shall judge the twelve tribes of Israel; wherefore, the twelve ministers of thy seed shall be judged of them; for ye are of the house of Israel.

And these twelve ministers whom thou beholdest shall judge thy seed.' (1 Ne. 12:9–10.) Then to those 12 Nephite ministers, the resurrected Lord said: '*Ye shall be judges of this people, according to the judgment which I shall give unto you, which shall be just. Therefore, of what manner of men ought ye to be? Verily I say unto you, even as I am.'* (3 Ne. 27:27; Morm. 3:19.)" (*MD*, pp. 398–99).

Although the Savior authorizes some righteous men to sit as common judges in Israel, he is the Chief Judge of all men.

John then sees **the souls of them that were beheaded for the witness of Jesus, and for the word of God, and which had not worshipped the beast, neither his image, neither had received his mark upon their foreheads, or in their hands.** As has been evident throughout Revelation, many will lose their lives in defense of the truth and the testimonies they possess. Satan will attempt to increase his areas of influence until the Lord comes again to deliver his people. The beast's only recourse against those who refused to worship him or those things he has brought forth was to slay them. If the righteous did not give in to his pressures and enticements, then he used his servants here upon the earth to slay the righteous. The Lord allowed such killings as a testimony against the wicked (see Alma 14:10–11). John saw that the righteous who died in defense of the gospel **lived and reigned with Christ a thousand years** during the Millennium. Would any price be too high to secure that type of blessing?

20:5. **The rest of the dead lived not again until the thousand years were finished.** "The rest of the dead" are those who had followed after the adversary and chose wickedness over righteousness. They are those whose works were such that they could not endure the presence of the Lord and were destroyed in the final battle. They shall not come forth until the end of the millennial reign, and then they shall come forth to receive their resurrection and telestial glory, or condemnation, because they were not "willing to enjoy that which they might have received" (D&C 88:31–32).

The Doctrine and Covenants explains the wait some will

endure: "And the saints that are upon the earth, who are alive, shall be quickened and be caught up to meet him. And they who have slept in their graves shall come forth, for their graves shall be opened; and they also shall be caught up to meet him in the midst of the pillar of heaven—They are Christ's, the first fruits, they who shall descend with him first, and they who are on the earth and in their graves, who are first caught up to meet him; and all this by the voice of the sounding of the trump of the angel of God. And after this another angel shall sound, which is the second trump; and then cometh the redemption of those who are Christ's at his coming; who have received their part in that prison which is prepared for them, that they might receive the gospel, and be judged according to men in the flesh. And again, another trump shall sound, which is the third trump; and then come the spirits of men who are to be judged, and are found under condemnation; And these are the rest of the dead; and they live not again until the thousand years are ended, neither again, until the end of the earth" (88:96–101).

Those who were faithful in the things of the Lord come forth to meet him and dwell with him during his sojourn here on earth. The Doctrine and Covenants says that "the day cometh that the Lord shall utter his voice out of heaven; the heavens shall shake and the earth shall tremble, and the trump of God shall sound both long and loud, and shall say to the sleeping nations: Ye saints arise and live; ye sinners stay and sleep until I shall call again" (43:18). **This is the first resurrection.** Obviously, those who had died for the cause of truth, who had voluntarily given up their lives as faithful witnesses, shall be resurrected and shall live in glory with the Savior upon the earth. Those who have been faithful, who are still alive, shall also be caught up to meet him and shall also dwell in glory with him for one thousand years here upon the earth.

*20:6.* **Blessed and holy is he that hath part in the first resurrection.** It is interesting to note that the JST renders the verse, "Blessed and holy *are they* . . ." Those who have part in the first resurrection are supremely blessed and happy, and are purified before the Lord. They have been found worthy to stand in his presence, to be glorified with him. They "shall be like him; for [they] shall see him as he is" (1 Jn. 3:2). Of those of the first resurrection the Prophet Joseph Smith recorded: "These are they whose names are written in heaven, where God and Christ are the judge of all. These are they who are just men made perfect through Jesus the mediator of the new covenant, who wrought out his perfect atonement through the shedding of his own blood" (D&C 76:50–70, specifically 68–69).

**On such the second death hath no power.** The second death is the death of the spirit, "to be cast into the lake of fire" (Rev. 20:14). Those who have part in the first resurrection shall not be affected by this second death. **They shall be priests of God and of Christ, and shall reign with him a thousand years.** This is the glory which awaits us if we are faithful: to be priests of God and of Christ, both the Father and the Son, and to reign with Christ in glory during the Millennium. Paul taught that we are "heirs of God, and joint-heirs with Christ; if so be that we suffer with him, that we may be also glorified together. For I reckon that the sufferings of this present time are not worthy to be compared with the glory which shall be revealed in us" (Rom. 8:17–18).

## Applicability

The first resurrection, the resurrection of the righteous, began when the Savior was resurrected from the dead. The main requirement to participate in such a glorious event is faithful membership in the Lord's Church. Many people have already received the assurance of participation in this event when they were told in their patriarchal blessings that they would be blessed to come forth in the morning of the first resurrection. Such a promise will come to pass in accordance with a person's faith and devotion to truth and righteousness. Even if one doesn't have this written in his blessing, the promises are guaranteed to those who receive the testimony of Jesus, believe on his name, are baptized, keep the commandments, overcome by faith, and are sealed by the Holy Spirit of Promise. The list of requirements is not intimidating to one who has sought to follow the Lord throughout his or her life. These are basic principles of obedient membership in the Church. Obedience to these principles will allow us to dwell in the millennial period.

<h2 align="center">REVELATION 20:7–10</h2>

7 And when the thousand years are expired, Satan shall be loosed out of his prison,

8 And shall go out to deceive the nations which are in the four quarters of the earth, Gog and Magog, to gather them together to battle: the number of whom is as the sand of the sea.

9 And they went up on the breadth of the earth, and compassed the camp of the saints about, and the beloved city: and fire came down from God out of heaven, and devoured them.

10 And the devil that deceived them was cast into the lake of fire and brimstone, where the beast and the false prophet are, and shall be tormented day and night for ever and ever.

**Verse Commentary**

*20:7–8.* **And when the thousand years are expired, Satan shall be loosed out of his prison.** Once the millennial reign is complete, all of the saving ordinances are performed for those who had not had the opportunity in mortality, and all other necessary things are fulfilled, then Satan shall be loosed once again. The bottomless pit will be opened and allow Satan and his forces to **go out to deceive the nations which are in the four quarters of the earth.** Satan immediately begins to attempt to deceive the children of men on the earth. His work will cover the entire earth and once again we find some who are willing to follow after him. In an 1877 address, Elder Orson Pratt said that "when the thousand years are ended, and Satan is again loosed, he will find a large number who have not been tempted by him, and he will use his cunning among them, and will succeed in leading more or less astray. He will gather up his numerous hosts from the four quarters of the earth, and will encompass the camp of the Saints. The Saints will then gather from abroad, as they now do, and they will have to pitch their tents while doing so; and Satan's army will also compass the beloved city to destroy the people of God; but fire will come down from God out of heaven, and will devour them" (*JD*, 19:176–78).

**Gog and Magog** are those forces of evil which came from the north and descended upon Israel in ancient times. In this situation they represent the nations of the earth which gather together to fight against the Lord and his servants, both prior to the Millennium (see Ezek. 38–39) and again at the end of the one-thousand-year period (see Rev. 20:7–9). It is in both of these battles that the wicked will be cast off from the earth. Temporarily placed in the bottomless pit after the first battle, they are cast off eternally to outer darkness following the second battle.

According to *The Life and Teachings of Jesus and His Apostles*, "John calls the hosts who follow Satan, Gog and Magog. These terms cause some confusion, for they are also used to refer to the leader of the final battle before the Millennium begins, which is commonly called the battle of Armageddon. The terms themselves come from Ezekiel 38, 39, where the battle of Armageddon is described in some detail. Most scholars believe that Ezekiel chose these names as symbols of great military prowess and wickedness.

"Joseph Fielding Smith clarifies the difference between the battle of Armageddon and the battle of Gog and Magog: '*Before the coming of Christ, the great war, sometimes called Armageddon, will take place* as spoken of by Ezekiel, chapters 38 and 39. *Another war of God and Magog will be after the millennium*.' (*Doctrines of Salvation*, 3:45.)" (pp. 468–69).

Satan will gather his forces **together to battle; the number of whom is as the sand of the sea.** The Doctrine and Covenants records the gathering of both the forces of good and of evil. "And Michael, the seventh angel, even the archangel, shall gather together his armies; even the hosts of heaven. And the devil shall gather together his armies; even the hosts of hell, and shall come up to battle against Michael and his armies. And then cometh the battle of the great God; and the devil and his armies shall be cast away into their own place, that they shall not have power over the saints any more at all. For Michael shall fight their battles, and shall overcome him who seeketh the throne of him who sitteth upon the throne, even the Lamb" (88:112–15).

This last battle is the adversary's final attempt to overthrow the Lamb.

*20:9.* **The forces of evil spread out upon the face of the land and then surround the camp of the saints . . . , and the beloved city.** The camp of the Saints and the beloved city represent the place where the righteous gather unto the Lord. The camp are those who have gathered out of the city walls to encompass and defend the city from the onslaught of wickedness that has encircled it. The beloved city refers to "the mount Zion which [the Lord] loved" (see Vincent, p. 561; Ps. 78:68).

**Fire came down from God out of heaven, and devoured them.** As Elijah called down fire from heaven to confound the priests (see 1 Kgs 18), God sends fire from heaven to engulf those who follow after Satan in this final great battle. The righteous no longer need to fight, for the power of the Lord has delivered them from the adversary.

*20:10.* **The devil that deceived them was cast into the lake of fire and brimstone, where the beast and the false prophet are, and shall be tormented day and night for ever and ever.** The devil himself is finally completely cast off. The great day of the Lord is at hand. All things are now prepared for the final judgment. It is interesting to note that when the battle of Gog and Magog takes place the devil is alone leading his forces—the beast and the false prophet were not allowed out of the lake of fire and brimstone. Satan is cast into the lake of torment forever. In the Book of Mormon Jacob describes the final residence of Satan and his hoard. "They who are righteous shall be righteous still, and they who are filthy shall be filthy still; wherefore, they who are filthy are the devil and his angels; and they shall go away into everlasting fire, prepared for them; and their torment is as a lake of fire and brimstone, whose flame ascendeth up forever and ever and has no end" (2 Ne. 9:16).

Wickedness is destroyed. The sufferings which the righteous have endured for approximately six thousand years are vindicated as Satan is cast into everlasting burnings.

## Applicability

Near the close of the millennial period we will see Satan loosed from his prison and he will once again seek to draw away the souls of men after him. He will gather up all of his forces and will surround the righteous one final time. At this time the Lord will fight the final battle and will cast off Satan forever. Though those who follow Satan are as numerous as the sand of the sea they are powerless against the goodness of God. They have openly rejected him who truly should be their leader, even Jesus Christ. For this choice they will be devoured by fire from heaven and will be cast off with Satan. It is imperative that we, too, understand that when we openly reject the commandments we put ourselves at risk of being cast off and losing the blessings promised to us.

## REVELATION 20:11–15

11 ¶ And I saw a great white throne, and him that sat on it, from whose face the earth and the heaven fled away; and there was found no place for them.

12 And I saw the dead, small and great, stand before God; and the books were opened: and another book was opened, which is the book of life: and the dead were judged out of those things which were written in the books, according to their works.

13 And the sea gave up the dead which were in it; and death and hell delivered up the dead which were in them: and they were judged every man according to their works.

14 And death and hell were cast into the lake of fire. This is the second death.

15 And whosoever was not found written in the book of life was cast into the lake of fire.

## Verse Commentary

*20:11.* **And I saw a great white throne, and him that sat on it, from whose face the earth and the heaven fled away; and there was found no place for them.** John now sees the Savior sitting upon the throne. He is the pure and righteous King and sits in judgment upon his throne. "For the Father judgeth no man, but hath committed all judgment unto the Son" (John 5:22). Once again we see an obvious distinction between God the Father and his Son Jesus Christ.

**There was found no place for them.** Even the heaven and the earth must become new and clean and pure before the Lord, especially as they prepare to become the final dwelling place for the souls of the righteous. "For all old things shall pass away, and all things shall become new, even the heaven and the earth, and all the fulness thereof, both men and beasts, the fowls of the air, and the fishes of the sea; And not one hair, neither mote, shall be lost, for it is the workmanship of mine hand" (D&C 29:24–25). The earth is cleansed. The great day for which it was prepared is finally at hand and it shall become a celestial kingdom, a tabernacle of the righteous.

*20:12.* The Judgment must now take place. John's words ring out clear and true as he describes who will stand before the Lord in judgment and what process the Lord will use to judge the people who come before him: **And I saw the dead, small and great, stand before God; and the books were opened: and another book was opened, which is the book of life: and the dead were judged out of those things which were written in the books, according to their works.**

The word *small* comes from the Greek *mikrŏs,* or *mikrŏtĕrŏs,* and means either small in size, quantity, or number; or, with respect to dignity, it can mean least, less, little, or small (see *Strong's,* Greek Dictionary, p. 48). The word *great* comes from the Greek *mĕgas,* or *megalŏi,* and means big, great, or strong (see *Strong's,* Greek Dictionary, p. 46). In this particular reference it would seem to indicate all of those people who are considered the well-known and famous people throughout history.

Concerning this verse the Prophet Joseph Smith taught the Church the following: "You will discover in this quotation that the books were opened; and another book was opened, which was the book of life; but the dead were judged out of those things which were written in the books, according to their works; consequently, the books spoken of must be the books which contained the record of their works, and refer to the records which are kept on the earth. And the book which was the book of life is the record which is kept in heaven; the principle agreeing precisely with the doctrine which is commanded you in the revelation . . . that in all your recordings it may be recorded in heaven" (D&C 128:7).

The Doctrine and Covenants continues to explain that the sealing power given to men on earth is part of what causes things to be recorded in heaven. "Whatsoever you record on earth shall be recorded in heaven, and whatsoever you do not record on earth shall not be recorded in heaven; for out of the books shall your dead be judged, according to their own works" (128:8).

No one is exempt. All people will have to be judged, and they will be judged based upon their actions while here upon the earth. They will be judged by their own lives, by their works while in this mortal sphere. Jacob teaches us that "when all men shall have passed from this first death unto life, insomuch as they have become immortal, they must appear before the judgment-seat of the Holy One of Israel; and then cometh the judgment, and then must they be judged according to the holy judgment of God" (2 Ne. 9:15).

The grace of the Lord Jesus Christ manifests itself in one form in that he gave his life that all men might be saved from the physical death brought about by Adam's transgression. All will be resurrected (see 1 Cor. 15:20–22), but the glory or resurrected state we will receive is dependent upon what we have done while here in this life, including faith and repentance in addition to more physical "works." The judgment will be based upon those things written of our mortal existence. This is one of the reasons why the phrase "the great and awful day of the Lord" is used. For the righteous it becomes a "great" day because they receive the reward for their acts of righteousness. To the wicked it becomes a "dreadful" day because they also receive the reward for their acts of wickedness.

*20:13–14.* **And the sea gave up the dead which were in it; and death and hell delivered up the dead which were in them.** All people who have ever lived upon the earth, even those who were swept off when the sea heaved beyond its bounds or who were cast into the pit with Satan and his servants, must come forth to stand before the Lord to be judged. Death and hell must deliver up their captive spirits. Jacob expounds, "And because of the way of deliverance of our God, the Holy One of Israel, this death, of which I have spoken, which is the temporal, shall deliver up its dead; which death is the grave. And this death of which I have spoken, which is the spiritual death, shall deliver up its dead; which spiritual death is hell; wherefore, death and hell must deliver up their dead, and hell must deliver up its captive spirits, and the grave must deliver up its captive bodies, and the bodies and the spirits of men will be restored one to the other; and it is by the power of the resurrection of the Holy One of Israel" (2 Ne. 9:11–12).

**They were judged every man according to their works.** Once death and hell have delivered up their captive spirits, the righteous and the wicked must be judged for the works they have performed while on the earth. The judgment is individual and each person is accountable for his own actions. We are not accountable for or punished for Adam's transgression, but only for the sins we have committed and not repented of (see A of F 1:2).

**And death and hell were cast into the lake of fire. This is the second death.** Alma taught Zeezrom and others about this second death. "Therefore God gave unto them commandments, after having made known unto them the plan of redemption, that they should not do evil, the penalty thereof being a second death, which was an everlasting death as to things pertaining unto righeousness; for on such the plan of redemption could have no power, for the works of justice could not be destroyed, according to the supreme goodness of God" (Alma 12:32). This is their punishment because they have put off the enticings of the Holy Spirit and have sought to follow after that spirit which entices men to do evil (see Mosiah 3:19). The Prophet Joseph Smith said, "A man is his own tormentor and his own condemner. Hence the saying, They shall go into the lake that burns with fire and brimstone. The torment of disappointment in the mind of man is as exquisite as a lake burning with fire and brimstone. I say, so is the torment of man" (*HC*, 6:314).

There are three scriptures found in the Book of Mormon and

Doctrine and Covenants which provide great insight to the reason behind the punishment imposed upon the wicked. The first comes from the Nephite prophet Jacob. "And assuredly, as the Lord liveth, for the Lord God hath spoken it, and it is his eternal word, which cannot pass away, that they who are righteous shall be righteous still, and they who are filthy shall be filthy still; wherefore, they who are filthy are the devil and his angels; and they shall go away into everlasting fire, prepared for them; and their torment is as a lake of fire and brimstone, whose flame ascendeth up forever and ever and has no end. O the greatness and the justice of our God! For he executeth all his words, and they have gone forth out of his mouth, and his law must be fulfilled" (2 Ne. 9:16–17). Next, Alma teaches, "For behold, if ye have procrastinated the day of your repentance even until death, behold, ye have become subjected to the spirit of the devil, and he doth seal you his; therefore, the Spirit of the Lord hath withdrawn from you, and hath no place in you, and the devil hath all power over you; and this is the final state of the wicked" (Alma 32:35). And finally, Joseph Smith recorded that "they who remain [meaning those not receiving of the celestial, terrestrial, or telestial glory] shall also be quickened; nevertheless, they shall return again to their own place, to enjoy that which they are willing to receive, because they were not willing to enjoy that which they might have received" (D&C 88:32).

*20:15.* John gives a great warning to all people as he says, **And whosoever was not found written in the book of life was cast into the lake of fire.** When we stand before the Lord for our final judgment all of our work must be completed, especially concerning those ordinances which take place in the temple to seal us to him. Continually throughout the book of Revelation we have seen the need for those who follow after God to have his name sealed in their foreheads. Why is this so vital? It is because only through the ordinances of the temple can a man or woman realize their full potential and becomes joint-heirs with Jesus Christ. Those who have not done these things, either in this life or in the Millennium have no promise. They do not enjoy the benefits of the sealing because they were not willing to enjoy those benefits; they receive the reward they were willing to receive (see D&C 88:26–32). They must be cast into a lake of fire, because that is the consequence or condemnation associated with failure to obey the law of the Lord. The Lord is bound by the requirements of justice.

## Applicability

We will be judged based upon our own obedience or disobedience. We will be judged for our own actions and not those of anyone else. We will stand before the throne and be judged by Jesus Christ. He is both our Judge and our Advocate. His atonement intercedes on our behalf. All men are equal as far as salvation from the grave. No man can brag or be prideful that his works have saved him—salvation comes by the grace of God. We are, however, accountable for our works and we will be judged by the Savior for the manner in which we have followed him.

The fruits brought forth by everyone, both small and great, and their obedience to the commandments of God will be the measuring stick for the glory to be received. It is not an arbitrary judgment where some of us are just lucky and found to be in the right place at the right time. No one will go to be judged until they have had sufficient opportunity to receive all of the ordinances of the gospel and fulfill all things which are required in the flesh. The most important warning comes in John's words that whosoever was not found written in the book of life was cast into the lake of fire. Once again, the choice is ours.

## SUMMARY

This chapter has taught some great doctrines of the plan of salvation, implemented from the foundation of the world. First, that Satan will be bound, not just that he will not be able to deceive the hearts of the children of men, but that he will actually be placed back in the bottomless pit for one thousand years. Second, there will be a period of one thousand years of peace upon the earth, during which those who are the Lord's at his coming will dwell in peace and righteousness and complete all of the necessary ordinances for them to stand before the Lord in judgment. Third, at the end of that thousand-year period Satan will be loosed for a short season and will attempt one final overthrow of the Lord and his kingdom. At that point Satan and all of the host who follow after him will lose the battle to Michael and the Saints, and will be consumed from off the earth by fire. Fourth, once all wickedness has been cleansed for the final time from the earth, the judgment begins. All people must come and stand before the Lord to be judged of their works while in the flesh. Those who have the seal of God in their foreheads will consider it a great day before the Lord. To those who have not been sealed, it is truly a dreadful day because no more labor can be performed. They have procrastinated the day of their repentance until it is too late. Fifth, we learn that those who are righteous and have overcome all things participate in the first resurrection. Sixth, those who have followed after the devil and his servants will end up suffering the second death, in that they will be cast out of the Father's presence and shall dwell with Satan in the lake of fire forever.

The most comforting doctrine of Chapter 20 is that evil will be completely swept off from the earth. We will not have to battle against its destructive ways forever! Probably the single most important doctrine of the book of Revelation is that the Lord will conquer. He will destroy his enemies and deliver his people. Those who are striving to stay on the path, to hold firmly to the iron rod, and to live their lives in accordance with his divine decrees need not fear. The way is prepared. To succeed, the righteous must have the "seal of God" (Rev. 9:4) placed in their foreheads. This is done by entering the temple and performing the necessary saving ordinances. It is never *too* late until the time of the final judgment.

What a great and glorious message awaits us! All wickedness is done away. Everything that has ever brought sorrow, discouragement, or lack of hope has now vanished away and we are left to see the glory of the Lord and to dwell in his presence. Those who are righteous need not fear the judgment of the Lord.

# 21

## The Celestial Earth and Heavenly City

With all old things having been done away and all things becoming new, the earth is prepared as an eternal dwelling place for the righteous. The glorious things spoken of by the prophets throughout the ages are now to come forth. The vision of the complete purification of the earth has come to a close. John's vision now focuses on a new heaven and earth. The earth is ready to host the holy city, the New Jerusalem, that shall come down from heaven.

All things were created spiritually before they were created physically. As a part of this creation and refinement, the earth, too, must go through a saving and purifying process. The earth was baptized at the time of the flood and was cleansed by fire previously in the vision. It is now ready to fulfill the purposes for which it was created: to be the celestial home of the faithful Saints.

The heavenly city is described in glorious detail. John sees it become the dwelling place of the Lord while here on the earth. There is no need for the sun, moon, or artificial light because the Savior is the light of the city. There is also no need of the temple because "the Lord God Almighty and the Lamb are the temple of it" (Rev. 21:22). Imagine what it will be like to dwell in the presence of the Father and the Son!

### REVELATION 21:1–7

1 ¶ And I saw a new heaven and a new earth: for the first heaven and the first earth were passed away; and there was no more sea.

2 And I John saw the holy city, new Jerusalem, coming down

from God out of heaven, prepared as a bride adorned for her husband.

3 And I heard a great voice out of heaven saying, Behold, the tabernacle of God is with men, and he will dwell with them, and they shall be his people, and God himself shall be with them, and be their God.

4 And God shall wipe away all tears from their eyes; and there shall be no more death, neither sorrow, nor crying, neither shall there be any more pain: for the former things are passed away.

5 And he that sat upon the throne said, Behold, I make all things new. And he said unto me, Write: for these words are true and faithful.

6 And he said unto me, It is done. I am Alpha and Omega, the beginning and the end. I will give unto him that is athirst of the fountain of the water of life freely.

7 He that overcometh shall inherit all things; and I will be his God, and he shall be my son.

## Verse Commentary

21:1. **And I saw a new heaven and a new earth.** As explained in the introduction, all old things have been done away and in their place we find a new heaven and earth. In a Melchizedek Priesthood manual titled *Church History and Modern Revelation*, President Joseph Fielding Smith taught, "We discover from the word of the Lord that the earth, like mankind upon it, is passing through various stages of development, or change. It was created and pronounced good. It partook of the decree of mortality coming through the fall. It is now passing through the telestial condition, in which telestial beings predominate and rule. It will then pass into the 'renewed,' or restored state, for a thousand years as a terrestrial earth and the abode of terrestrial inhabitants. Then comes the end. The earth like all creatures living on it must die. Then it will, like all creatures, receive its resurrection and be celestialized because it obeys its law" (1:295).

**And the first earth . . . passed away; and there was no more sea.** With the passing of the first earth, drastic changes affect the land—there is no more sea! There are many interpretations of the meaning of this phrase, embracing both literal and figurative applications. Figuratively, the sea may represent the place from whence came the beast (see Rev. 13:1). If there was no more sea, then there would also be no beast nor wickedness. Literally, the celestial earth becomes an orb with one single landmass "like it was in the days before it was divided" (D&C 133:24). Nothing more has been revealed on this particular verse.

*21:2.* **The holy city, new Jerusalem, coming down from God out of heaven, prepared as a bride adorned for her husband.** The coming forth of the New Jerusalem as a bride expresses the beauty of the union of the marriage covenant. John meticulously describes the luster and beauty of the dwelling place of the righteous Saints (see Rev. 21:10–27). The city will be intact as it comes down from heaven, just as the city of Enoch was when it was taken up into heaven (see Moses 7:69).

The city of Enoch will be joined with the New Jerusalem that will be built in America. Describing what is meant by "New Jerusalem," Elder Bruce R. McConkie says, "To envision what is meant by this title [New Jerusalem] we must know these five facts:

"1. Ancient Jerusalem, the city of much of our Lord's personal ministry among men, shall be rebuilt in the last days and become one of the two great world capitals, a millennial city from which the word of the Lord shall go forth.

"2. A New Jerusalem, a new Zion, a city of God shall be built on the American continent.

"3. Enoch's city, the original Zion, 'the City of Holiness, . . . was taken up into heaven.' (Moses 7:13–21.)

"4. Enoch's city, with its translated inhabitants now in their resurrected state, shall return, as a New Jerusalem, to join with the city of the same name which has been built upon the American continent.

"5. When this earth becomes a celestial sphere 'that great city, the holy Jerusalem,' shall again descend 'out of heaven from God,' as this earth becomes the abode of celestial beings forever. (Rev. 21:10–27.)" (*DNTC,* 3:580–81).

*21:3.* John hears **a great voice out of heaven saying, Behold, the tabernacle of God is with men, and he will dwell with them, and they shall be his people, and God himself shall be with them, and be their God.** The tabernacle is more than just a building representing the workings of the Lord, or his presence. In this case, it is the dwelling place of God with his people. As promised throughout scripture, the people become one with God, and God will be with them. The Doctrine and Covenants teaches that the righteous "reside in the presence of God, on a globe like a sea of glass and fire, where all things for their glory are manifest, past, present, and future, and are continually before the Lord. The place where God resides is a great Urim and Thummim. This earth, in its sanctified and immortal state, will be made like unto crystal and will be a Urim and Thummim to the inhabitants who dwell thereon, whereby all things pertaining to an inferior kingdom, or all kingdoms of a lower order, will be manifest to those who dwell on it; and this earth will be Christ's" (130:7–9). And Ezekiel prophesied that the city would be called, "The Lord is there" (Ezek. 48:35).

21:4. **And God shall wipe away all tears from their eyes; and there shall be no more death, neither sorrow, nor crying, neither shall there be any more pain.** The very things which bring tears to the eyes and suffering to the hearts of the children of men shall be done away. Can we even begin to fathom what life will be like to dwell in the presence of the Lord and not experience death, sorrow, crying, or pain? All of those things which caused such suffering among men **are passed away.** Death is vanished away, the Savior has opened the portal for death to be vanquished. Sorrow, or mourning and grief, shall be gone as we experience the joy and happiness of residing in the presence of our Lord. Without death, sorrow, and pain there will be no more tears flowing from our eyes.

21:5. The proclamation then comes forth from the throne, **Behold, I make all things new.** Through the power of the resurrection all old things are done away and all things become new. Paul explains, "So also is the resurrection of the dead. It is sown in corruption; it is raised in incorruption: It is sown in dishonor; it is raised in glory: it is sown in weakness; it is raised in power: It is sown a natural body; it is raised a spiritual body" (1 Cor. 15:42–44).

John is also commanded, **Write: for these words are true and faithful.** Bible scholar Marvin R. Vincent says, "The proper order of the Greek is the reverse, as Rev[ised], *faithful and true*"

(p. 564). The words John is commanded to write are those coming from the throne, and in that sense they are coming from he who is "Faithful and True" (Rev. 19:11). They are the words of the Lord, and the proclamation he is about to make, which John is to write, is a culmination of the plan of salvation.

*21:6–7.* The Savior now says from the throne, **It is done.** The work, all things that had been prepared from the foundation of the world, is now complete. All that the Father gave him to do has been fulfilled. **I am Alpha and Omega, the beginning and the end.** At the beginning of the revelation (see Rev. 1:8), John was introduced to Jesus Christ with this same affirmation, and now at the ending of all things the phrase "Alpha and Omega" is used again. Jesus Christ is the beginning and ending of all things.

**I will give unto him that is athirst of the fountain of the water of life freely.** Christ is the source of the living waters. From him comes life eternal. Recall the story of the woman at the well. "Jesus answered and said unto her, Whosoever drinketh of this water shall thirst again: But whosoever drinketh of the water that I shall give him shall never thirst; but the water that I shall give him shall be in him a well of water springing up unto everlasting life" (John 4:13–14). The Savior also promised Joseph Smith that "unto him that keepeth my commandments I will give the mysteries of my kingdom, and the same shall be in him a well of living water, springing up unto everlasting life" (D&C 63:23).

**He that overcometh shall inherit all things; and I will be his God, and he shall be my son.** What glorious promises from on high! We shall inherit all things! All that the Father has shall be ours and we shall sit with him in his glory. Consider the powerful words that John has just received from his Father. President Joseph Fielding Smith taught that we are the literal children of God. "The scriptures inform us that we are the *offspring of God.* [Acts 17:29; Heb. 12:9.] He has called upon us to address him as *Father:* not in some mythical sense, but literally as our Father. It was in this manner that Jesus taught his disciples to pray, [Matt. 6:9] and when he appeared to Mary after his resurrection, he said to her, 'Touch me not; for I am not yet ascended to *my Father:* but go to *my brethren,* and say unto them, I ascend unto *my Father,* and *your Father;* and to my God, and your God.' [John 20:17.] Does not this indicate family organization?" (*DS,* 2:66). The Doctrine and Covenants teaches that through the priesthood we can all inherit the Father's kingdom. "For whoso is faithful unto the obtaining these two priesthoods of which I have spoken, and the magnifying their calling, are sanctified unto the renewing of their bodies. They become the sons of Moses and of Aaron and the seed of Abraham, and the church and kingdom, and the elect of God. And also all they who receive this priesthood receive me, saith the Lord; For he that receiveth my servants receiveth me; And he that receiveth me receiveth my Father; And he that receiveth my Father receiveth my Father's kingdom; therefore all that my Father hath shall be given unto him" (84:33–38).

We are joint-heirs with Jesus Christ. As joint-heirs we share all that is to be received. Paul taught that "the Spirit itself beareth witness with our spirit, that we are the children of God: And if children, then heirs; heirs of God, and joint-heirs with Christ; if so be that we suffer with him, that we may be also glorified together. For I reckon that the sufferings of this present time are not worthy to be compared with the glory which shall be revealed in us" (Rom. 8:16–18).

President Joseph Fielding Smith capsulized this entire concept saying, "He who receives this great gift shall be *like Jesus Christ* [1 John 3:1–3], not only in bodily form, but also *a son of God;* he 'shall *inherit all things,*' and the Father has said, 'I will be his God, and he shall be my son' [Rev. 21:7]. *Eternal life is God's life.* It is that gift by which the righteous not only dwell in his presence, but by which they become *like him*" (*DS,* 2:217).

### Applicability

Paul wrote, "These all died in faith, not having received the promises, but having seen them afar off, and were persuaded of them, and embraced them, and confessed that they were strangers and pilgrims on the earth. For they that say such things declare plainly that they seek a country. And truly, if they had been mindful of that country from whence they came out, they might have had opportunity to have returned. But now they desire a better country, that is, an heavenly: wherefore God is not ashamed to be called their God: for he hath prepared for them a city" (Heb. 11:13–16). The "better country" has descended from heaven. The Lord has abolished sorrow, pain, and suffering. Those who were faithful, those who received the gospel on faith and clung tenaciously to its precepts, will be blessed of the Lord. They will reside in the heavenly city and will drink from the fountain of life, becoming sons and daughters of God. This is our opportunity.

Paul's teachings help us to understand why we cannot remember the glory that we previously experienced in the presence of the Lord. If we had been able to remember what it was like in our Father's presence, there is a great probability that we would have desired to go back there instead of continuing forward to face the challenges of mortality. But we have overcome, we inherit all things and the heavenly glory shall be ours. We shall partake of the waters of life freely and shall never thirst.

## REVELATION 21:8

8 But the fearful, and unbelieving, and the abominable, and murderers, and whoremongers, and sorcerers, and idolaters, and all liars, shall have their part in the lake which burneth with fire and brimstone: which is the second death.

### Verse Commentary

*21:8.* John is reminded of the judgments that await the wicked. **The fearful, and unbelieving, and the abominable, and murderers, and whoremongers, and sorcerers, and idolaters, and all liars, shall have their part in the lake which burneth with fire and brimstone: which is the second death.** The unrepentant will receive their just reward. They shall be given over to that spiritual death which is hell, the second death. As to things which are spiritual, they shall die.

However, these people will not suffer forever. "These," the Lord has said, "are they who shall not be redeemed from the devil until the last resurrection, until the Lord, even Christ the Lamb, shall have finished his work" (D&C 76:85). Only those who become sons of perdition will be denied an inheritance after the last resurrection. The Lord has said that sons of perdition "shall return again to their own place, to enjoy that which they were willing to receive, because they were not willing to enjoy that which they might have received" (D&C 88:32).

## Applicability

Once again the wicked receive a warning to turn from their corrupt ways or they will receive a judgment that is commensurate with their actions. This is not meant to cause one to repent out of fear; it is a warning from our loving Father. He must tell us the consequence of sin so that we are fully aware of what must come upon us if we choose to follow Satan. God's plan requires that man have their agency. Lehi taught that "men are free according to the flesh; and all things are given them which are expedient unto man. And they are free to choose liberty and eternal life, through the great Mediator of all men, or to choose captivity and death, according to the captivity and power of the devil; for he seeketh that all men might be miserable like unto himself" (2 Ne. 2:27).

The choice of inheritance in the kingdoms of glory, or of being cast into a lake of fire and brimstone, is truly ours to make. We must be careful in this brief existence to make the choice which will lead us to eternal happiness.

## REVELATION 21:9–27

9 ¶ And there came unto me one of the seven angels which had the seven vials full of the seven last plagues, and talked with me, saying, Come hither, I will shew thee the bride, the Lamb's wife.

10 And he carried me away in the spirit to a great and high mountain, and shewed me that great city, the holy Jerusalem, descending out of heaven from God,

11 Having the glory of God: and her light was like unto a stone most precious, even like a jasper stone, clear as crystal;

12 And had a wall great and high, and had twelve gates, and at the gates twelve angels, and names written thereon, which are the names of the twelve tribes of the children of Israel:

13 On the east three gates; on the north three gates; on the south three gates; and on the west three gates.

14 And the wall of the city had twelve foundations, and in them the names of the twelve apostles of the Lamb.

15 And he that talked with me had a golden reed to measure the city, and the gates thereof, and the wall thereof.

16 And the city lieth foursquare, and the length is as large as the breadth: and he measured the city with the reed, twelve thousand furlongs. The length and the breadth and the height of it are equal.

17 And he measured the wall thereof, an hundred and forty and four cubits, according to the measure of a man, that is, of the angel.

18 And the building of the wall of it was of jasper: and the city was pure gold, like unto clear glass.

19 And the foundations of the wall of the city were garnished with all manner of precious stones. The first foundation was jasper; the second, sapphire; the third, a chalcedony; the fourth, an emerald;

20 The fifth, sardonyx; the sixth, sardius; the seventh, chrysolite; the eighth, beryl; the ninth, a topaz; the tenth, a chrysoprasus; the eleventh, a jacinth; the twelfth, an amethyst.

21 And the twelve gates were twelve pearls; every several gate was of one pearl: and the street of the city was pure gold, as it were transparent glass.

22 And I saw no temple therein: for the Lord God Almighty and the Lamb are the temple of it.

23 And the city had no need of the sun, neither of the moon, to shine in it: for the glory of God did lighten it, and the Lamb is the light thereof.

24 And the nations of them which are saved shall walk in the light of it: and the kings of the earth do bring their glory and honour into it.

25 And the gates of it shall not be shut at all by day: for there shall be no night there.

26 And they shall bring the glory and honour of the nations into it.

27 And there shall in no wise enter into it any thing that defileth, neither whatsoever worketh abomination, or maketh a lie: but they which are written in the Lamb's book of life.

## Verse Commentary

*21:9–10.* One of the seven angels (see Rev. 16:1–17) comes to John and says, **Come hither, I will shew thee the bride, the Lamb's wife.** An angel who previously had a vial of the wrath of God now introduces the bride. In contrast to the great whore that John saw earlier, when he was taken into the wilderness (see Rev. 17:1–3), John now sees the bride, the wife of the Lamb. Instead of being taken into the wilderness, he is carried away **in the spirit to a great and high mountain.** The mountain represents the temple of the Lord. Ezekiel had a similar experience when he was allowed to see the heavenly city (see Ezek. 40:2), as did Nephi (see 1 Ne. 11:1).

John is shown **that great city, the holy Jerusalem, descending out of heaven from God.** The holy Jerusalem, the city of peace that has known so little of it, descends from a divine presence to become a holy abode for the righteous Saints upon the earth. All things must go through a refining process before they can inherit or participate in celestial glory. Jerusalem, like all creation, must all pass through the refiner's fire in order to be prepared for the glory which will permeate it in the eternities.

*21:11.* **Having the glory of God** is not just speaking of reflecting the brightness of God, but of having the divine "presence of the God of glory himself" (see Vincent, p. 565). The next verses (11–27) are John's physical and spiritual descriptions of the heavenly city. The Apostle uses the glorious, bright, and vivid radiance of the many jewels to describe the beauty of the city. **Her light was like unto a stone most precious, even a jasper stone, clear as crystal.** As a gem gives off a luster and brilliance of indescribable beauty, the glory which emanates from the New Jerusalem is as stunning as light reflected through crystal. The Doctrine and Covenants describes the beauty of the holy city and of the restored earth. "The angels do not reside on a planet like this earth; But they reside in the presence of God, on a globe like a sea of glass and fire, where all things for their glory are manifest, past, present, and future, and are continually before the Lord. The place where God resides is a great Urim and Thummim. This earth, in its sanctified and immortal state, will be made like unto crystal and will be a Urim and Thummim to the inhabitants who dwell thereon, whereby all things pertaining to an inferior kingdom, or all kingdoms of a lower order, will be manifest to those who dwell on it; and this earth will be Christ's" (130:6–9).

*21:12–13.* The city **had a wall great and high, and had twelve gates.** The heavenly city is open to each of the twelve tribes and they have their **names written** on the gates. **At the gates twelve angels** seem to stand watch, ensuring that all who enter are worthy to do so. Gates are used to restrict entrance to places. At the gates, only those who are worthy are permitted to enter. Nephi taught that the gates to the kigndom of God are the ordinances of the priesthood. "Wherefore, do the things which I have told you I have seen that your Lord and your Redeemer should do; for, for this cause have they been shown unto me, that ye might know the gate by which ye should enter. For the gate by which ye should enter is repentance and baptism by water; and then cometh a remission of your sins by fire and by the Holy Ghost" (2 Ne. 31:17).

Each of the twelve tribes of Israel are to enter through the gate marked with their name. There are two ways that we become part of the house of Israel: 1) through direct lineage or, 2) by adoption into one of the tribes. Obviously, only those who have the proper sealings and ordinances will be allowed to pass by the angels who stand as sentinels at the entrances to the city. Brigham Young gives further insight into this concept when he taught the following principle about the endowment: "Your *endowment* is, to receive all those ordinances in the House of the Lord, which are necessary for you, after you have departed this life, to enable you to walk back to the presence of the Father, passing the angels who stand as sentinels, being enabled to give them the key words, the signs and tokens, pertaining to the Holy Priesthood, and gain your eternal exaltation in spite of earth and hell" (*JD,* 2:31).

**On the east three gates; on the north three gates; on the south three gates; and on the west three gates** are written the names of the twelve tribes. Ezekiel informs us that the east gates bear the names of Joseph, Benjamin, and Dan. The north gates are those of Reuben, Judah, and Levi. The three southern gates have the names of Simeon, Issachar, and Zebulun, and the western gates bear the names of Gad, Asher, and Naphtali (see Ezek. 48:31–34).

Like the walls that surround current temples, John sees a wall that encircles the entire heavenly city, the New Jerusalem being a temple to the Most High God.

*21:14.* **The wall of the city had twelve foundations, and in them the names of the twelve apostles of the Lamb.** The wall of the city is based upon the foundation of apostles and prophets with Jesus Christ being the chief cornerstone (see Eph. 4:11–14). The foundation of priesthood authority is evident in all aspects of the heavenly city. The twelve gates, angels, tribes, and Apostles all represent the order of the priesthood. Elder Bruce R. McConkie, commenting on the use of the names of the Twelve Apostles, says "that their names—as well as those of all who endure valiantly in the cause of truth and righteousness—shall be had in honorable and everlasting remembrance in the presence of God and his saints" (*DNTC*, 3:587–88).

*21:15.* The angel which speaks with John has **a golden reed to measure the city, and the gates thereof, and the wall thereof.** In Revelation 11 a reed was used to measure the temple and the altar of those who were about to be martyred. Now, the entire heavenly city will be measured. All martyrs and faithful Saints will dwell in this beautiful city. The golden color of the reed symbolizes the enduring nature of this city that will remain standing forever.

*21:16.* **And the city lieth foursquare, and the length is as large as the breadth: and he measured the city with the reed, twelve thousand furlongs.** Four is the number of geographic fulness and sufficiency (see Symbols Guide). Being squared represents an eternal geographic completeness that is shown to be exact by the measurements. An angel from on high must measure the unimaginable proportions of the heavenly city. The size of the city is enormous and its constitution is perfect. Richard

Draper asserts that "as great as John is, he is yet mortal and imperfect. The task of measuring the height, depth, and breadth of celestial perfection is beyond any mortal man's capability" (p. 236).

**The length and the breadth and the height of it are equal.** The heavenly city is a perfect cube in its shape, representing exactness, order, and reflection. All who dwell within the walls of the city will be as their Lord and King. They will reflect the light of Christ and will embody perfection and glory.

*21:17.* **[The angel] measured the wall thereof, an hundred and forty and four cubits.** The wall surrounding the city is a representation of priesthood power. Its measurement, in conjunction with its foundation upon the Apostles of the Lamb, stands as a testament to the power of God. The number 144 indicates a consolidation and magnification of all priesthood power (see Symbols Guide).

*21:18.* John is handicapped by mortal language as he tries to describe the city's heavenly appearance. **The building of the wall of it was of jasper: and the city was pure gold, like unto clear glass.** Pure gold reflects the eternal quality of the city. Clear glass is indicative of the earth being "like a sea of glass" through which all things become apparent, past, present, and future (see D&C 130:7–9).

*21:19–20.* John sees precious stones representing each of the twelve tribes of Israel. The twelve types of stone each have a different beauty and luster. They sparkle in the light shining forth from the heavenly city. The stones John names are jasper, sapphire, chalcedony, emerald, sardonyx, sardius, chrysolyte, beryl, topaz, chrysoprasus, jacinth, and amethyst. (For further explanations on the gems and their colors, see Vincent, pp. 567–69.)

Each of the stones represents the glory and beauty of each of the twelve tribes of Israel. The kingdom of God on the earth is exceptionally beautiful.

*21:21.* **And the twelve gates were twelve pearls; every several gate was of one pearl.** Each of the gates through which people enter are represented by a pearl. The Savior said that "the kingdom of heaven is like unto a merchant man, seeking goodly pearls: Who, when he had found one pearl of great price, went and sold all that he had, and bought it" (Matt. 13:45–46). Those who enter this celestial city have "sold all that [they] have" through their devotion to God.

**The street of the city was pure gold, as it were transparent glass.** The Prophet Joseph Smith and Oliver Cowdery while in the Kirtland Temple saw the Lord standing on a pavement of gold. "The veil was taken from our minds, and the eyes of our understanding were opened. We saw the Lord standing upon the breastwork of the pulpit, before us; and under his feet was a paved work of pure gold, in color like amber" (D&C 110:1–2). The magnificence of the city is such that gold is used to pave the roads in the heavenly kingdom.

21:22. **And I saw no temple therein: for the Lord God Almighty and the Lamb are the temple of it.** There is no need of the temple. Why? Because temples are constructed to provide a place of purity on the earth that the Lord can come to. The entire city will be pure and worthy of the Lord's presence during the Millennium. He will frequent all sectors of the city. The structures which are built as houses of the Lord here on earth are extremely sacred. It is a glorious blessing to be able to enter into the temple of the Lord as we dwell in our mortal probation. Our Heavenly Father has truly blessed us with a grand and glorious opportunity, the likes of which very few of us fully comprehend.

Elder Bruce R. McConkie writes, "Temples, now and during the millennium, are to prepare men for a celestial inheritance. When that glorious goal is gained, heaven itself becomes a temple. The holy of holies in the Lord's earthly houses are symbols and types of the Eternal Holy of Holies which is the highest heaven of the celestial world" (*DNTC*, 3:588).

21:23. **And the city had no need of the sun, neither of the moon, to shine in it: for the glory of God did lighten it, and the Lamb is the light thereof.** There is no need of reflected light such as the sun or moon because the Savior is the light and the life of the world and provides the glorious light to illuminate the heavenly city.

*21:24.* **And the nations of them which are saved shall walk in the light of it: and the kings of the earth do bring their glory and honour into it.** In contrast to those pre-millennial nations of the earth that worshipped the beast and the kings who refused to worship the Lord, at this time we find all of the nations and their kings coming into the city and giving their praise and glory to the Lord. Their lives are illuminated by the light coming forth from the Lord. He is the glorious center of this celestial dwelling place.

*21:25–26.* **And the gates of it shall not be shut at all by day: for there shall be no night there.** There is no need to close the gates because of nightfall, for there is none. The gates are continuously open for all those who desire to enter in. There is no concern over wickedness. All wickedness is done away and the glory of God rules the city eternally. It is eternally a celestial home for the righteous.

**And they shall bring the glory and honour of the nations into it.** All nations shall flow into it and as they come they will sing praises, and glory, and honor unto him that sits upon the throne (see Rev. 4:8–11; 5:12–14; 7:9–17; 11:17; 15:3–4).

*21:27.* **And there shall in no wise enter into it any thing that defileth, neither whatsoever worketh abomination, or maketh a lie: but they which are written in the Lamb's book of life.** There is no concern for the wicked things of the world. All of the things which represent wickedness have long since passed away and only the good things of the earth remain, throughout eternity. Where God is, wickedness cannot come. The only ones who will have entry into this heavenly realm are the righteous.

## Applicability

The heavenly city! This is the glory that we hopefully all desire: to have admittance through the gates of the heavenly city, the New Jerusalem, and to dwell in the presence of the Father and the Son. We will not be dependent upon the sun or the moon to light our way anymore, because the Lamb will be the light. Nothing which defiles will enter in. There will be joy and gladness for all who have proven themselves worthy through their obedience to the gospel of Jesus Christ. Righteous kings and nations shall bring their glory and honor into the city. The praises of the Lord will ring out as we extol him who provided the supreme sacrifice that enabled us to return home, even Christ the Lamb.

## SUMMARY

Throughout Revelation we have heard promises "to those who overcome all things." Chapter 21 shows a complete fulfillment of those things. There is only joy and gladness in the hearts of the righteous who inherit this earth in its celestial state. Imagine, we will actually, once again, be in the presence of the Father and the Son. We will be like they are, having perfected, immortal, resurrected bodies. We will become joint-heirs with Christ (see Rom. 8:17) in kingdoms of glory, worlds without end. We will sit on thrones (see Rev. 3:21) and dwell in the perfect holy city. At times it seems so impossible! Yet as we consider the numerous blessings and miracles that have already taken place in our lives, it is evident that with God nothing is impossible (see Luke 1:37; 18:27).

There are great blessings in store for those of the house of Israel. The Lord will remember and keep his covenants. Although there are times in life when we may question whether it is all worth it, if we persevere we will recognize that the Lord shows us fragments of eternity as he blesses our lives and the lives of others who are faithful. As long as we have faith, keep the commandments, and endure to the end we truly "shall have eternal life, which gift is the greatest of all the gifts of God" (D&C 14:7). Consider this promise from the Doctrine and Covenants, "Verily, verily, I say unto you, ye are little children, and ye have not as yet understood how great blessings the Father hath in his own hands and prepared for you; And ye cannot bear all things now; nevertheless, be of good cheer, for I will lead you along. The kingdom is yours, and the blessings thereof are yours, and the riches of eternity are yours. And he who receiveth all things with thankfulness shall be made glorious; and the things of this earth shall be added unto him, even an hundred fold, yea, more" (78:17–19).

So many blessings await us if we are faithful. We cannot allow challenges and hardships in this life to cloud our eternal perspective.

# 22

# THE FINAL PROMISED BLESSINGS
# AND WARNING

The events and principles defined in Revelation have been shown to prophets of all dispensations. Nephi, for example, was allowed to see many of the things shown to John. Nephi, however, was told not to write of what he saw. "But the things which thou shalt see hereafter thou shalt not write; for the Lord God hath ordained the apostle of the Lamb of God that he should write them. And also others who have been, to them hath he shown all things, and they have written them; and they are sealed up to come forth in their purity, according to the truth which is in the Lamb, in the own due time of the Lord, unto the house of Israel" (1 Ne. 14:25–26).

This final chapter is a beautiful compendium of the many promised blessings which await those who are faithful. The curse that came upon mankind and the earth at the time of the Fall is completely taken away. Once again we can partake of the fruit of the tree of life in the midst of the paradise of God. That thing which was desired by Adam, Lehi, Nephi, and all of the prophets throughout the ages is finally brought to pass as promised in Revelation 2:7. Not only are we allowed to partake of the fruit of the tree of life, but we are also allowed to drink of the waters of life freely.

Finally, we receive a warning to not add to or take from the words of the book of this prophecy or "God shall take away his part out of his book of life, and out of the holy city, and from the things which are written in this book" (Rev. 22:18–19). Many have mistakenly supposed that this warning is concerning the whole Bible and have said that there can be no further revelation coming from God, but the warning is actually referencing the singular book of Revelation. We are commanded not to add to or take from the revelation which John received and shared as part of his mission.

It is my prayer that as you read this final chapter you will further strengthen your testimony of the blessings which await the faithful followers of Christ. There is only one person who can truly decide which path you will follow—you! Recall the words of Samuel the Lamanite: "And this to the intent that whosoever will believe might be saved, and that whosoever will not believe, a righteous judgment might come upon them; and also if they are condemned they bring upon themselves their own condemnation. And now remember, remember, my brethren, that whosoever perisheth, perisheth unto himself, and whosoever doeth iniquity, doeth it unto himself, for behold, ye are free; ye are permitted to act for yourselves; for behold, God hath given unto you a knowledge and he hath made you free. He hath given unto you that ye might know good from evil, and he hath given unto you that ye might choose life or death; and ye can do good and be restored unto that which is good, or have that which is good restored unto you; or ye can do evil, and have that which is evil restored unto you" (Hel. 14:29–31).

## REVELATION 22:1–5

1 ¶ And he shewed me a pure river of water of life, clear as crystal, proceeding out of the throne of God and of the Lamb.

2 In the midst of the street of it, and on either side of the river, was there the tree of life, which bare twelve manner of fruits, and yielded her fruit every month: and the leaves of the tree were for the healing of the nations.

3 And there shall be no more curse: but the throne of God and of the Lamb shall be in it; and his servants shall serve him:

4 And they shall see his face; and his name shall be in their foreheads.

5 And there shall be no night there; and they need no candle, neither light of the sun; for the Lord God giveth them light: and they shall reign for ever and ever.

**Verse Commentary**

*22:1.* John is now shown **a pure river of water of life, clear as crystal, proceeding out of the throne of God and of the Lamb.** In the paradise of God the Saints are given the waters of life and the fruit of the tree of life. Whosoever would drink from the waters or eat from the fruit is made a partaker of eternal life, a gift that proceeds out from the throne of God and the Lamb. All of the evidence in Revelation emphasizes that the Father and Son are separate and distinct beings, but that they have one purpose: "the immortality and eternal life of man" (Moses 1:39).

This water reflects the brightness of the throne from whence it comes, as it is clear and bright as crystal. If the very things the righteous are partaking of are bright and clear, it seems that our whole souls will be filled with light (see D&C 50:24; 93:36–37).

*22:2.* **In the midst of the street of it, and on either side of the river, was there the tree of life, which bear twelve manner of fruits.** The tree of life is one of the most prominent features in the heavenly city. Jesus Christ is the tree of life and the fruit of the tree is eternal life. In the vision which Nephi had regarding the tree of life the focus is on the Savior and his works among men. He saw the tree of life in the center of the field and the straight and narrow path and rod of iron leading directly to it. This glorious and beautiful tree is in direct opposition to the great and spacious building: the former represents Jesus Christ and his righteousness, the latter represents Satan and his wickedness (see 1 Ne. 11). In Nephi's vision, the tree of life was on one side of the river of filthiness and the great and spacious building was on the other. Here, the river runs pure and clean, and the tree of life is found on both sides of it.

The "twelve manner of fruits" may represent the priesthood (see Symbols Guide), the tribes of Israel, or the blessings of the gospel. In other words, they represent the things of the Lord.

The tree **yielded her fruit every month** meaning that the people could partake of the fruit continually. This is not an ordinary tree that produces only during a certain growing season—the tree of life is everbearing.

**The leaves of the tree were for the healing of the nations.**
The leaves may represent two ideas. First, leaves depict spring-
time and a newness of life. As such, the leaves of the tree of life
represent the healing, that is, the growth and purity of the
nations united under Christ. A newness of life is achieved
through the atonement of our Savior. Secondly, leaves sprout
from the tree; they are the offspring of the tree, as we are the offspring of the Lord (see Mosiah 15:1–4).

22:3. **And there shall be no more curse.** What a beautiful
blessing! The curse which was placed upon the earth is no
longer. The curse of death was removed from Adam and his
posterity by the resurrection of Jesus Christ. But the earth has
had to endure the curse that "thorns also, and thistles shall it
bring forth" instead of voluntarily producing fruits of the earth
(Moses 4:23–25). Imagine the release that the earth will feel!
Elder McConkie writes, "In the beginning the Lord cursed the
ground; decreed that Adam should eat of its fruits in sorrow all
his days; and placed Cherubim and a flaming sword to keep
him from eating of the tree of life while yet in his sins. (Gen. 3.)
Now the curse is removed; all men who attain celestial glory
have free access to the tree of life and partake of all the goodness
of God" (*DNTC*, 3:589).

**The throne of God and of the Lamb shall be in it; and his
servants shall serve him.** We continue to see a separation of the
Father and the Son even as they occupy one throne. Revelation
teaches that the Father and the Son are not one in person but are
one in purpose. All that the Son does in rule, judgment, and
honor resembles what the Father would do. The throne is in the
midst of the paradise of God. Because the Savior overcame all
things he is "set down" with the Father in his throne (see Rev.
3:21). In gratitude, faithful Saints serve their Savior and Master.
The throne John sees is surrounded by those who worship and
serve the Father and Son for their great goodness in providing
the plan of salvation.

22:4. **And they shall see his face; and his name shall be in
their foreheads.** As previously noted, "we shall be like him; for
we shall see him as he is" (1 Jn. 3:2; see also D&C 38:7–8). The

Lord himself told Peter, "I go and prepare a place for you, I will come again, and receive you unto myself; that where I am, there ye may be also" (John 14:3; see also 1 Thes. 4:17).

Having his name in our foreheads is to be marked as one of Christ's own, to be marked as one who has accepted him. This we do through the covenant of baptism in which we "take upon [us] the name of [the] Son, and always remember him and keep his commandments" (D&C 20:77), a covenant that we remake each time we partake of the sacrament. As we meet the Savior and see his face, all of our thoughts will be of him and of his mercy towards us. Imagine how blessed we will feel to be in the presence of the Savior and the Father once again to "go no more out" (Rev. 3:12).

22:5. **And there shall be no night there; and they need no candle, neither light of the sun; for the Lord God giveth them light: and they shall reign for ever and ever.** Imagine what the love of Christ will do for us as it provides all of the life-giving light that we will need. The power of God is such that there is sufficient light to supply each with the brightness and glory that there is no need for other light and the night will not exist anymore. In this blessed and holy state we shall reign with the Father and the Son for ever and ever. I am humbled in my attempt to express what truly lies before us as exalted children of a Heavenly Father who loves us and desires that each of us become like him. We will be like the Father and the Son for we were created in their image. "Every man who reigns in celestial glory is a God to his dominions" (*TPJS*, p. 374).

## Applicability

The curse placed upon the earth and mankind will be removed in preparation of the celestial kingdom. We shall once again have free access to the tree of life and the fountain of living waters. We will dwell in the presence of the Lord. We will see his face and know that he is. All of the blessings we have desired for such a long time are finally ours to keep for eternity. We have fought the fight, finished the course, and kept the faith;

for this purpose there is laid up for us an eternal glory and the opportunity to rule and reign with our Father and his Son forevermore. What a glorious blessing!

## REVELATION 22:6–21

6 ¶ And he said unto me, These sayings are faithful and true: and the Lord God of the holy prophets sent his angel to shew unto his servants the things which must shortly be done.

7 Behold, I come quickly: blessed is he that keepeth the sayings of the prophecy of this book.

8 And I John saw these things, and heard them. And when I had heard and seen, I fell down to worship before the feet of the angel which shewed me these things.

9 Then saith he unto me, See thou do it not: for I am thy fellowservant, and of thy brethren the prophets, and of them which keep the sayings of this book: worship God.

10 And he saith unto me, Seal not the sayings of the prophecy of this book: for the time is at hand.

11 He that is unjust, let him be unjust still: and he which is filthy, let him be filthy still: and he that is righteous, let him be righteous still: and he that is holy, let him be holy still.

12 And, behold, I come quickly; and my reward is with me, to give every man according as his work shall be.

13 I am Alpha and Omega, the beginning and the end, the first and the last.

14 Blessed are they that do his commandments, that they may have right to the tree of life, and may enter in through the gates into the city.

15 For without are dogs, and sorcerers, and whoremongers, and murderers, and idolaters, and whosoever loveth and maketh a lie.

16 I Jesus have sent mine angel to testify unto you these things in the churches. I am the root and the offspring of David, and the bright and morning star.

17 And the Spirit and the bride say, Come. And let him that heareth say, Come. And let him that is athirst come. And whosoever will, let him take the water of life freely.

18 For I testify unto every man that heareth the words of the prophecy of this book, If any man shall add unto these things, God shall add unto him the plagues that are written in this book:

19 And if any man shall take away from the words of the book of this prophecy, God shall take away his part out of the book of life, and out of the holy city, and from the things which are written in this book.

20 ¶ He which testifieth these things saith, Surely I come quickly. Amen. Even so, come, Lord Jesus.

21 The grace of our Lord Jesus Christ be with you all. Amen.

## Verse Commentary

*22:6–7.* The angel then said to John, **These sayings are faithful and true: and the Lord God of the holy prophets sent his angel to shew unto his servants the things which must shortly be done. Behold, I come quickly: blessed is he that keepeth the sayings of the prophecy of this book.** The angel is speaking here by divine investiture of authority as he speaks in the name of the Lord, as though he were the Lord. Elder McConkie states that the meaning of "quickly" is "not soon, but in a quick manner; that is, with speed and suddenness after all of the promised conditions precedent have occurred" (*DNTC*, 3:590).

"This book" does not mean the Bible, but rather the singular book of Revelation. He has not spoken of the Bible as a part of his work to this point so there is no reason that we should suppose that he would change at this moment and include the whole of the Bible. The prophecy of this book is all that has been revealed to John. Revelation is a guide to enable us to enter the celestial kingdom. Elder Bruce R. McConkie explains: " 'This book' is the Book of Revelation. All who keep its sayings shall, for instance, know that revelation is to continue after New Testament times; that the gospel was destined to come again in the latter-days by angelic ministration; that glory and honor and exaltation await those who overcome the world and are true and faithful in all things; and that Christ the Lord shall receive glory and honor, power and might, now and forever" (*DNTC*, 3:591).

*22:8.* **John saw these things, and heard them. And when [he] had heard and seen, [he] fell down to worship before the feet of the angel which shewed [him] these things.** John is so overcome with the Spirit and radiance of what he has just seen and heard that he feels inclined to kneel before the angel in a sense of reverence and respect for this holy being before him (see Rev. 19:10).

*22:9.* The angel forbids him. **See thou do it not: for I am thy fellowservant, and of thy brethren the prophets, and of them which keep the sayings of this book: worship God.** This angelic ministrant, with such good tidings of great joy, is a fellowservant of John and is one of his prophetic brethren. To all those who keep the sayings of the book of Revelation there is one specific message which is uttered time and again: Worship God!

*22:10.* In the first part of Revelation, John saw a book that was sealed and could not be opened except by one who was found worthy to do so. Here he is told **Seal not the sayings of the prophecy of this book: for the time is at hand.** The purpose of the revelation is to make men aware of the dealings of God from the beginning of time down through the culmination of all things. John is not to seal the book so that men can be informed of what lies ahead prior to the Second Coming. Revelation proclaims to all that the Lord will be the victor, even though it may seem that the battle is lost.

*22:11.* In the midst of all of these glorious blessings we are again reminded of the terrible consequences of those who choose to disobey the commands of God. **He that is unjust, let him be unjust still: and he which is filthy, let him be filthy still.** It is impossible for God the Father, or for Jesus Christ, to save men in their sins (see Alma 11:36–37). If man refuses to repent then he must remain in that sinful and filthy state until he has paid the price for the sins he has committed (see D&C 19:16–20). Mercy cannot rob justice.

Then comes the reminder of the promise for obedience. **And he that is righteous, let him be righteous still: and he that is holy, let him be holy still.** Alma explained this principle to his son Corianton: "And now behold, is the meaning of the word restoration to take a thing of a natural state and place it into an unnatural state, or to place it in a state opposite to its nature? O, my son, this is not the case; but the meaning of the word restoration is to bring back again evil for evil, or carnal for carnal, or devilish for devilish—good for that which is good; righteous for that which is righteous; just for that which is just; merciful for that which is merciful" (Alma 41:12–13).

*22:12.* Another reminder from the Lord: **Behold, I come quickly; and my reward is with me, to give every man according as his work shall be.** Although there are many who profess that all one must do is "confess that Jesus Christ is their Savior," it is obvious that the Lord requires obedience to his commandments. His reward is not arbitrary. It is based upon obedience to certain principles of the gospel. The Doctrine and Covenants teaches, "There is a law, irrevocably decreed in heaven before the foundation of this world, upon which all blessings are predicated—And when we obtain any blessing from God, it is by obedience to that law upon which it is predicated" (130:20–21).

All will receive their just reward for the things that they have performed while in this flesh. The payment, or reward, will be meted out justly for the service rendered. We are saved by grace, and exalted by obedience.

*22:13.* **I am Alpha and Omega, the beginning and the end, the first and the last.** A reiteration of exactly who Christ is and what his mission entails (see also Rev. 1:8, 11; 21:6). He is truly the beginning and ending of the fulfillment of our Heavenly Father's plan.

*22:14.* The promised blessings are stressed again and again: **Blessed are they that do his commandments, that they may have the right to the tree of life, and may enter in through the gates into the city.** Obviously, it is not enough to merely believe in the Lord. We are required to "do" his commandments, and if we do we will be able to partake of the tree of life and will have entrance into the heavenly city. Marvin R. Vincent suggests that "they that do his commandments" should be read as "they that wash their robes" (p. 573). Perhaps by keeping or "doing" his commandments we acknowledge the atonement of Jesus Christ and allow his blood to cleanse our garments.

Nephi and numerous other prophets wrote that those who keep the commandments of the Lord will prosper while those who do not will be cut off from his presence (see 1 Ne. 2:20–22). The brother of Jared (see Ether 1:42), Moses (see Ex. 3:8), Lehi and Nephi (see 1 Ne. 2:20), and Joseph Smith (see D&C 38:18–20) all obtained a land of promise for their peoples because of their obedience to the Lord's commandments. Through faithfulness and keeping the commandments we pass by the angels standing as sentinels at the gates of the city and are allowed to enter our own land of promise, even the celestial kingdom.

*22:15*. **For without are dogs, and sorcerers, and whoremongers, and murderers, and idolaters, and whosoever loveth and maketh a lie.** Just a brief reminder of the judgment which comes upon the wicked. This list represents those who are cast out of the Father's presence because they were wicked continually and are now called dogs rather than men (see also Rev. 21:8). In the Mosaic law dogs were considered unclean, and were "depicted as animals with voracious appetites . . . and powerful enemies of man" (Eerdman, p. 290). The last classfication, those who love and make a lie, condemns those who feel there is no harm in telling a lie (see 2 Ne. 28:7–9). He who "loveth and maketh a lie" most surely offends the Lord.

*22:16*. The Savior now witnesses of the truthfulness of the message: **I Jesus have sent mine angel to testify unto you these things in the churches. I am the root and the offspring of David, and the bright and morning star.** We find the Savior declaring that there have been two witnesses of his right to the throne. The angel was sent to bear witness, and now he bears witness of who he is. He is "the root and offspring of David." Elder McConkie explains how Christ can be both the root and the offspring of the most significant king of Israel: "The Son of David was also David's Lord. Christ established David and was the source of his power; and through David's lineage the Great God received his mortal body" (*DNTC*, 3:592).

The "morning star" was promised as one of the blessings to the faithful Saints who overcame (Rev. 2:28). Those who are faithful shall receive the "morning star" or, in other words, the constant companionship of the Savior. They will dwell in his presence.

*22:17*. We now find two further testimonies of all that has been spoken. **The Spirit and the bride say, Come. And let him that heareth say, Come. And let him that is athirst come. And whosoever will, let him take the water of life freely.** No one will be forced to partake of the fruit of the tree of life or of the water of life. It is an invitation to all, from the Spirit and the Church, to come and partake of the wonderful blessings of the gospel. Whosoever will may partake and enjoy the blessings of their decision to come into the fold of God. Consider a similar statement offered by Moroni: "Yea, come unto Christ, and be perfected in him, and deny yourselves of all ungodliness; . . . and love God with all your might, mind and strength, then is his grace sufficient for you, that by his grace ye may be perfect in Christ; and if by the grace of God ye are perfect in Christ, ye can in nowise deny the power of God. And again, if ye by the grace of God are perfect in Christ, and deny not his power, then are ye sanctified in Christ by the grace of God, through the shedding of the blood of Christ, which is in the covenant of the Father unto the remission of your sins, that ye become holy, without spot" (Moro. 10:32–33).

*22:18-19.* The final warning comes with strength and power to all who would read the prophecies of John. Here John bears testimony of all that has been revealed to him: **For I testify unto every man that heareth the words of the prophecy of this book, If any man shall add unto these things, God shall add unto him the plagues that are written in this book: And if any man shall take away from the words of the book of this prophecy, God shall take away his part out of the book of life, and out of the holy city, and from the things which are written in this book.**

Failure to heed the warnings will result in a loss of all that has been promised to those who are faithful. Moses spoke similarly when he commanded, "Ye shall not add unto the word which I command you, neither shall ye diminish ought from it, that ye may keep the commandments of the Lord your God which I command you" (Deut. 4:2; see also 12:32). These warnings are specific to the books of Deuteronomy and Revelation. The Lord is at liberty to add whatever he pleases—and he has and does through prophets (see Amos 3:7). The prohibition that John attaches to Revelation applies to scheming people who, in attempts to get gain or influence, may write scripture unto themselves.

*22:20.* **He which testifieth these things saith, Surely I come quickly. Amen.** The Lord's promises are sure. He will come, though it be at an hour when we are least expecting it. John responds to the Lord by saying, **Even so, come, Lord Jesus.** An invitation on behalf of all mankind, for the Savior of the world to return and deliver us from the adversary.

22:21. The final blessing pronounced by John, a prophet of God and an Apostle of the Lord Jesus Christ, invokes the saving mercies of the Lord upon each of us. **The grace of our Lord Jesus Christ be with you all. Amen.**

### Applicability

Numerous testimonies have come from the mouths of prophets, apostles, angels, and Saints who dwell among us. It is our opportunity and obligation to make proper choices in our lives. Such choices will enable the Father to pour down blessings from heaven upon our homes and our families. The book of Revelation is full of promised blessings which the Father and Son desire to send forth upon the righteous. But it is also full of warnings to those who practice wickedness. The message of Revelation is that those who are faithful and true, following Jesus Christ who is "Faithful and True" (Rev. 19:11; 21:5), shall overcome all things and dwell in celestial glory. We will dwell in the light, power, and glory of our Heavenly Father and elder brother Jesus Christ. What joy we will experience!

### SUMMARY

The celestial city has been aptly described in the previous chapter and the blessings which have been reviewed time and again are ultimately brought to pass. The Saints shall dwell in the presence of the Father and the Son. The curse upon the earth is removed. The Savior provides all the light that we need. We will enjoy the companionship of the Savior. We shall see him and shall realize that all of his promises are fulfilled. As participants in the heavenly, then earthly, celestial city we shall enjoy the prosperity which comes about from living faithful lives while in this mortal probation. Consider similar words written by the Prophet Joseph Smith as he finished recording the revelation of the degrees of glory: "This is the end of the vision which we saw, which we were commanded to write while we were yet in the Spirit. But great and marvelous are the works of the Lord, and the mysteries of his kingdom which he showed unto us, which surpass all understanding in glory, and in might, and in dominion; Which he commanded us we should not write while we were yet in the Spirit, and are not lawful for man to utter; Neither is man capable to make them known, for they are only to be seen and understood by the power of the Holy Spirit, which God bestows on those who love him, and purify themselves before him; To whom he grants this privilege of seeing and knowing for themselves; That through the power and manifestation of the Spirit, while in the flesh, they may be able to bear his presence in the world of glory. And to God and the Lamb be glory, and honor, and dominion forever and ever. Amen" (D&C 76:113–19).

May the Lord bless you with similar understanding of the many hidden treasures of knowledge that are available to those who diligently seek him. You are guaranteed that to him who seeketh, the Lord shall reveal "great treasures of knowledge, even hidden treasures" (D&C 89:19; see also 101:32–34).

# EPILOGUE

I hope this book has provided you with a testimony that the Lord will fulfill his promises and deliver his people in the battles against the adversary. As we are faithful to the covenants we have made, especially those made in the house of the Lord, we have the assurance that we will be victorious. We were sent here to prepare ourselves to return to the Lord's presence. The responsibility to do so is ours.

The Lord has promised us that we would find "great treasures of knowledge, even hidden treasures" (D&C 89:19). Please remember that hidden treasures require that one look and search for them. A mystery is a mystery only because it is unknown and we may not have sufficient knowledge to readily explain what is termed the "mystery." As the Lord blesses and enlightens your understanding you will begin to comprehend more of his mysteries and will gain a greater testimony that this is his work.

I realize that there are still many things left undone for you to search out, but I believe that if you keep the focus of Revelation in your mind and remember whose revelation it is, you will comprehend that all things bear witness of Christ and of his power and glory. I would now counsel you to follow the advice of the Lord to Enoch the prophet: "Behold my Spirit is upon you, wherefore all thy words will I justify; and the mountains shall flee before you, and the rivers shall turn from their course; and thou shalt abide in me, and I in you; therefore walk with me" (Moses 6:34).

It is my humble prayer that after having studied through

this book, *The Book of Revelation: Plain, Pure, and Simple,* your understanding of the book of Revelation will be increased along with your desire to be obedient to the commandments of God. This is the revelation of Jesus Christ. He is our Lord and our King, the literal Son of God. It is my testimony that we can one day become like our Heavenly Father and dwell in his presence, sit upon thrones as he does, and be like him in every way.

Also a brief note of caution. Do not search after those things which have not yet been revealed. They will be made known in the Lord's own due time. Avoid speculation. Protect yourself against "looking beyond the mark" and missing the target altogether. We will not be held accountable for the things which the Lord has not revealed.

I pray that this book has inspired you with the determination and desire to stay on the straight and narrow path and to continue on in the faith and grace of the Lord Jesus Christ, until we all shall meet "before the pleasing bar of the great Jehovah" (Moro. 10:34). May the Lord bless and prosper you in all of your activities and guide you unto the riches of eternity.

# Symbols Guide

## Numbers

**1.** The number 1 represents the beginning of all things. It is often used in the context of the "first," the "first fruits," or the "First-born," and may refer to place, time, or rank.

**3.** Three symbolizes the Godhead, the Trinity of Deity, and perfection. It is considered a perfect number because it has a beginning, a middle, and an end. The beginning is 1, 2 is the middle, and 3 is the end. All three numbers are unified within the number 3, yet each is separate and distinct. Though representing the Father, Son, and Holy Ghost, 3 is also used by the adversary to represent the dragon, beast, and serpent.

**4.** The number 4 represents mankind and the geographic fulness of the earth. It occurs in the "four points of the compass," the "four winds," and the "four corners of the earth." Whenever 4 is added to or multiplied by another number it portrays the geographic fulness of that number.

**6.** Six is the number of incompleteness or imperfection. In triplicate (666) the number is used to represent the name of the beast.

**7.** As a sum of 3 (representing the Godhead) and 4 (representing mankind and geographic fulness), 7 represents perfection. Its use implies a full, complete joining together of all things in heaven and on the earth.

**10.** Ten represents a completeness and is often multiplied with other numbers for emphasis.

**12.** The number 12 represents the priesthood and completeness. Anytime the number 12 is multiplied by another number, it symbolizes an increase in power and covenant responsibility.

**40.** Forty is used symbolically to represent geographic fulness or sufficiency, or a lengthy period of time.

**144.** The number 144 is the product of the priesthood's number (12) multiplied by itself. This number represents the combination of the Aaronic and Melchizedek Priesthoods, thereby representing all priesthood power.

**666.** The number of the beast, 666, a triple rendering of the imperfect 6, represents the great imperfection inherent in evil.

**1000.** One thousand is used to denote power, strength, and magnitude. Anytime it occurs, by itself or as a multiple of another number, it symbolizes greatness and vastness.

## COLORS

*White.* Purity and victory
*Red.* Blood or violent death
*Black.* Death by famine, plague, and pestilence
*Pale (pale green).* Death or hell
*Purple.* Royalty, honor, and wealth
*Green.* Life or truth
*Gold.* Riches, value, or incorruptibility
*Rainbow.* Covenants

## TERMINOLOGY

*Babylon.* The world and its ways
*Beasts.* Unknown unless specified
*Bow.* Battle, war
*Candlesticks.* Servants of God, carriers of the light
*Cloud.* The presence of God
*Crowns.* Authority, glory, exaltation, royalty, rule
*Dragon.* Satan
*Eyes.* Sight, light, knowledge
*Horns.* Symbols of power
*Horse.* Battle, power
*Keys.* Authority, access, control, responsibility

*Lamb.* The Savior, an offering
*Palm fronds.* Symbols of joy and celebration
*Sea of Glass.* Celestialized earth, Urim and Thummim
*Sword.* Power, war, revelation
*Thunder.* Power and strength
*Wings.* Mobility, speed

## APPROXIMATE PERIODS OF THE SEALS

*1st Seal.* 4000 B.C. to 3000 B.C.
*2nd Seal.* 3000 B.C. to 2000 B.C.
*3rd Seal.* 2000 B.C. to 1000 B.C.
*4th Seal.* 1000 B.C. to Christ's Birth
*5th Seal.* Christ's Birth to A.D. 1000
*6th Seal.* A.D. 1000 to A.D. 2000
*7th Seal.* A.D. 2000 to A.D. 3000

## HELPFUL SOURCES

Achtemeier, Paul J., ed. *Harper's Bible Dictionary.* San Francisco: HarperCollins Publishers, 1985.
Buttrick, George A., ed. *The Interpreter's Dictionary of the Bible.* 4 vols. Nashville: Abingdon Press, 1962.
Douglas, J. D., ed. *New Bible Dictionary*, 2nd ed. Wheaton, Illinois: Tyndale House Publishers, 1982.

# BIBLIOGRAPHY

Benson, Ezra Taft. *The Teachings of Ezra Taft Benson*. Salt Lake City: Bookcraft, 1988.

Buttrick, George A., ed. *The Interpreter's Bible*. 12 vols. Nashville: Abingdon Press, 1957.

"Diana, Zeus, Athena." In Microsoft *Encarta*. Funk and Wagnalls Corp., 1994.

Draper, Richard D. *Opening the Seven Seals*. Salt Lake City: Deseret Book Co., 1991.

Eerdman, William B., et al. *The Eerdman's Bible Dictionary*. Ed. Allen C. Myers. Grand Rapids, Michigan: William B. Eerdman Publishing Co., 1987.

Fallows, Rt. Rev. Samuel, ed. *The Popular and Critical Bible Encyclopedia*. Chicago: Howard-Severance Co., 1903.

Gates, Susa Young. "The Temple Workers' Excursion." *The Young Woman's Journal*, Vol. 5, no. 11, pp. 505–16.

Jamieson, Robert, A. R. Fausset, and David Brown. *A Commentary Critical and Explanatory on the Whole Bible*. Grand Rapids, Michigan: Zondervan, 194?.

*Journal of Discourses*. 26 vols. Liverpool: F. D. Richards and Sons, 1851–86.

Kimball, Spencer W. *Faith Precedes the Miracle*. Salt Lake City: Deseret Book Co., 1973.

*The Life and Teachings of Jesus and His Apostles*. Salt Lake City: The Church of Jesus Christ of Latter-day Saints, 1978.

McConkie, Bruce R. *Doctrinal New Testament Commentary*. 3 vols. Salt Lake City: Bookcraft, 1965–73.

————. *Mormon Doctrine*, 2nd ed. Salt Lake City: Bookcraft, 1977.

————. "Understanding the Book of Revelation." *Ensign*. Salt Lake City: The Church of Jesus Christ of Latter-day Saints, Sept. 1975, pp. 85–89.

McConkie, Joseph Fielding. *Gospel Symbolism*. Salt Lake City: Bookcraft, 1985.

Mounce, Robert H. *The Book of Revelation*. Grand Rapids, Michigan: William B. Eerdman Publishing Co., 1977.

*New Testament Seminary Teacher Outline*. Salt Lake City: The Church of Jesus Christ of Latter-day Saints, 1987.

Nibley, Hugh. *Approaching Zion*. Salt Lake City: Deseret Book Co., 1989.

Rushdoony, Rousas John. *The Institutes of Biblical Law*. The Presbyterian and Reformed Publishing Co., 1973.

Smith, Joseph Fielding. *Answers to Gospel Questions*. 5 vols. Salt Lake City: Deseret Book Co., 1957–66.

————. *Church History and Modern Revelation*. 4 vols. Salt Lake City: Deseret Book Co., 1946–50.

————. *Doctrines of Salvation*. 3 vols. Salt Lake City: Deseret Book Co., 1954–56.

Smith, Joseph, Jr. *History of the Church of Jesus Christ of Latter-day Saints*, ed. B. H. Roberts. 7 vols. Salt Lake City: The Church of Jesus Christ of Latter-day Saints, 1932–51.

————. *Teachings of the Prophet Joseph Smith*. Comp. Joseph Fielding Smith. Salt Lake City: Deseret Book Co., 1976.

Strong, James. *The New Strong's Exhaustive Concordance of the Bible*. Nashville: Thomas Nelson Publishers, 1990.

*Times and Seasons*, vol. 55. Nauvoo, Illinois: John Taylor, 1844.

Vincent, Marvin R. *Word Studies in the New Testament*. 4 vols. Peabody, Massachusetts: Hendrickson Publishers, 1887.

Vine, W. E. *Vine's Expository Dictionary of Old and New Testament Words*. Old Tappan, New Jersey: Fleming H. Revell Co., 1981.

*The New Lexicon Webster's Encyclopedic Dictionary of the English Language*. New York: Lexicon Publications, 1989.

# INDEX

Meschach, 140
Michael, 22, 70, 123, 239, 247–48, 255
Millennium, 78, 111, 118, 196, 222, 237, 238–55
Milligan, George, *Vocabulary of the Greek Testament*, 224
Millstones, 217, 220, 221
Minerva (Roman goddess), 19
Miracles, 147, 180, 234
Missionaries, 62, 219
Missionary work, 153–55
Missouri, 149
Money, 207
Moon, symbol of the, 119, 256
Mormon, on the Spirit of Christ, xiii–xiv, 167–68
Morning star, symbol of the, 25–26, 125, 282
Moroni, 70, 154, 156
    on grace, 283
Moroni statue, 154
Moses, 8, 9, 32, 59, 70, 83, 109, 128, 131, 147, 166, 168, 169, 180, 185, 261, 281
Mothers, honoring, 114
Moulton, James H., *Vocabulary of the Greek Testament*, 224
Mounce, Robert H., on Christianity in Smyrna, 17
    on "holdeth and walketh," 14
    on the seven letters, 43
Mountains, 185, 197, 265
Mount of Olivet, 149
Mount Zion, 148–51, 248
Mourning, 211, 213, 215, 234, 259
Movies, 22, 39, 112, 203
Murder, 218, 262
Music, 39, 112, 217, 218
Musicians, 217
Mysteries, 9, 46, 51, 52, 54, 101, 191–92, 195, 260, 286

— N —

Names, confessed by Jesus Christ, 29, 30
    new, 20–21, 33, 40–41, 42, 229
    recorded in the book of life, 41
    written on the gates, 266
Naphtali, 267
Napoleon, 145
Nations, 184, 247, 270, 276
Natural calamities, 81–82, 185
Natural disasters, 78–79
Natural man, 112
Nature, forces of, 88

Nauvoo, Ill., 121
Nebuchadnezzar, 136
Nephi, on agency, 115–16
    on church of Satan, 201–2
    on the gates, 266
    on gathering armies, 199
    on John the Revelator, 102
    on judgment, 242–43
    on obedience, 281
    on past feelings, 178
    protected for mission, 140
    punishment of people of, 95
    on the rod of iron, 230–31
    on Satan's influence, 97
    saw the same things as John, 10
    on the tree of life, 40, 75
    vision of, 273
    on worldliness, 191
Nephites, three, 105, 115
Nero, 136
New Jerusalem, 33, 42, 128, 167, 225, 256, 258–71
New name, 21–22, 33, 40–41, 42, 229
Nibley, Hugh, on Babylon, 156
    on segregation, 208
Nicolaitans, 15, 20, 21, 22
Noah, 59, 70, 83, 88, 128, 131
Noble and great ones, 52
Numbers. *See individual numbers*

— O —

Oath and covenant, 48
Oaths, secret, 192
Obedience, 13, 167, 232, 246, 281
Oil, symbol of the, 7, 60
Olivet, Mount of, 149
Olive trees, symbol of the, 109
One thousand six hundred, symbol of the number, 163
*Opening the Seven Seals* (book), x
Opposition, 84–85, 129, 136
Ordinances, 40, 41, 76, 192, 227, 246
Organizations, 193
Ostracism, 33
Outer darkness, 234, 247
Overcoming, 15–16, 18, 21–22, 25–26, 33, 37–38

— P —

Paganism, 11, 19–20, 31, 190, 197
Pain, 148, 259, 262
Pale horse, symbol of the, 60–61, 289
Palm fronds, 74, 290